TIES THAT BIND?

Graham Walker is Emeritus Professor of Political History at Queen's University Belfast. He has published widely in the subject areas of Irish and Scottish history and politics, and the politics of sport.

Dr James Greer's publications have focused on the political history of Ulster unionism, the modern Troubles, British and Irish labour, and Irish Presbyterianism. His research has also explored the politics of European integration in Northern Ireland, and literature and popular culture in twentieth-century Northern Ireland.

TIES THAT BIND?

Scotland, Northern Ireland and the Union

GRAHAM WALKER & JAMES GREER

IRISH ACADEMIC PRESS

First published in 2023 by
Irish Academic Press
10 George's Street
Newbridge
Co. Kildare
Ireland
www.iap.ie

978 1 78855 817 4 (Paper)
978 1 78855 131 1 (Ebook)
978 1 78855 171 7 (PDF)

A CIP catalogue record for this book is
available from the British Library.

Typeset in Calluna 11.5/18 pt

Cover design by Fiachra McCarthy

Irish Academic Press is a member of Publishing Ireland.

Contents

Introduction

This is a study of the political relationship between Scotland and Northern Ireland, both in historical and contemporary perspective. It will attempt to show that both places have been politically, as well as culturally, entwined, even if this has often been unacknowledged and seldom explored in any depth. As the political commentator Newton Emerson has observed, it is remarkable how little Scotland features in contemporary Northern Ireland's politics, and vice versa.[1] This is remarkable given the extent to which the cultural affinities spanning the 'narrow sea', and the folk history which surrounds them, have fostered a set of assumptions about the closeness of this relationship. It was indeed an awareness of these unreflective assumptions, and the belief that they were preventing proper appreciation of the changing nature of Scottish and Northern Irish societies and the new political dynamics of the time, that led one of this book's authors to reappraise the relationship at a juncture when Northern Ireland was emerging from a quarter-century of political violence. The resulting book's title – *Intimate Strangers* – was carefully chosen to convey the paradoxical character of an historically rich and multi-layered, yet politically ambiguous, association.[2]

The present study takes stock after another quarter-century of political change, which has profoundly affected Scotland and Northern Ireland and has ensured that both places have been central to debates and speculation over the future of the United Kingdom (UK). It is a period that has also reinforced the significance of the relationship between Scotland and Northern Ireland within the broader context of the management of relationships and interactions across Britain and Ireland and 'these islands'.

This book will demonstrate that there are a number of connecting themes to be explored in an up-to-date appraisal of Scotland–Northern Ireland ties, and that these are essentially political. They include the issue of devolved government within the UK state, and in particular the way in which the Scottish and Northern Irish questions have driven the agenda of devolution and constitutional change in the UK from the 1970s. Relatedly, the sense in which British identity has been most keenly contested and intensely debated in Scotland and Northern Ireland is another theme discussed, with due reference to the upsurge in the scholarly literature in this and the wider subject area of identity politics.

In the twenty-first century, devolution provided a new context for public discussion in Scotland of old questions of religious divisions and the extent and nature of sectarianism. This was a theme that clearly brought Scotland into a frame of comparison with Northern Ireland; issues around sectarianism in Scotland have roots in Irish influences in Scottish life and have fed off the conflict in Northern Ireland. In this book it will be argued that the impact of the independence debate in Scotland has given a new twist to this phenomenon. Moreover, it will be contended that the narrowing of political preoccupations in Scotland around the constitutional question, and the contemporary language and discourse of politics between 'Unionists' and 'Nationalists', are all redolent of Northern Ireland and have brought to light political similarities long obscured.

The political landscape on which Scottish and Northern Irish issues currently play out has been re-cast by the transformative effects of 'Brexit', the decision made in a UK-wide referendum in 2016 to leave the European Union (EU). The challenges posed by Brexit and by the vote of both Scotland and Northern Ireland being at variance with the rest of the UK will be addressed. It will also be shown how the protracted negotiations between the EU and the UK since the Brexit referendum have exposed competing priorities, new fault-lines and new alliances both within and between Scotland, Northern Ireland and Westminster.

All these themes are explored against the background of the deep historical and cultural links and bonds that bring together Scotland and Northern Ireland. It is a relationship which has always been a close one culturally, but an awkward and problematic one politically. This book illuminates the complexities of the relationship and poses pertinent questions about its future in a period of intense political turbulence and uncertainty.

CHAPTER ONE

Shared History Across the Narrow Sea

I n an obituary of Ian Adamson, physician, scholar and politician, it was claimed that he regarded Ulster as 'an interface between Ireland and Scotland'.[1] Adamson's published work, moreover, had controversially advanced the theory that the original inhabitants of Ulster were a people called the 'Cruthin', who were driven out by the Gaels and took refuge in Scotland. Adamson was concerned with emphasising the antiquity of the Ulster–Scottish relationship and the ancient distinction between Ulster and the rest of Ireland, and he also contributed to scholarly deliberations on the ancient kingdom of Dalriada, which had spanned both Ulster and the outlying islands and western seaboard of Scotland.[2] A variation on Adamson's 'interface' metaphor has been provided by the literary scholar Edna Longley in her identification of Ulster, or the north of Ireland, as a 'cultural corridor, a zone where Ireland and Britain permeate one another'.[3]

Such characterisations stress the unique positioning of Ulster within the context of the British Isles, and its historic role as both contested territory and a cultural melting pot. They remind us especially of the constant interaction and traffic of peoples between Ulster and Scotland, which dates back to the earliest times, and of the singular character of a relationship scarred by wars, famines and religious friction, yet enhanced by resilience, toil and mutual bonding and support. The North Channel, as the late eminent historian Jonathan Bardon put it, was 'a conduit, a routeway where peoples and cultures constantly blended'.[4] The Presbyterian historian Finlay Holmes has written in a similar vein:

> Geography and history have combined to link the peoples of what we now call Scotland and Ireland closely together. The Mull of Kintyre, which can be seen from Ireland on a clear day, is only twelve miles from the coast of Co. Antrim. Over the centuries, the narrow channel between the two countries has been the bridge for people and ideas moving in both directions ... Thus, long before the Plantation of Ulster, Scotland and the North of Ireland were closely linked ... History and geography have combined to make Ulster as much a Scottish as an Irish province.[5]

Notwithstanding earlier Scottish settlements and conquests, such as that of the Gaelic Lord MacDonnell in the Antrim Glens, the movement of Scots into Antrim and Down in the early seventeenth century, followed by the organised settlements of both Scots and English authorised by King James I (or James VI of Scotland), formed a transformative period in the history of these islands.[6] This settlement process was itself deeply rooted in the wars, religious revolutions, social unrest, political rebellions and invasions between, and within, the three kingdoms of England, Scotland and Ireland. These conflicts placed Ireland at the centre of a broader European turmoil emanating from the Protestant Reformation and the imperial ambitions of France, Spain and England.

The plantation scheme was uneven and certainly did not result – as may have been hoped by the King – in a homogeneously loyal community of subjects. Many native Gaelic-speaking Irish remained. Religiously, too, while the planters were Protestant, and zealously so in the case of those from Scotland where the sixteenth-century Reformation had taken a Calvinist shape, the native Irish generally clung to the Catholic faith. Religious division and resentment over the loss of land produced a rebellion, in 1641, on the part of the Gaelic Irish; massacres took place and the blood of the settlers flowed. Only the arrival of help from Scotland rescued the plantation from going into reverse. The entry into Ulster of a 10,000-strong Scottish army under Robert Monro, dispatched in 1642 to stamp out the native Irish uprising and protect the Scots settlers, secured Ulster-Scot settlements; many of these soldiers themselves remained and settled. Moreover, as historian David Stevenson argues, 'Under its [Monro's army] patronage, Presbyterianism became so firmly rooted in Ulster that it proved impossible to eradicate, in spite of intermittent official hostility in the generations that followed ... and Presbyterianism was to be the main agency which preserved the Ulster-Scots as a separate interest in Ireland.'[7]

Nevertheless, there were many settlers who fled back to Scotland to escape the violence, and this was to be a feature of the remaining decades of the century: as political turbulence ebbed and flowed across the three kingdoms, people moved, out of a survival instinct, back and forth across the 'narrow sea'. In the 'killing times' of the 1670s and 1680s in Scotland, for example, many Covenanting Presbyterians, hunted by Royal forces, took refuge in Ulster.[8] As the historian of migration Bryan Fanning has argued, most emigrants and immigrants who left or came to Ireland across the centuries journeyed under circumstances that were not of their choosing; they were, moreover, supported by family members who had already come to, or left, Ireland.[9] Even more Scottish Presbyterians settled in Ulster during the political upheavals of the 1690s, so that by the end of the century there had been a demographic makeover of the province that would decisively steer the course of future relationships across the British Isles.[10]

For generations the Scots in Ulster regarded themselves as essentially a cross-channel extension of Scotland, and their descendants have not let go of a sense of Scottish identity, as the popular usage of the term 'Ulster-Scots' continues to indicate.[11] Outside of the 'official' plantation, therefore, the success and growth of Scots communities in the east of Ulster was built upon established links between the two islands. The foundation of these connections and the numerical strength of the Scots in Antrim and Down, however, was in contrast to the isolation experienced by settlers further west and south. This was reflected in Presbyterianism's later repeated willingness in these two counties to assert its own political will, contrasted with the primacy those from other areas gave to defending themselves from a position of minority insecurity.

The extent to which Ulster became a Presbyterian haven through waves of Scottish incomers troubled the hierarchy of the established Anglican Church of Ireland, as well as the Catholic

Irish. The penal laws, brought into force in 1704, infringed the civil liberties of Presbyterians as well as Catholics, prevented them from holding public office, and declared as invalid marriage sacraments conducted by the Presbyterian churches. The eighteenth century would see substantial emigration to America on the part of Ulster Presbyterians precisely on account of these disabilities and impediments, and in their new homeland they would be dubbed the 'Scotch-Irish' and embody the ethos of 'God's Frontiersmen'.[12]

In the eighteenth century there was highly significant interaction between Scotland and Ulster around education. Sons of Ulster farmers who could afford to proceed to higher learning, and were barred from Trinity College Dublin, did so at Scottish universities, particularly that of Glasgow. There, many were taught by a fellow Ulsterman, Francis Hutcheson (1694–1746), whose moral philosophy, scholarly writing and preaching has been widely praised and recognised for its catalytic effects on what became known as the 'Scottish Enlightenment' of the later eighteenth-century period. Hutcheson was a colleague of David Hume and a tutor to Adam Smith; another of his students, Francis Alison, would spread his ideas across the Atlantic at a time of political ferment which culminated in the American Revolution. Hutcheson influenced political radicalism both at home and abroad: as the historian A.T.Q. Stewart has observed, his ideas were 'startlingly modern'.[13] His opposition to slavery and support for the right of resistance to private and public tyranny, along with his development of the Lockean doctrine of contractarianism, or conditional allegiance to monarchs and governments, made him an outstanding intellectual figure. Moreover, his advocacy of governance in pursuit of the greatest happiness for the greatest number of people anticipated the contributions of later thinkers, such as Jeremy Bentham.[14]

Hutcheson's political thought was evident in the surge of radicalism in Ireland at the close of the eighteenth century. In this period in Ulster, growing Presbyterian economic power and cultural confidence had combined with popular demands for land reform and religious freedoms to create a flowering of political radicalism. Vitally, and without precedence in Irish affairs, sections of this radical opinion openly sought alliance with Catholic Ireland. It is important to note that they did so while still maintaining what they saw as the democratic and spiritual superiority of their form of Protestantism. A common refrain of Presbyterian radicals of the time was the assertion that increased liberty for all of Ireland's citizens would encourage the decline of Catholicism, which they regarded as being in opposition to the Age of Reason. Nonetheless, the radicals' support for Catholic emancipation and desire to 'unite Protestant, Catholic and Dissenter' was transformative in Ireland.[15]

Ulster Presbyterians were at the forefront intellectually, and numerically in the north, of the Society of United Irishmen, which was formed in 1791 and would launch a rebellion against British rule in 1798. Among these leaders was William Drennan, a son of one of Hutcheson's closest friends, Thomas Drennan. Other legendary figures in the Society, such as Henry and Mary Ann McCracken, had forebears who had been Covenanters in Ayrshire.[16] Echoing their American kin, a citizens' militia was to prove central to the development of the Northern radicals' conception of self-government. Initially established as defensive state-sanctioned militias in 1778 due to fears of French invasion, the Irish Volunteers evolved in the 1780s into a vehicle for radical demands and community organisation challenging the state. Through the period of this evolution, the radicalisation of the demands and the methods of the Society of United Irishmen in the 1790s, and up to the 1798 rebellion itself, the state responded with a mixture of reform and repression.

This response, allied to the increasingly radical demands of some within the movement for reform, began to divide Presbyterian opinion. When the rebellion began in May 1798 in Dublin, the response from the Ulster United Irishmen was slow and divided. The eventual June Ulster rebellion was – tellingly – essentially restricted to the Presbyterian majority areas of Antrim and Down, and it produced short-lived victories. During the rebellion, Ulster Presbyterian sympathies remained divided. A significant minority openly supported the loyalist cause, a section supported only some of the radicals' objectives, while others supported the radical platform but not violent rebellion as a means of achieving it.[17]

There was significant interaction between the United Irishmen and like-minded radical societies in Scotland in this 'Age of Revolution', and there is a suggestion that the ideals of equality before the law, challenging inherited power and seeking a government more representative of the people were carried into the Scotland of the early nineteenth century, if in muted form, by way of those who sought refuge after the rebellion was ruthlessly suppressed by the forces of a British state fearful of the spread of revolution from France.[18] Culturally we can see Ulster-Scots origins and the legacy of the rebellion entwined in the work of radical weaver poets, such as James Orr and David Herbison, who worked in the textile industry and wrote much of their verse in the Scots language of Robert Burns; they were immortalised in the twentieth century and beyond by those from a Protestant dissenting back-ground anxious to keep their spirit and memory alive.[19]

The United Irishmen's rebellion remains the most dramatic example of Protestant–Catholic unity in pursuit of a constitutional goal in modern Irish history and, as such, it has endured as an inspiration for Irish republicans in more recent times. However, the circumstances that produced the events of 1798 and the 'Protestant, Catholic and Dissenter' message of the United Irish leader Wolfe Tone need to be carefully distinguished from the very different political, cultural and religious ingredients of modern Irish nationalism from the mid-nineteenth century onwards. This national movement was the result of an Irish nationalist consciousness, effectively restricted to the Catholic community, and of grievances against governance within the new United Kingdom (following the Act of Union of 1801) that the increasingly coherent community of Protestants in Ulster did not generally share. This is not to underplay the substantial denominational and political differences between 'Dissenters' and the Church of Ireland that continued throughout the nineteenth century and beyond, especially with regard to land ownership, tenants' rights, and representation in the professions and politics, but by the Victorian era these intra-Protestant divisions increasingly became viewed by all but a minority as issues to be resolved within the framework of the Union.

In essence, the growth of the Lagan Valley as an industrial powerhouse during the nineteenth century, and the remarkable expansion of key sectors such as linen, shipbuilding and engineer-ing, came to represent an economic dividing line within Ireland and a firm basis for the further cultivation of a distinctive northern or 'Ulster' outlook. In this connection the new forms of cross-channel trade in coal, steel and iron reinforced the old Ulster–Scottish ties: Belfast and Glasgow, as Bardon has written, 'together formed a thriving commercial and industrial hub'.[20] Shipbuilding on the Clyde and in Belfast was a modern industrial reflection of the Ulster–Scottish corridor, with the narrow sea continuing to act as a bridge rather than a barrier. In detailing the dynamism and extraordinary growth of this economic hub in the years between 1890 and the First World War, the economist Sidney Pollard bluntly stated: 'It is no accident that transatlantic liners were built on the Clyde or its extension, Belfast.'[21] At its peak in 1914 this 'extension', the two shipyards of Belfast, was responsible for 8 per cent of global shipping output.[22] The broader economic development of Ulster in those years was the material foundation for the deepening of allegiances that a majority of Ulster people felt towards the Union, and also highlighted the region's role in the engine-room of British global and imperial power. In an Irish context, the religious and cultural distinctiveness of Ulster was now reinforced by uneven economic development.

One of the most significant Presbyterian ministers in nineteenth-century Ulster, the Reverend Henry Cooke, repudiated the 'Great Liberator' Daniel O'Connell's campaign for Repeal of the Union with the assertion: 'Look at Belfast and be a Repealer if you can.'[23] For Cooke, the spread of industry and manufacturing was the fruit of the Union, and his accompanying message to Protestants of all denominations to join together and defend it became increasingly influential. For many Protestants, the extent to which O'Connell's campaigns for Catholic emancipation – successfully won in 1829 – and Repeal had politicised Catholic Ireland and provided a basis for the growth of nationalist sentiment induced caution and conservatism. Despite a controversial public image and clashes with authority, the Orange Order, a Protestant fraternal organisation formed in 1795, grew into a popular movement ready to lend political support in the cause of preserving the Union. Ironically, it had opposed that Union at the outset, on account of the expectation that it would bring about immediate Catholic emancipation.

In an illuminating study of Islandmagee, County Antrim, the historian Donald Akenson charts the history of this most culturally Scottish of Ulster communities between the two political milestones of the 1798 rebellion and the Irish revolution of 1916–21. He argues that, although the community was sympathetic to the former rebellion, by the middle of the nineteenth century its orientation was decidedly towards acceptance of the Union. Like most of Ulster, Islandmagee was not calamitously affected by the Great Famine which ravaged the south and west of Ireland especially; its economy was relatively stable, there were employment and educational opportunities in nearby Belfast, and there was a collective will to preserve the integrity of its Ulster-Scots identity.[24] The community of Islandmagee is a microcosm of what was happening throughout Ulster at that time, with Presbyterian communities that had previously been antagonistic, or agnostic, towards the Union increasingly seeing their culture, security and futures through a unionist lens.

North Channel Flows: Migrations, Industry, Culture

The nineteenth and early twentieth centuries saw a continuation – on a larger scale – of the two-way movement in people between

Scotland and Ireland. Some two-thirds to three-quarters of Irish immigration into Scotland over this period was Catholic, and the most voluminous influx occurred in response to the Famine of the late 1840s. The combination of their numbers and their religion made them unwelcome in the eyes of many in Scotland, and they endured much poverty and hardship. However, much of the emigration from Ireland to Scotland in the early nineteenth century was of the largely Ulster Protestant weaving class, and substantial numbers of Protestants did go to Scotland later in the century as employment opportunities seemed more plentiful. On top of this it is important to note that the back-and-forth pattern of population of earlier times was still reflected in the seasonal migration of potato-pickers or 'tattie-howkers' from Donegal, and workers who moved from Belfast to the Clyde and vice-versa depending on shipyard orders. The Protestant Irish in general did not suffer the extremes of poverty of the Catholic Irish, but there is, nevertheless, considerable evidence of Protestant Irish poverty in Glasgow in the 1860s and 1870s, and many more of the earlier Protestant migrants had been seasonal labourers and unemployed weavers than is usually recognised.[25]

The Orange Order took root in Scotland, as in Ulster, in the aftermath of the failure of the 1798 rebellion, and seems to have been set up by Scottish soldiers returning from Ireland, where they had been instrumental in suppressing the insurrection.[26] The Order could in some areas take on the character of a support society for impoverished Irish Protestant migrants, just as in others it took on a role helping forge paternalistic links between workers and bosses.[27] Overall, however, it was a more proletarian organisation than in Ireland, where it received significant landlord patronage. It may also have been particularly significant as a rallying point for those non-Presbyterian migrants to Scotland who, if they were Episcopalian, tended to find the Scottish variant of their denomination uncongenial in its more 'high church' character.[28]

The Irish, both Catholic and Protestant, provided much labour for Scotland's industrial development, and their heavy presence in coal mining shaped the working-class culture of Lanarkshire, Ayrshire, West Lothian and Stirlingshire.[29] They brought their tribal allegiances with them and late nineteenth-century industrial Scotland witnessed periodic 'Orange and Green' disturbances in towns such as Motherwell, Coatbridge, Airdrie, Greenock and parts of Glasgow.

The impact of Scots on Ulster's flourishing industrial enterprises has only recently been examined in scholarly detail.[30] What this work highlights is the way that Scottish entrepreneurs put their stamp on these industries: the Barbour family in linen manufacture; James Mackie in engineering; William Ritchie, the founding father of Belfast shipbuilding; and the Workman family, which also became synonymous with shipping. Industrial Belfast was shaped by family connections and intermarriage between prominent Scottish and Irish business-oriented families involving a number of talented and wealthy Scots. Furthermore, these Scottish industrialists and merchants made their presence felt in the world of local politics and in bodies such as the Chamber of Commerce and Harbour Commission. The associational culture of the Scottish elite in Belfast involved substantial interaction with the host community: this was a social and cultural context that reflected Ulster's deep attachments to Scotland, which were demonstrated, for instance, in mutual celebrations of the memory of Robert Burns. These business elites and the prosperous raised the profile of the Ulster–Scottish relationship, but it should not be forgotten that there were also numerous working-class Scots attracted to Ulster on account of less costly food and accommodation. For example, Scottish women made up notable sections of the workforce in rope-working and textiles.

The Ulster–Scottish corridor also provided Belfast with Isabella Tod, the Edinburgh-born founder of the first Irish Women's Suffrage association, who moved to Ulster as a young woman. Increasingly, through the avenues of Church organisations, the voluntary sector, local government and party politics, Presbyterian women like Tod became the backbone of many social campaigns. A trailblazer for women in Irish and British public life, Tod was one of the founders of the Belfast Women's Temperance Association and campaigned for girls' access to education. Liberal in her politics, Tod was one of those who broke with the Liberal Party of William Gladstone, and she co-founded the Belfast branch of the Liberal Unionist Association in 1886. This Liberal schism emerged over the issue that was to dominate Irish and British politics for the next generation: Home Rule for Ireland. In 1887 Tod, who opposed the idea, wrote an article stressing that the history of Ireland was one of successive colonisations, and that too much attention was paid to the Plantation of the early 1600s and not enough to the 'interfusion of races', which went on before and carried on afterwards. She clearly viewed Irish nationalist arguments as reductionist in this respect, and thus likely to produce sectarian divisions which would hamper progressive change.[31]

Home Rule 'All Round' and the Presbyterianisation of Ulster Unionism

From the 1880s through to 1920, Irish Home Rule was the most contentious political issue affecting the whole of the United Kingdom.[32] It was an issue that disrupted party politics and led to realignments along the lines of support or opposition to the measure. It triggered a broad debate about the future of the UK and its constitution, encouraging intense discussion of ideas, such as 'Home Rule All Round': in effect a new 'federalised' union with devolved parliaments in each constituent nation. At the close of the twentieth century, interest in this 'federal idea' saw a revival, with the introduction of devolved administrations for Scotland, Wales and Northern Ireland.[33] However, the key questions that arose during debates over Irish Home Rule have remained pertinent right up to the present day, and the Ulster–Scottish – or Scotland–Northern Ireland – relationship has remained central to them.

Before the Home Rule controversy, politics in the north of Ireland had roughly reflected the Tory–Whig/Conservative–Liberal polarisation of the rest of the UK.[34] Liberal support among Ulster Presbyterians was substantial, although it did not quite rival Scotland, where the out-workings of the 'Great Disruption' of 1843 – the break from the Church of Scotland by those opposed to state interference in religious affairs, and their formation of the 'Free Church of Scotland' – saw dissenting energies flow in the direction of a Liberal Party that also drew much of its strength from Non-Conformists in England. However, in both Scotland and Ulster there developed, as Andrew Holmes has argued, a distinctive Presbyterian version of a Whig British identity, which asserted that British civil and religious liberty was established by John Knox in the sixteenth century, developed by the Covenanters in the seventeenth century, and confirmed by William III in the 'Glorious Revolution'.[35]

The Irish Home Rule cause was adopted by Liberal Prime Minister William Gladstone in 1885. Those throughout Ireland who were not supportive of the proposed constitutional change – 'unionists' – mobilised in opposition, and defiance was strongest in Ulster. There, a pan-Protestant front emerged in response to Gladstone's conversion to Home Rule: they depicted any such measure as presenting a perilous threat to their British citizenship, to their economic interests and to their religious freedom. They regarded the Irish nationalist movement, led so astutely by Charles Stewart Parnell, as essentially an instrument of Catholic Church power and Gaelic cultural hegemony.

Several figures from an Ulster-Scot background emerged around the Home Rule controversy to make a significant impact on the battle of ideas and arguments. Of these, perhaps Thomas Sinclair ranks highest. From a Belfast merchant family, Sinclair was representative of the largely Presbyterian business interests that were to be so vital to the construction of a broad cross-class unionist alliance comprising landlords, industrialists, merchants, farmers, agricultural labourers and industrial workers. Sinclair was instrumental in forming the Ulster Liberal Unionist Association, as was Thomas Andrews, a linen magnate and father of the Thomas of *Titanic* fame, and John Miller Andrews, future Prime Minister of Northern Ireland. For such men, their Liberal political heritage cannot be over-stressed: Sinclair and other prominent anti-Home Rule Liberals, such as Isabella Tod, had supported Gladstone's disestablishment of the Church of Ireland in 1869 and the land reform act of 1870, regarding the removal of landed privilege, the expansion of educational opportunities and improvements in living standards as moral imperatives.[36] However, at the heart of their political ideals was a devout belief in the Union, as it then stood, to deliver social and economic betterment, and protect cherished liberties. It was this ideal that Ulster Liberals like Sinclair believed Gladstone had betrayed by pursuing Irish Home Rule.

Sinclair's mentor in his student days was James McCosh, Professor of Logic and Metaphysics at Queen's College Belfast, and later President of Princeton College in the USA. McCosh was a towering intellectual figure who had been strongly influenced by the Scottish Enlightenment philosophers, who, in turn, owed a great debt, as noted previously, to Francis Hutcheson.[37] Through his links with McCosh, Sinclair can be viewed as being in a line of political and philosophical thought that connects the intellectual advances of the mid-eighteenth century to the 'Ulster Crisis' of the First World War years, and representing an essentially liberal-enlightenment cast of mind.[38]

Sinclair's concern with social problems and moral improvement constituted a form of evangelical paternalism very typical of the Victorian age, which also carried with it a concern about socialist ideas spreading to the working classes. In Ulster, socialism made tentative inroads in the late nineteenth century through the emergence of branches of the Independent Labour Party (ILP), the growth of trade unions and the efforts of local Labour pioneers, such as William Walker, Alexander Bowman and an archetypal 'Ulster Scot' Robert Smillie, who was to become famous in Scotland as the 'miners' champion'.[39] Smillie was a colleague of Keir Hardie, who founded the Scottish Labour Party in 1888, a forerunner of the ILP which took firm root in industrialised Scotland along with the North of England.[40] The ILP, indeed, can be viewed as being a connecting political strand in Ulster–Scottish relations between the 1890s and the 1920s, and central to the development of a Labour politics which was authentically pan-UK in its scope and appeal. That the 1906 Labour Party conference was held in Belfast symbolises this scope, as well as the heavily unionised and militant nature of the workforce in Belfast and the region's central place within a British industrial political economy. The life and activism of Margaret McCoubrey (1880–1956) is a further example of how Scottish–Ulster migration and ties were significant to the development of labour politics in Ulster. Born in Glasgow, McCoubrey settled in Belfast after marrying a local trade unionist and became a significant figure in Ulster's campaign for women's suffrage, a peace campaigner during the First World War, an elected Belfast Labour councillor, and General Secretary of the Ulster Co-operative movement.[41]

Returning to Thomas Sinclair, his major significance lies in the extent to which anti-Home Rule arguments came to be expressed in a particular Ulster-Scot's voice. The unionist campaign against Home Rule was a triumph of bridge-building across Protestant denominational and social class divisions and brought together the Conservative and Liberal political traditions. Yet it should be remembered that those like Sinclair from a Liberal and Presbyterian background had to work hard to convince fellow Liberals and Presbyterians in Scotland, as well as Non-Conformists in England, that Ulster was sincere in her objections to Home Rule, fearing that it would become the basis for a future Catholic ascendancy.

Their task in this respect was complicated by the support given to Home Rule by a small but vocal group of Presbyterians led by the Reverend James Armour of Ballymoney.[42]

There were in fact limits to the amount of support in Scotland, and in Britain more widely, that the unionists could achieve in respect of those for whom the Liberal cause ran deep. In 1888, two years after Gladstone's first Home Rule Bill, which was defeated in the House of Commons, the Reverend Hugh Hanna, a prominent minister in Belfast and a firebrand and controversial preacher, wrote to a Scottish friend in regretful terms that 'the half million Scottish Presbyterians in Ireland might in the crisis that had threatened them ... expect that an appeal to their kinsmen in Scotland would not be in vain – that Scotchmen owning a common ancestry and a common faith would not desert their friends in Ireland in the hour of their need.' While grateful for the support that was offered, Hanna was more concerned about the lack of it from those fellow Presbyterians who appeared to be unmoved by the Ulster appeals.[43]

Over the subsequent Home Rule dramas up to the outbreak of the First World War, the politics of 'kith and kin' turned out not to be straightforward.[44] Support for Ulster's stance was strongest among the business (and to some extent professional) elites of the west of Scotland, who were the backbone of Liberal Unionism there,[45] and those workers in industrial centres influenced by the Orange Order.[46] In rural and small-town Scotland, where Gladstonian Liberalism remained dominant and the Free Church's opposition to landed privilege was an article of faith, there was much less sympathy for a cause that could still appear to be controlled by Conservative Party priorities and driven by sectarian antagonisms. Nevertheless, it should be acknowledged that Liberal Unionists like Sinclair made every effort to stress that they had supported Catholics in the past in their struggles for equality, and they were certainly not sacrificing their long-held Liberal principles, such as support for land reform and tenant rights.[47] Sinclair also stressed his Covenanting roots and invoked the example of Scottish Presbyterians coming to their co-religionists' aid during the Irish rebellion that broke out in 1641. A charismatic Presbyterian land reformer, T.W. Russell, made an impassioned plea to a Scottish audience in 1886 using language carefully crafted to appeal to common historical ties and sacrifices: 'Three hundred years ago Ulster was peopled by Scottish settlers for State reasons. You are bound to remember this. These men are bone of your bone, flesh of your flesh. The blood of the Covenanters courses through their veins; they read the same bible, they sing the same Psalms, they have the same church polity.'[48]

The climax of Ulster's stand against Home Rule could be said to have been the mass signing of the 'Ulster Solemn League and Covenant' of 1912. This document, pledging resistance to the implementation of the Third Home Rule Act passed by the Westminster House of Commons, was modelled consciously on the Scottish National Covenants of 1638 and 1643, and can be viewed as further evidence of the 'Presbyterianisation' of the unionist campaign against Home Rule and the use of an Ulster-Scots history and cultural distinctiveness to bolster the sense of an Ulster identity constructed to confound the all-Ireland claims of Irish nationalism.[49] Sinclair, indeed, is widely credited with crafting the resonant text of the Ulster Covenant, with its stress on Home Rule's threat to 'the material well-being of Ulster', to 'our civil and religious freedom' and 'our citizenship', and its promise to band together 'throughout this our time of threatened calamity ... to defeat the present conspiracy to set up a Home Rule Parliament in Ireland'.[50] The Covenant gestured to that long history of contractarian political thought identified with the Ulster Protestant community:[51] the idea of loyalty only given on the basis of the state's protection of the community's interests and welfare. This was a disposition unappreciated in metropolitan governing circles, yet the notion of a contract or covenant has arguably been at the heart of the way the UK Union has functioned and held together over time, and is also applicable to Scotland and Scottish interpretations of the Union.[52]

As well as unionists in Ulster, the Covenant was signed by Ulster-born domiciles in Britain, with signatories in Scotland accounting for almost 60 per cent of the total outside of the province itself.[53] Support from high-profile contemporary Scottish figures, such as the novelist and politician John Buchan, helped disguise the disappointment felt over those Scots Presbyterians, mostly from the Free Church (which had been viewed as their 'sister church' by Ulster Presbyterians since its inception in 1843), who prioritised their Liberal political loyalties over those to their co-religionists. In a speech in 1912 in the Scottish Borders, Buchan referred to the Ulstermen as 'a race comprised of men of our own blood and our own creed', before proceeding to argue: 'If Home Rule Ireland is a nation, how on earth can you deny the name to the Ulster Protestants? Indeed, they have a far higher title to it. They are one blood and one creed; they have such a history behind them as any nation might be proud of.'[54]

Ulster unionists refused inclusion in a unitary Irish democracy. Their first line of argument was that the unit of democratic decision-making should be that of the UK as a whole – they claimed in 1912 that Home Rule had never been explicitly put to the electorate; however, increasingly, they felt obliged to argue their case in terms of holding distinctive democratic rights, in the manner of Buchan's reasoning, as the alternative 'nation' in Ireland. Mapping on to these respective positions were inclusive arguments on the one hand about the benefits of UK citizenship for all, and, on the other, exclusivist assertions of 'rights' for Ulster based on distinguishing ethnic characteristics, particularly that of Protestantism.[55]

Both these lines of argument were pertinent to the question of British identity. In both Ulster and Scotland, civic and ethnic conceptions of Britishness can be discerned, overlaid by perceptions of the British Empire as providing moral purpose, opportunities for religious missions, opportunities for spreading notions – perceived today as highly problematic – of 'progress' and 'civilisation', and ways of securing Britain's global 'greatness'. Scottish involvement in the Empire has been shown to have been particularly pronounced in terms of military service, employment in the colonies, missionary zeal and economic exploitation.[56] Undoubtedly, the extent to which Scots could use the Empire to make their mark internationally was, until the second half of the twentieth-century, a source of great national pride and of continuing support for the Union and the idea of a 'British' partnership that was working in all interests.

In Ulster and Scotland there were many at the outset of the twentieth century who would have believed in the idea of a cohesive

British nation, forged through the shared history of the previous three centuries. There would also have been those who viewed Britain or the UK as a composite identity uniting four different national units, albeit that the Irish one was divided within itself about the nature of the relationship to the others. However, in the pivotal era of the Irish Home Rule controversies, which gave rise to much deliberation about the constitutional character of the whole UK and its future, the Scots' sense of their identity and their 'destiny' was expansive and secure in comparison with the edginess, the defensiveness and the foreboding evinced by Ulster unionists and loyalists, however determined and defiant they were in confrontation with Irish nationalism.[57]

Irish Partition and Twentieth-century Scotland

The outbreak of the First World War placed Irish Home Rule on hold. Thousands from both unionist and nationalist backgrounds in Ireland joined up to fight. In Scotland, the recruiting figures were the most impressive, proportionately, in the whole of the UK.[58] As the war on the continent turned into an attritional slog, seismic events at home ensured a dramatically altered post-war political context.

The Easter Rising in Ireland in 1916, and the way the British government responded to it, brought about a mass movement for independence focused on the Sinn Féin party. The leaders of the rebellion who had been executed, including James Connolly, the Edinburgh-born son of Irish immigrants to Scotland, assumed the status of martyrs.[59] The War of Independence, fought between the Irish Republican Army (IRA) and war-weary British troops and undisciplined auxiliary forces, finally ceased in 1921, and a treaty was signed between the Irish representatives and the British government. The twenty-six county Irish Free State emerged the following year during a brutal civil war, which ranged those who accepted the Treaty against those who considered it a betrayal.

If the Easter Rising was viewed as a blood sacrifice for the honour of nationalist Ireland, then the thousands of Ulster Protestants, part of the 'Ulster Division' of the British Army, who perished at the Battle of the Somme a few months later, took on a similar role in popular unionist memory.[60] If nationalists raised the stakes in the post-war era, then unionists simply hardened their determination to remain within the UK and were ready to claim that their losses in the service of the crown could allow for no other fate.

The Irish question was dealt with in 1920–22 through the expedient of partition. The Government of Ireland Act of 1920 outlined a scheme for the setting-up of two 'Home Rule' or devolved parliaments in Ireland: one for a six-county northern unit, the other for the rest of the island. A Council of Ireland was also provided in the expectation that the two administrations would work together and ultimately become one, still within the UK. The 1920 Act was, in effect, another attempt to achieve Irish Home Rule. However, in the circumstances of the changed political aspirations and the turmoil of the War of Independence, such an arrangement could not be workable in nationalist Ireland. Thus, prior to the establishment of the Free State, the new 'Northern Ireland' came into being in 1921, the first example of devolution in the history of the UK. Sectarian violence, especially in the early months of 1922, scarred the new political entity's birth.[61]

The settlement of the Irish question had important political consequences for Scotland. It could be argued that it freed Scotland to develop along wider British left–right lines, to be part of a class-based political system. It made it easier for the Labour Party – which had grown during and after the war – to appeal across the Protestant–Catholic religious divide of west-central, industrial Scotland, and simultaneously constrained the Conservatives – known then and until 1965 as the 'Unionists'[62] – from making much sectarian capital out of the Irish issue and the out-workings of partition. As Labour edged aside a divided Liberal Party to become the main progressive force in British politics, it assumed the character of an urban, working-class alliance throughout Britain, and effectively a unionist party on the constitution. The socially disadvantaged Catholic community (of Irish descent) in industrial Scotland became solidly Labour on account of the party's advocacy of working-class interests and its ability to satisfy the Catholic Church that it would defend the Education Act of 1918. The latter legislation, passed by the coalition government headed by Lloyd George, provided for full state support for Catholic schools and was denounced by sections of Protestant opinion including the Orange Order, the growth of which in Scotland in the post-war years was striking.[63]

Scottish Labour had been supportive of land reform, but that issue, which had been the basis in the late nineteenth and early twentieth century for joint Scottish–Irish radicalism, saw its profile decline within the predominantly urban British political context of the 1920s onwards. In this sense there was a disconnect politically between Scotland and Ireland compared to the days of land agitators from both places, such as Michael Davitt and John Murdoch. Moreover, these notable episodes of Irish–Scottish rural radicalism had encompassed the mainly Catholic nature of the land agitation in Ireland and the mainly Calvinist crofters of Scotland.[64]

As Scotland's politics became increasingly shaped around the two-party, class-based structure of the Westminster-dominated world, much of its interaction with the new political entity of Northern Ireland was curtailed. Northern Ireland, while still represented in the House of Commons, pursued a political path centred on the continuing struggles between unionists and nationalists over the constitutional question; a local party system operated to the disadvantage of those, like the small Labour Party in the region, who sought to replicate the left–right pattern that had taken hold across the water.

This did not mean that the ethnically charged political preoccupations of Northern Ireland did not echo in Scotland. In the inter-war period, a form of popular Protestant politics did register there and bore many similarities to Ulster;[65] however, these political manoeuvres were fragmented and were kept in check by a Conservative 'Unionist' Party anxious not to be religiously confined in its appeal. Moreover, as Bruce has contended, there was little opportunity for tribal leaders in Scotland to engage in the 'pork-barrel' politics that came to characterise Northern Ireland. The governing unionists in the region had patronage resources to draw on to reward supporters that were simply not available in Scotland.[66]

It needs to be appreciated that social and cultural divisions and tensions in Scotland did not map straightforwardly onto political positions as they did in Northern Ireland, and that economic and class concerns were able to cut across sectarian appeals in a way that they would not in the six counties. Northern Ireland was cut adrift from British party politics and a 'zero-sum' Orange versus Green political culture afforded little room for secular appeals of any kind. Yet religious sectarianism in Scotland ran deep in the inter-war years, particularly in Glasgow and the west of the country, though not exclusively: an Edinburgh-based party, 'Protestant Action', chalked up some local government election successes for a brief period in the 1930s. Several historians have brought to light the anti-Irish Catholic campaign carried on by elements of the Church of Scotland and some leading public figures in this period; there was, indeed, something of a panic whipped up around perceptions of Irish Catholic immigration and its supposed effects on the country's character, values and morals.[67] In a memorandum by a health department civil servant at the Scottish Office in 1933 it was observed that 'under normal conditions an annual accession of about 2,000 immigrants from Ireland would be immaterial but with trade and industry heavily depressed, as it has been during the past ten years, even that number must have had an effect in aggravating an otherwise difficult situation'.[68] The same official then went on to add a point about immigrants who found work having 'kept others out of work', and that if they had not found work 'they have probably added to the burden of expenditure on public assistance'. Such readings of the impact of Irish immigration could, and did, feed prejudices and resentments.

Such tensions as were clearly manifest in inter-war Scotland over Irish matters were also connected to the phenomenally high rate of emigration from Scotland. As Angela McCarthy has pointed out, emigration from Scotland in this period was proportionately higher than any other European country – almost half a million Scots emigrated beyond Europe during the 1920s. In Scotland there was understandable concern about the effects of such a loss of, in most cases, skilled and young working people. McCarthy's case studies also testify to the significance of sectarian tensions in Scotland at this time: one interviewee recalled that the Irish Troubles had 'split Scotland right down the middle', while another likened the Lanarkshire steel town of Motherwell to Belfast.[69] Escaping religiously rooted animosities that clearly drew on the Irish question should form part of any explanation of the remarkable outflows of people in this era.

The economic downturn of the early part of the 1920s and the slump that hit many of Scotland's heavy industries – and those, it might be said in passing, of the newly constituted Northern Ireland – led many to emigrate and can be said to have exacerbated communal tensions that had been stoked by the spill-over of the Irish Troubles to Scotland in the 1920–22 period. This was when IRA activity in Scotland resulted in clashes with the authorities, leading in one instance to the killing of a police officer in a raid on a prisoner van in the east end of Glasgow.[70] After another shooting incident in 1920 in Bothwell, Lanarkshire, the county clerk wrote to the under-secretary of state for Scotland to say that it was the work of a group 'in sympathy with the Sinn Féin movement', who had been planning to raid a drill hall for arms.[71] Another correspondent to the under-secretary wrote in 1922 about the town of Paisley in Renfrewshire:

At the outbreak of war the young men of the Catholic religion in Paisley enlisted in greater proportion than the rest of Paisley's inhabitants; they were then apparently loyal, but their attitude has changed since the Dublin Rebellion of 1916, and while many support Collins and the Free State, De.Valera [*sic*] and his Republic have many supporters, and the majority of both sides are against the crown and constitution of this country.[72]

The impact of the Irish Troubles of the early 1920s in Scotland, and the sense in which this set the tone for the socially discordant inter-war period, has yet to be fully appreciated by historians.

Indeed, given the bleak economic context, the demoralising loss of so many people to emigration, the lingering bitterness of the Irish question, and controversies over education and mixed marriages (another echo of Ulster, where the socially divisive effects of the Catholic Church's 'Ne Temere' decree only added to sectarian strife),[73] it might be contended that Scotland actually did well to contain religious-based antagonism and to ensure that scapegoating and calls for Irish people to be sent back home were rebuffed. For every sectarian rabble-rouser there were more tolerant voices. A case in point is the constituency of Motherwell, which elected an anti-Catholic candidate to Westminster in 1923, only to reject him a year later by electing a Presbyterian minister standing for Labour, who took a stance against the fanning of sectarian flames and who held onto the seat until the different circumstances of the advent of the national government in 1931.[74] It needs to be acknowledged that the mainstream political parties in Scotland held the line in relation to defusing tensions. Maybe, too, it was Scotland's good fortune in this respect that her political development should have taken place within the broader, more capacious context of the British state; local tribal and sectarian squabbles rarely achieved any British-wide political profile or purchase.[75]

The contrast with the political conditions in Northern Ireland was stark. There, restless radical spirits felt constrained and frustrated by the rival communal imperatives, even if some – particularly writers with deep Scottish cultural affinities – kept alive the dissenting impetus of days gone by.[76] It was also a major point of contrast with Ireland – North and South – that Scotland's own 'national question' was politically muted between the wars. Although bills for a Scottish Home Rule parliament were introduced and debated at Westminster during the 1920s – and the most far-reaching of these was in the name of the Motherwell Labour victor of 1924 – they were talked out and easily defused. This spurred a small group of culturally attuned nationalists, including the poet Hugh MacDiarmid, to form the Nationalist Party of Scotland (NPS) in 1928. However, this party's independence demands were watered down to the 'Home Rule within the Empire' stance of the Scottish National Party (SNP), which came into being in 1934 after the fringe fundamentalists such as MacDiarmid had been ejected. It would only be during the Second World War and immediately afterwards that the Scottish question would make political waves, and then in the form of a campaign for devolution rather than independence.[77]

In the meantime, some, like MacDiarmid, looked to Ireland for inspiration in a spirit of Celtic solidarity. However, as Bob Purdie has demonstrated, Scottish nationalists could make little sense of the Civil War of 1922–23 in Ireland and its profound legacy for the subsequent politics of the Irish Free State. Scottish nationalist visitors to Ireland tended only to see what they wanted to see – usually a kind of romantic Gaelic idyll – and ignored the rest.[78] Again it is important to stress how Scotland's largely social class-based political odyssey was at variance with Northern Ireland, where the constitutional or 'national' question dominated politics to the virtual exclusion of everything else, and with the Irish Free State, where the politics of the national question lingered in the shadow of the Civil War and where there was a largely rural economy with no significant urban proletariat driving class politics.

The Second World War saw Northern Ireland share the experience, notably the catastrophic trauma of the Blitz by German bombers, with the rest of the UK, while the South of Ireland remained neutral. This broadened and deepened the gulf between North and South in Ireland, a development compounded by the extension to Northern Ireland of the Attlee Labour government's post-war welfare state reforms. Indeed, the combination of the UK's part in the defeat of Nazi Germany and the sense of a 'people's peace' to match the 'people's war' provided a signal boost to British identity: notions of common sacrifice rewarded with common social security tightened the bonds of Union.[79]

De Valera at Ibrox

On a Saturday afternoon in October 1948, 105,000 football fans crammed into Ibrox stadium in Glasgow for an 'Old Firm' clash between Rangers (the home team) and Celtic, a rivalry to a large extent defined since the First World War by sectarian identities and allegiances shaped by Irish political divisions.[80] Among the massive throng was none other than former Irish Taoiseach Éamon de Valera, whose Fianna Fáil party had just lost power in Southern Ireland – or 'Éire' as it was then officially called – after sixteen years in office. De Valera, an ascetic figure whose preferred form of amusement was mathematical puzzles, was reported to have left the stadium after twenty minutes of play. Clearly his attendance was a token gesture and an acknowledgement of Celtic FC's symbolic importance to the Catholics in Scotland of Irish descent, even if, ironically, it had to be on hostile territory, with 'Dev' the official guest of Rangers FC.

A veteran of the Easter Rising and the tumultuous events leading to the partition of Ireland, de Valera was in Scotland for other, political, business. It was another stop in the global tour he had embarked upon since losing office, an enterprise designed to refurbish his credentials as 'tribal chief' and the main figurehead of nationalist opposition to partition. By the time of de Valera's arrival in Scotland, a concerted anti-partition campaign – spearheaded by the Anti-Partition League (APL) formed in late 1945[81] – was in full swing; moreover, the new Irish Taoiseach, John Costello, who headed up a coalition government, had declared it his intention to break the connection with the British Commonwealth and officially change the status of the South to that of a Republic. Costello signalled this while in Canada in September, when he also arrogated to himself the title 'Prime Minister of all Ireland', 'no matter what the Irish in the North say'.[82] This was blatant populist politics and reflected, in addition to the traditional nationalist disregard for the views of Ulster unionists, a post-war climate of anti-partitionist militancy in which the various Irish political parties tried to outdo each other in their rhetoric and declared intentions. Costello at this time also expressed the consensus view of mainstream Irish nationalism that Ireland could only enter into a defence pact with western European countries when partition was abolished. With memories of Éire's neutrality in the Second World War (and de Valera's gratuitous offer of condolences over Hitler's death to the German Legation in Dublin) still niggling in

Washington and London especially, this was political brinkmanship of a notably risky kind.[83]

It backfired. Irish nationalists could not have chosen a worse time to petition governing circles in Britain and the USA. Both were well disposed at this juncture to Northern Ireland on account of the latter's involvement in the war, the sacrifices made with the rest of the Allies, the horrors of the Nazi Blitz endured, and the crucial strategic importance of Northern Ireland as a military and naval base in the conduct of the war.[84] In the wake of the Holocaust and the massive international traumas and upheavals occasioned by the war, grievances over the Irish border could, and did, appear disproportionate and self-indulgent. It hardly helped their cause that the APL was led by political figures who were anti-Semitic yet actually compared the treatment of Catholics in Northern Ireland with that of Jews in Hitler's Germany.[85]

The British Labour government of the period was certainly unresponsive to the anti-partitionist campaign and was angered by the peremptory decision to cut ties with the Commonwealth. In 1949, in order to clarify its position, the UK government passed the Ireland Act. This piece of legislation acknowledged the new Irish Republic and provided for the maintenance of citizenship rights for Irish nationals in Britain and special trading arrangements.[86] However, to the fury of nationalist Ireland, it also reinforced the position of Northern Ireland within the UK, stating that only if the Stormont Parliament so voted would the British link be broken. This represented the single greatest blow to the anti-partition campaign, coming as it did from a government in London they had fondly imagined would look favourably on their objective, given Labour's past history of support for Irish unity.

The APL had also hoped – as it turned out, in vain – that galvanising the Irish (and Irish descent) communities in British cities – whose vote was traditionally vital to Labour – would prove a winning stroke.[87] Glasgow and the surrounding area was one such key location. The APL, indeed, was very active in the area, with branches in Glasgow, Lanarkshire, Renfrewshire and Dunbartonshire. On the evening of 17 October, the day after the match at Ibrox, de Valera addressed a packed St Andrew's Hall in Glasgow, flanked, significantly, by sympathetic Glasgow Labour MPs, Alice Cullen, who represented the Gorbals, and John McGovern, who represented Shettleston. Following condemnation of the unionist government in Northern Ireland and a demand to be given back 'the natural unity of our own country', de Valera then gave notice to those in Northern Ireland – the unionist majority – that they would have to choose whether to be Irish or British, and that if they did not choose the former then, he exclaimed, 'in God's name will you go to the country that your affections lie in!'[88] What de Valera appears to have been urging, therefore, was that Ulster Protestants should get on the boat to Scotland, England or Wales and stop holding up the 'natural' process of Irish territorial unity. It may be wondered if he was not also hinting that they were undermining the ethnic – Catholic and Gaelic – homogeneity of the nation. Certainly, the APL was widely considered to have stood for both Catholic militancy and Gaelic cultural primacy.[89] Leading APL figures in the late 1940s and early 1950s also channelled the Catholic Church's condemnation of communism, as well as uttering blatantly sectarian and anti-Semitic sentiments.[90] Even in very recent and contemporary times, the idea of overpowering or in some way removing an 'alien' obstacle to Irish unity still circulates in some Irish nationalist and republican quarters.[91]

Sympathy for de Valera and anti-partitionists in general was scarce in the Scottish press of the day. *The Glasgow Herald* considered him profoundly mistaken in his apparent belief that Britain could be persuaded to initiate moves towards Irish unity. The editorial went on to point out that declaring a Republic hardly helped the nationalist objective in relation to the unionists of Northern Ireland: 'Union with Eire associated with the Commonwealth would be difficult to achieve: union with an Eire separated from the Commonwealth would be unthinkable.'[92]

The Scottish connection around the anti-partition controversies was also not neglected by Ulster unionists in their efforts to counter the APL. In September, before de Valera's visit, Prime Minister Basil Brooke gave an interview to *The Scotsman* newspaper in which he observed that 'the Scots are hardheaded, and so is the Ulsterman. He's got your blood in him.' Perhaps conscious of the way political life had developed differently in Scotland to Northern Ireland, Brooke also took pains to say that working men in Northern Ireland were 'Unionists not Tories', citing one of his cabinet ministers, the trade unionist and Labour-minded William Grant, as an example of this.[93] One week after de Valera's headline-grabbing trip to Ibrox and speech in Glasgow, a counter-demonstration was held in the city at which one Northern Ireland MP told the audience that 'your traditions are the same as ours', and another accused the Catholic Church of seeking domination over the whole island of Ireland.[94]

A visit to Scotland, some fifty years later, by de Valera's grandson, Éamon Ó Cuív, provides an interesting footnote to this episode. The political context this time was the immediate post-Good Friday Agreement period, when hopes for a permanent peace in Northern Ireland, reconciliation between Protestant and Catholic communities, and imaginative interconnections and co-operation across 'these islands' were high. Ó Cuív was a guest of a Scottish Office minister, Labour's Calum Macdonald, and both spoke enthusiastically about the historical and cultural links between Scotland and Ireland. Macdonald, a Presbyterian Gaelic speaker from the Western Isles, was well positioned to voice the expansive temper of the times: 'We in Scotland feel acutely the pain of Northern Ireland since so many Scots have strong links on both sides of the historical divide. As Gaels, we have natural affinity with the Irish dimension, while as Scots, many have links with the Protestant and Unionist community.' 'It is essential', Macdonald continued, 'the new political announcements are founded on respect for people of different traditions.'[95]

At the *fin de siècle* moment of this later 'de Valera' visit to Scotland, there was genuine openness towards a new era of relationships between the different parts of these islands, in particular Scotland's relationship with both parts of Ireland. It appeared that new alignments were in the offing, that old cultural affinities were being rediscovered and reactivated in a new atmosphere of political tolerance and co-operation. The UK was decentralising and embarking on a new age of devolution, while an historic conflict in Northern Ireland appeared to be ending. It seemed a world away from the time 'Dev' took his seat at Ibrox for the 'Orange versus Green' sporting echo of the Irish question in Scotland and thought about his address to his 'tribe' the following day.

CHAPTER TWO

Scotland, Northern Ireland and Devolution

In a recent scholarly intervention in the debate around 'Brexit' and the UK's departure from the EU, the historian David Reynolds made reference to what he called the 'Pocock Principle'. Drawing upon the seminal work of historian J.G.A. Pocock, Reynolds defined this as the contention 'that the four countries of the UK have not only acted individually to create the conditions of their separate existences but, by their interactions, have also modified the conditions of each other's existence'.[1] The point about modifying interactions is best illustrated in a political sense through scrutiny of arguments for and against constitutional change in the UK. These arguments have a long and, at times, tortuous history, and Home Rule, or devolution as it came to be called, has been the main organising theme since the late nineteenth century. In turn, debates over devolution have overwhelmingly been given impetus and direction by either Irish or Scottish concerns.[2]

The UK polity has developed out of a series of unions, most notably the Anglo-Scottish Union of 1707 and the British–Irish

Union of 1800. The Irish dimension to the UK was reduced, in 1922, to that of the political entity of Northern Ireland, a construction defined in legal terms by the Government of Ireland Act of 1920. Northern Ireland, from June 1921, constituted the first example of devolution within the UK. Although the fashioning of Northern Ireland was largely the result of the wish of British statesmen to remove the 'Irish Question' from British politics, the Irish dimension to the UK in the form of the new Northern Ireland was to prove enduringly significant as constitutional matters periodically re-emerged in political discourse. Meanwhile from the 1960s there has been a restlessness surrounding questions of the stability, durability and future of the UK Union to which Scotland has been central.

The UK, in a manner of speaking, has been a singularly pluralist union. A common term to describe it for many scholars and politicians over recent decades is 'Union State', a usage derived from the conceptual work of political scientists.[3] The term is meant to signal the substantial extent to which, in the UK, integration has been less than complete, and that pre-Union rights and institutional infrastructures survived to preserve varying degrees of national and regional autonomy. 'Union State' indicates that the UK encompasses a great deal of administrative, institutional and, since the turn of the twenty-first century, governmental diversity. 'Union State', or 'State of Unions' or 'plurinational Union' as preferred by some scholars,[4] is certainly more appropriate for the UK than the label most often attached during the twentieth century, namely 'Unitary State'. This last term has been misleading in its suggestion of a level of integration and administrative and institutional uniformity that has not been the case in reality.[5]

The 'Union State' concept alerts us to the way that Scotland's place in the UK has been accompanied by the retention – since 1707 – of distinctive national institutions: the law, the education system and the established Presbyterian Church. From 1885 Scottish distinctiveness was further accentuated by the creation of the Scottish Office, and during the twentieth century the Scottish Office's role was expanded to the point where Scotland was said to enjoy a system of 'administrative devolution'. One Scottish academic wrote a landmark study prior to the radical devolutionary reforms of the British Labour government in the late 1990s, suggesting that Scotland enjoyed more effective autonomy than some regional governments of federal states such as Germany.[6] Another scholar, Bernard Crick, went as far as to say that the UK during the twentieth century operated along the lines of 'de facto' federalism.[7]

The 'Wicked Issues' of Devolution

When, on taking office in 1886, William Gladstone embarked on his quest to deliver Home Rule for Ireland, he instigated a wave of debate and discussion over constitutional arrangements for the UK that still resonates in the early twenty-first century. Home Rule meant an Irish legislative body with powers over a range of domestic responsibilities. To borrow from the definition of devolution set out by British constitutional academic Vernon Bogdanor, it involved the transfer to a subordinate elected body on a geographical basis of functions then exercised by the Westminster parliament.[8] Technically, therefore, Home Rule or devolution is not federalism in the strict sense of supreme power being divided and shared. Nevertheless, the term 'federal' came to be loosely used in the arguments for and against constitutional change which occupied so much political attention in the late nineteenth- and early twentieth-century period. More specifically, the 'federal idea' invaded political discourse in this era around arguments for the extension of the Home Rule principle to the other national components of the UK, namely England, Scotland and Wales.[9]

'Home Rule All Round', as it was to become colloquially known, would have meant parliaments or elected assemblies for the four national parts of the UK with an 'Imperial' parliament at Westminster dealing with issues of foreign affairs and defence. In this era, such responsibilities would have focused to a great extent on the management of the Empire, a concern very much at the forefront of British political life. Those in favour of a constitutional shake-up along the lines of 'Home Rule All Round' argued that removing the burden of dealing with so much domestic legislation from Westminster would lead to greater governmental efficiency at home on the one hand, and, on the other, more time and freedom to devote to the Empire and foreign affairs in general. Moreover, it was the reformers' belief that such change would better recognise the essential multinational character of the state: it would resolve the Irish question and modernise the entire UK into the bargain.

Gladstone's motivation was to 'pacify Ireland', but his pursuit of Irish Home Rule proved to be the catalyst for a political debate about a much grander project. Indeed, as Alvin Jackson has argued, his vision has remained influential and relevant right up to the present day: 'He devised a constitutional proposition which still has importance – the paradox that the United Kingdom could best be sustained through devolution.'[10] It has thus become commonplace to think of the Blair government's constitutional changes of the late twentieth century in terms of bringing the 'Gladstonian' vision of the late nineteenth century to fruition.

If we can use 'Gladstonian' as a form of shorthand for a conceptualisation of the UK in the form of a 'Union State', then we might equally take 'Diceyan', from the constitutional lawyer and thinker Albert Venn Dicey, as a synonym for the 'Unitary State' strand of political thinking of the Home Rule era of the late nineteenth and early twentieth centuries that was to exert a similarly enduring influence on the future as its Gladstonian counterpart. Dicey supplied the core arguments against Irish Home Rule and any extension of the devolution principle to other parts of the UK. Irish Home Rule and subsequent 'federalisation' of the UK, he contended, would destroy the sovereignty of parliament – the doctrine underpinning the constitution.[11] For Dicey and the constitutional conservatives, both his contemporaries and their later counterparts, any such devolutionary or 'federal' tinkering would weaken the unity of the UK and lead to friction between the parliaments. Their conception of the state was that of a unitariness forged over two centuries. Moreover, in the eyes of the 'Diceyans', Home Rule for the constituent parts of the UK would send a dangerous signal to the Empire that Britain no longer had the appetite for strong central governance and global leadership.

These rival 'Gladstonian' and 'Diceyan' concepts of the UK shaped debates of a constitutional nature from the late nineteenth century onwards. However, Irish Home Rule itself posed some difficult questions about the workability of devolution that have also proved long-lasting. These so-called 'wicked issues' have related primarily to representation and finance,[12] although the question of the accommodation and treatment of minorities – which was so problematic in the Irish case – can be regarded as another.[13]

The representation issue boiled down to the creation of a potential anomaly in the event of devolution being granted to one part of the UK, as Gladstone wished to do in relation to Ireland, even if this might only be a first step towards a more radical decentralisation of power throughout the UK. The question arose as to whether, in the event of a parliament being set up in Dublin for domestic matters, Irish MPs would still sit at Westminster and, if so, would they be able to vote on issues which had been devolved to Ireland but not to the rest of the UK? Gladstone had actually opted to remove Irish representation at Westminster in his first Home Rule Bill, introduced in 1886 and defeated in the House of Commons. However, he took the opposite course in his second Bill, introduced in 1893 and eventually rejected by the House of Lords, and provided for their retention. The latter decision was taken on the basis of Irish objections that the main taxation powers would still rest in London and that the principle of 'no taxation without representation' should be adhered to.

However, even if Irish MPs were still able to take their seats, should they be able to vote on non-Irish affairs? This question has echoed through the decades any time devolved government has raised its head: it was to manifest itself in relation to the arrangements for Northern Ireland as a separate political entity from 1921 until 1972, and it was to be bitterly fought over in the context of parliamentary and public debates surrounding proposed schemes of devolution for Scotland and Wales during the 1970s. Indeed, it was in this decade that the matter was popularly termed 'The West Lothian Question' in acknowledgement of the untiring efforts to raise and forensically scrutinise it on the part of the Labour MP for that constituency, the fiercely anti-devolutionist Tam Dalyell.[14]

In relation to finance, questions surrounding the calculation of an 'Imperial Contribution' to be made by Ireland following Home Rule, and the estimation of her likely tax revenues, bedevilled Gladstone's schemes and foreshadowed the problems that would arise when Northern Ireland was finally given devolved powers. Financial matters were always bound to be the most fraught set of issues pertaining to relations between central government and a devolved territory. Indeed, arguments about fiscal autonomy and block grants would characterise the way devolution impacted British politics in the late twentieth century, particularly in respect of Scotland.[15]

There was a significant Scottish dimension to the debates over constitutional change that were such a feature of the late nineteenth- and early twentieth-century period. The separate Scottish Office was established in 1885, primarily to address complaints that Scottish business was not being dealt with adequately by the Home Office, but it also reflected the timeless sensitivities on the part of many Scots about the Union as a partnership and not an English takeover. There were those who wished to go further and agitate for Scottish Home Rule – an association was set up in 1886 for this purpose – although this was to be strictly in the context of 'Home Rule All Round' and for the overall strengthening of the UK Union.[16] Scottish Home Rulers were somewhat jealous of the attention given to Ireland in this period and could also feel resentful about the proportionately greater representation of Irish MPs compared to Scottish MPs in the House of Commons. In the event, the Scottish case was consistently overshadowed by the Irish one, from the political turmoil caused by Gladstone's bills to the threats of civil war and rebellion in Ulster in response to the third Irish measure introduced by Asquith's Liberal government in 1912. The 'Ulster Crisis' in fact stimulated another bout of the 'Home Rule All Round' debate, which featured particularly significant contributions from Frederick Scott Oliver, a Scottish patriot, Empire enthusiast and unionist.[17] At the core of these arguments was the contention that the Irish question in all its complexity could be resolved while 'federalising' the whole UK. In addition, the 'wicked issues' of representation and finance that had been highlighted by the Irish Home Rule bills could be tidied up by a more comprehensive scheme. A measure for Scottish self-government did make progress through the House of Commons the following year, but it ultimately fell victim to the coming of war.

Essentially, political priorities in this period were constructed around the much more intense pressure applied by the Irish demands, and the extent to which a Home Rule measure was deemed necessary to defuse a growing separatist nationalism that had no counterpart at this time in Scotland. Scottish concerns were focused on acquiring what they thought their national status and identity entitled them to within the Union. National feeling in Ireland was in general much less influenced by notions of partnership; rather, there was a pronounced sense of their national identity having been suppressed and disparaged. However, Ireland also involved the Protestant community concentrated in Ulster, whose opposition to Home Rule had been clearly evident from 1886 and whose determination to resist following the removal of the House of Lords veto in the Parliament Act of 1911 looked set to trigger a constitutional and societal crisis until the outbreak of the First World War placed all such matters on hold. Even when deliberations on Home Rule for everyone resumed at the end of the war – a Speaker's conference involving parliamentarians and civil servants took place in 1919[18] – resolving the Irish question still took precedence. It may also have been the case that the political violence and upheaval which accompanied the partition of Ireland and the setting up of Northern Ireland as a devolved part of the UK and the Irish Free State as a dominion somewhat discouraged the Scots from addressing matters of radical constitutional reform in the ensuing years.

It should, nonetheless, be noted that Scottish Home Rule Bills were a feature of successive parliamentary sessions in the 1920s. These were introduced by Scottish Labour MPs, Labour having inherited the mantle of the pro-Home Rule cause from the Liberals. However, it quickly became clear that, notwithstanding the strong self-government sentiments espoused by compelling political figures such as James Maxton – a 'Red Clydesider' who served as chairman of the ILP for a number of years – the Labour leadership (in a national sense) was more attracted to the developing two-party competition with the Conservatives within a unitary British political framework. Labour's leader, and first prime minister during 1924, Ramsay MacDonald, typified this change of course. In 1924, while Labour was in power as a minority government, a bill proposing Home Rule for Scotland within a federal Britain was introduced and debated but failed to pass due to opponents wasting parliamentary time. Many Scottish Labour MPs were furious at the stymying tactics of opponents, but MacDonald was untroubled.[19] In 1927 an attempt was made to drive through a measure providing for Dominion Status for

Scotland and the withdrawal of Scottish MPs from Westminster. These bold moves were too much even for most Scottish Labour members, and the bill met the same fate as the earlier measure. Agitation for Scottish self-government from this point to the end of the Second World War was largely confined to various small cultural groups and individual mavericks, and to the National Party of Scotland, which came into being as a result of disillusionment with Labour and parliamentary tactics in 1928, and the SNP that effectively subsumed and succeeded it in 1934.[20]

Northern Ireland: The UK's First Example of Devolution

The Government of Ireland Act of 1920 was in effect a fourth Irish Home Rule scheme. It was drawn up to provide two devolved parliaments in Ireland – one for a six-county Northern unit, and one for the rest of the country. It also provided for a Council of Ireland through which both devolved administrations could work together on issues of common concern leading, in time, to the two merging into one devolved parliament and government for Ireland within the UK. The scheme thus involved a dynamic towards unity: partition was intended to be temporary. Fiscal powers of a very limited nature were granted by the Act in the expectation that more could be devolved as North and South worked in harmony. Moreover, the 'federal' thinking which had infiltrated debate over the Irish question was alive in the 1920 Act and was reflected in the views of the chairman of the committee which framed its provisions, Walter Long.[21] The Act was intended to produce an example of devolution at work, between historic foes to boot, that would commend itself to the rest of the UK and bring similar developments in the shape of parliaments for England, Scotland and Wales. The 'Home Rule All

Round' arguments of the era since the 1880s were thus brought to bear at a critical constitutional juncture.

Nevertheless, the visionary intentions of the 1920 Act were to be frustrated. The parliament meant for Dublin stood no chance of being established in view of the transformation in the public mood following the 1916 Easter Rising, and in the context of the War of Independence in the South between 1919 and 1921. 'Home Rule' as a cause was dying out by the time of the 1918 general election, which resulted in an overwhelming endorsement in the majority of Ireland of the separatism of Sinn Féin. The Council of Ireland, despite Northern willingness to make it work, never sat. The Anglo-Irish Treaty of December 1921 marked a new form of settlement for the twenty-six county South in the form of an Irish Free State with Dominion Status.

This left the new political entity of 'Northern Ireland' as the sole outcome of the original project. Instead of being a precursor to the 'federalising' of the UK, Northern Ireland was to take on the character of a constitutional anomaly: a territory with a distinctive legislature, executive and party system, yet still represented in the House of Commons and very much a part of broad UK calculations around government expenditure and international and foreign policy matters. Northern Ireland thus brought to the fore the 'wicked issues' that had arisen previously out of the prospect of Irish Home Rule proceeding on its own as a separate constitutional measure.

While Northern Ireland continued to send MPs to Westminster, the twelve members, plus one representing the Queen's University 'constituency', was significantly short of the number the new entity was entitled to on the basis of population.[22] It was later argued, by Northern Ireland's Prime Minister Terence O'Neill among others, that the lower number of MPs represented a 'trade off' for Northern Ireland possessing its own devolved institutions and powers, and it therefore provided a constitutional precedent to be followed, as indeed it was in the case of Scotland shortly after the devolutionary measures adopted there at the end of the twentieth century. However, following the curtailing of devolution amidst the political turmoil of the late 1970s in Northern Ireland, its allotment of MPs was increased to seventeen.[23]

Perhaps even more important in respect of constitutional convention, the question arose, as devolution began to be put into practice, of whether the thirteen Northern Ireland MPs would be allowed to vote on issues pertaining to the rest of the UK. Given the small numbers involved, this did not seem at the time to present a major anomaly and the MPs' voting rights were not in any way curbed or limited. Indeed, it was seen as part of the 'bargain' reached in the context of Northern Ireland being in a semi-detached political condition. Nonetheless, the matter did make political waves in the 1960s, when Harold Wilson's Labour government had a perilously small overall majority and the Ulster Unionist MPs voted habitually with the Conservative opposition; the question was a 'West Belfast' one before it became a 'West Lothian' one in the 1970s parliamentary dramas.[24]

The emergence of this issue in the 1960s also brought into the light the 'gentleman's agreement', reached as early as 1922, that devolved Northern Ireland business would not be discussed at Westminster. This was a convention that inhibited interventions from the centre that might have been justified on the grounds of upholding the spirit of the 1920 Act around the fair treatment of all sections of Northern Irish society. Such was the reluctance of the British political parties to become involved in Irish affairs after partition that self-interest could be said to have trumped the common good of the UK as a polity, and Northern Ireland's devolution experiment was tarnished by discriminatory practices against the Catholic and nationalist minority, particularly by unionist-controlled local councils with whose business the Northern Ireland government was always in turn unwilling to interfere. These varieties of governmental neglect and disconnect underlay the problem of communal division in Northern Ireland over national allegiance and ethno-religious identity.

Financial matters also brought to light questions of political choices and priorities with implications for UK devolution more broadly. The Government of Ireland Act, designed as has been stressed for a very different outcome, left Northern Ireland in control of only a number of minor taxes, with the major ones, such as customs and excise and income tax, being reserved to the central Exchequer in London, which then decided on the new entity's share. Out of both 'transferred' and 'reserved' tax revenues, Northern Ireland was expected to finance its services and, on top, pay the 'Imperial Contribution', which had been part of the original Irish Home Rule plans. These terms had been drawn up at a time when the heavy export industries of the Lagan Valley region were flourishing; however, boom gave way to slump in the early 1920s and mass unemployment ensued. The Northern Ireland government thus faced the prospect of having to honour unemployment insurance claims, as well as maintaining a level of other welfare benefits, such as health insurance and old-age pensions, in line with the rest of the UK. To do so under the constraints it inherited would have led to bankruptcy. In addition, Northern Ireland came into being against a backdrop of political instability and sectarian violence. As a result, security costs were high, but again the new entity was expected to pay these costs out of its own tax intake. For example, when the Labour government was in office in 1924 it refused to pay the costs of the supplementary police force, the Ulster Special Constabulary, the continuance of which the Northern Ireland government deemed essential to the state's security; this was notwithstanding the extent to which the 'Specials' had contributed to the sectarian outrages of the 1921–22 period, when disorder was at its peak and the viability of the new state was in jeopardy. Uncertainty about Northern Ireland's survival had also fed off the prospect of a Boundary Commission, written into the Treaty of 1921 that produced the Irish Free State. If any significant revisions were suggested by this commission to the border between North and South, it could further undermine the Northern state economically and call into question its capacity to function.

The Unionist government elected in 1921 and led by James Craig, took the view that London was obliged to put the devolved arrangements that it had contrived for its own ends onto an even keel. Although there were those in governmental circles in Belfast who were inclined to regard their relationship with the centre in a federal spirit, and who were acutely conscious of London's wish to be rid of troublesome Irish matters of whatever kind, Craig and the bulk of his cabinet were determined to fight for what they viewed as their British citizenship entitlements. Central to this stance was a pragmatic recognition of the need for the Unionist Party to be able to reassure its working-class supporters that they would not be treated unfairly relative to their counterparts across the water.

This was politically imperative for Ulster unionism in order to retain its cross-class, expansive character as a movement, which was so evident in the fight against Irish Home Rule and which was viewed as equally vital to ensuring that Northern Ireland would remain part of the UK.[25]

In the event, the Northern Ireland government persuaded London to revisit the devolution financial settlement. An arbitration process concluded in 1925, recasting the 'Imperial Contribution' as a final rather than a first charge on the Northern Ireland Exchequer; moreover, agreement was reached to integrate Northern Ireland into the UK unemployment insurance fund.[26] These changes were reinforced by further agreements in 1938 and 1946, which had the effect of shifting the financial basis of Northern Ireland from being 'revenue-based' to being 'expenditure-based' – in other words increasingly reliant on subventions from the centre. Writing in 1950, a former senior civil servant in the Northern Ireland Ministry of Finance remarked that 'the parliament of Northern Ireland stands on foundations whose supports it has itself gradually knocked away', and icily claimed that 'Northern Ireland is in many aspects converted into a new brand of Crown colony though it maintains the state and trappings of an independent legislature.'[27] A distinguished scholar of devolution was to comment much later that 'Northern Ireland was created with the forms of tax devolution but the reality of utter dependency.'[28]

Such jaundiced appraisals of the Northern Ireland experience of devolution have shaped much of the historical analysis of the region and have led to a tendency among scholars to disregard, or marginalise, Northern Ireland as a freakish exception in discussions of devolution more broadly. Many have been persuaded that there has been little of value to learn from the example of Northern Ireland. Yet, as the deliberations of the Royal Commission on the Constitution (1968–73) – the 'Kilbrandon Commission' as it became known – made clear, there was much in the Northern Ireland experience, particularly around financial arrangements, that was to have relevance for devolution for Scotland and Wales. For example, the recommendation of this Commission (at least in the majority report) that devolved assemblies for both places should be funded by a block grant and be 'expenditure-based' was influenced by the Stormont (Northern Ireland parliament) precedent.[29]

By adopting a 'step by step' policy of alignment with the rest of the UK in the area of welfare benefits and citizenship entitlements, Craig and his government were insisting on the right of Northern Ireland still to be part of the broader UK 'pool' when it came to the sharing of resources and assistance. Craig argued that Northern Ireland still had the right to be treated in the manner of other parts of the UK that were suffering economically. This indeed was the 'social insurance' aspect to the UK Union highlighted by academics and commentators.[30] Indeed, the Northern Ireland case can be linked to the much later debate in Scotland during the independence referendum of 2014, when the former Labour Prime Minister Gordon Brown made a telling intervention in the campaign around this very idea of the 'pooling and sharing' of resources as the hallmark of a socially progressive Union. Donald Dewar, who was responsible for the legislation which brought a Scottish parliament into being and who became Scotland's first 'First Minister' in 1999, commented approvingly in 1970 about how taxation and state services in Northern Ireland 'kept in step' with the rest of Britain.[31] Critical commentaries about Northern Ireland being a 'drain' on the British public purse fail to appreciate how the UK has worked as a broad multi-national construct to 'pool and share' and redistribute resources to meet social and economic challenges. A Royal Commission on Scottish Affairs conducted between 1952 and 1954 made clear the advantage Scotland possessed relative to England and Wales regarding expenditure on domestic services.[32]

The Craig governments – and those of his successors through to O'Neill in the 1960s – used the constitutional arrangements unionists had been given primarily to affirm Northern Ireland's place in the Union. Hence the emphasis on a 'step by step' approach in relation to social services as a means of minimising the disjunctive effects of devolution, namely the detachment of Northern Ireland politically from Westminster (despite the thirteen MPs) and from the British party system. (None of the mainstream British parties, Conservative, Labour or Liberal, organised or stood for election in Northern Ireland.) The significance of 'step by step' was, indeed, heightened in the post-Second World War era, when Northern Ireland shared in the Labour government's welfare state measures, including family allowances and the establishment of the National Health Service. The implementation of such measures further tied Northern Ireland into the UK even in a period when it was a devolutionary outlier.

Post-war Scotland and Devolution Questions

In a political sense, the setting-up of devolved structures in Northern Ireland had the effect of distancing it from Scotland, along with the rest of Britain, for decades, although there were clear echoes of Ulster's sectarian divisions in inter-war Scotland.[33]

It wasn't until the post-Second World War years that Scottish attention turned to the Northern Ireland experience of devolution and the question of whether it was a model worth emulating.

By the outbreak of the war in 1939, the 'administrative devolution' arrangements in Scotland had significantly expanded. The Minister for Scotland, created back in 1892 following the Scottish Office's establishment, was upgraded to the full rank of Secretary of State for Scotland in 1926. Government business pertaining to Scotland was increasingly carried on in Edinburgh rather than London, and a strong sense among officials of fighting Scotland's corner soon became apparent. Such developments, it might also be noted, were driven in particular during the 1930s by a Conservative Secretary of State, Walter Elliott.[34] Indeed Elliott typified the care taken by the 'Unionists', as they were popularly called in Scotland, to acknowledge national identity feelings and observe the partnership spirit of the Union.

Scottish interests were thus spoken for in the Cabinet, unlike Northern Ireland's, and if the Secretary of State was a skilled political operator, a strong argument could be made for the benefits of the system for Scotland. In the Second World War, albeit in those emergency conditions, the redoubtable Tom Johnston, a Labour politician, used the levers at his disposal to deliver a range of progressive measures and to trial innovations, as in the field of public health provision, with fruitful consequences for the future.[35] In the 1960s another Labour Secretary of State, Willie Ross, also showed what shrewd bargaining at the top table might achieve, this time in areas such as new industrial investment.[36]

On the other hand, few secretaries of state possessed the skill sets of Johnston and Ross, and several failed to cope with the wide range of responsibilities that were attached to the office. Further-more, although the Scottish Office represented a distinct pattern of administration and could function effectively as a pressure group within the wider British system, there were also clear limits to its powers and influence. Crucially, it carried no significant financial clout and was ultimately dependent on Treasury decisions. Perhaps, above all, the administrative devolution possessed by Scotland lacked visibility: policy was debated and decided on behind closed doors and unelected civil servants were in effect given licence to do what they thought was good for the people. This factor of the lack of democratic accountability was a hardy annual of critics of the system, and a key reason why demands for a Scottish parliament resurfaced after the war, and again – with even greater political impact – in the 1960s and 1970s.

While the collective sacrifices of the Second World War years undoubtedly fortified feelings of British identification and overall allegiance, fears of a distinctive Scottish identity being threatened by the centralising impulse of the Labour government after 1945 saw an upsurge in popular Home Rule agitation. In 1947 a cross-party body, the Scottish National Assembly (SNA), emerged, which later organised the signing of a covenant in favour of a Scottish parliament with tax-raising power. This covenant was said to have acquired over two million signatures.[37]

The covenant movement did not shy away from citing Northern Ireland and Stormont as an example to follow, if in a general rather than a precise fashion.[38] Delegations were sent to Belfast to meet government ministers, and a plebiscite was organised in 1949 in Kirriemuir in the east of Scotland, the outcome of which was an emphatic vote in favour of 'a Parliament like that of Northern

Ireland'. Scottish newspapers produced articles examining various features of the Stormont system and generally concluded that devolution had been a success: 'What Ulster can make work so can we in Scotland' ran the headline of one high-circulation paper. To an important extent, the loyalist outlook of the majority in Northern Ireland was appreciated in Scotland, as was its contribution to the war effort. Public opinion in Scotland – if the press is taken as a guide – seemed to see no tension between a degree of self-government and a broader British affiliation. The monarchy was perhaps as revered in Scotland at this time as it was by the unionist community in Northern Ireland.

Such was the impact of the Covenant and the stirrings of Home Rule sentiment that officials in the Scottish Office got to work on briefing papers on how devolution had worked in Northern Ireland. These papers, not surprisingly, highlighted the tortuous development of financial relations between London and Belfast, and the implications of the new era of the welfare state, with its range of expensive social security services, for any Scottish scheme which sought to follow the Stormont precedent. The Labour government in London indeed saw demands for Scottish devolution as a serious inconvenience. There was an unduly fearful perception, at least at this juncture, of them being driven by nationalism, as well as reservations over the potential disruption to the government's mission to deliver social progress and fairness for the working class throughout Britain. The government did not want Northern Ireland's arrangements reproduced for Scotland, and the Scottish Secretary of State at the time, Arthur Woodburn, focused on strengthening the existing administrative devolution arrangements, including an extension to the remit of the Scottish

Grand Committee.[39] By the early 1950s, as the welfare state provisions bedded in and Britain stepped out of the shadows of wartime deprivation, the steam effectively evaporated from the Scottish Home Rule movement.

However, this post-war devolutionary episode brought Scotland and Northern Ireland together in government policy deliberations, and – to an extent – in public debates about the shape of the UK and the Union in the new post-war world. The Labour government clearly considered further devolution within the UK to be at odds with its plans for social reconstruction, notwithstanding those in the party in Scotland who were part of the broad-based movement for change. Perhaps opportunistically, the unionists in Scotland flirted with Home Rule in this era, with warnings about Labour's central planning leaving no scope for Scottish self-expression.[40] And it was also the case that Labour feared the loss of Scottish seats at Westminster in the event of a Scottish parliament, leading to the chances of the party winning power in the future being significantly reduced. Devolution for Scotland, as an inquiry into Scottish finances in 1952 was to indicate, would likely have been beset by difficulties around the granting of taxation powers and the maintenance of social welfare payments in the manner of Northern Ireland from the outset. Scotland, too, benefited substantially from state subventions and redistribution of revenues, and shared with Northern Ireland the problems that over-reliance on a heavy export-oriented economic base would soon bring.

As there were unionists in Scotland prepared to entertain a parliament for Scotland in the context of a centralist-minded Labour government, so too in Northern Ireland there were unionists who advocated greater autonomy for their parliament, even, in the case of some, to the point of support for a form of Dominion Status. The ruling Unionist Party was in fact preoccupied with the matter in the post-war years, before fears of a Labour government being antagonistic to Ulster's position in the Union were largely removed by the Ireland Act passed at Westminster in 1949. This measure, drawn up as a response to the South's declaration of a republic and withdrawal from the Commonwealth, appeared to give reassurance to unionists in its stipulation that Northern Ireland would remain part of the UK unless the Stormont Parliament voted otherwise. In retrospect, the 1949 Act, and this its most quoted clause, need to be seen as of a piece with the Labour government's desire to close down any wider discussion of devolution and constitutional tinkering, and to prevent further deliberation about Northern Ireland's system of government, despite much backbench pressure to do so over matters of discrimination against the minority nationalist community.[41] Thus the constitutional convention of 1922 was adhered to, and the Ulster unionists permitted, with grave long-term consequences, to retain such outdated practices as the property-based ratepayer local government franchise.

Nevertheless, a number of academic studies of the Northern Ireland devolution experiment appeared in the 1950s, and most were concerned to draw lessons for the possibility of Scotland following in the region's footsteps.[42] Some took the view that Stormont offered a hopeful precedent, while others, including the constitutional legal expert F.H. Newark, who was later to sit on the Royal Commission set up in the late 1960s, counselled caution and were inclined to argue that devolution had made little difference to people's lives. In a review of a landmark collection of scholarly essays on the Northern Ireland experience, former

Scottish Secretary of State Arthur Woodburn contended that the Ulster system had been 'a doubtful privilege economically', and suggested that Northern Ireland, like Scotland, should be content with devolution of administrative functions.[43]

The End of the Old Stormont and the Failure of 1970s British Devolution

Constitutional matters and questions about the future of the UK re-entered the political sphere emphatically in the late 1960s. An apparent upsurge in Scottish and Welsh nationalism produced dramatic by-election victories for the Plaid Cymru party in Wales in 1966 and the SNP in 1967. Economic factors and protest votes may have been the main reasons for these results, but there was also a sense of the Union coming unstuck. This has been linked in various analyses to the loss of empire, but this factor was probably peripheral.[44] Social and cultural changes in Britain, involving the weakening of traditional institutions and values, seem to have contributed more heavily to the restless mood that was so emblematic of the era globally.[45]

The Labour government at Westminster, in office from 1964, felt less confident than its post-war predecessors about simply staring down apparent constitutional dangers. The government was also acutely aware that its strength in Scotland and Wales was instrumental in its ability to win power. In 1968, therefore, it appointed a Royal Commission, under the chairmanship of Lord Crowther, to inquire into the possibilities of constitutional reforms, in particular devolution for Scotland and Wales. The Commission, steered to its final report in 1973 by Lord Kilbrandon, has an important place in late twentieth-century political history.

The organisation of the Commission's remit coincided with the outbreak of serious disturbances in Northern Ireland around civil rights protests. It was decided to involve Northern Ireland in the commission's deliberations, and the Ulster Premier Terence O'Neill was even permitted to alter the terms of reference. Clearly, it was felt that the one existing example of devolution could not be omitted from an inquiry whose main focus was devolution. As a Home Office official put it in correspondence with O'Neill:

> It is not simply that the divisions of responsibility between our Parliaments and governments [have] been the subject of a good deal of questioning here and that the unique constitutional pattern set up by the 1920 Act must clearly be in the greatest interest in such an inquiry; more important is the consideration that we can no longer profitably deal with questions of government within the United Kingdom, piecemeal, country by country. We need to look at the whole.[46]

O'Neill, it should be acknowledged, had long been an enthusiast for devolution, and, on becoming prime minister in 1963, embarked on various initiatives designed to show that Northern Ireland was more prepared than hitherto to exercise the powers at its disposal in an inventive manner.[47] It was his tragedy that his positive outlook in this regard should come into collision with the defensiveness of unionist 'ultras' and the unbreakable scepticism of many in the nationalist community that Northern Ireland could ever be reformed effectively. Nonetheless, it is interesting to speculate about the prospects of Northern Ireland undergoing progressive renewal in the context of a 'Home Rule All Round' constitutional shake-up in the UK arising out of the Royal Commission's ultimate findings. The law-and-order crisis from the summer of 1969, necessitating the sending of British troops to the streets of Belfast and Londonderry, and the subsequent development of the 'Troubles', duly put paid to such a scenario.

Yet the crisis in Northern Ireland and the search for a solution was nevertheless to intersect with the issue of devolution for other parts of the UK, especially Scotland, as debates and controversies around both developed over the subsequent decade. As the historian David Powell has pointed out: 'the need to confront the problems of Northern Ireland after a long period of neglect had focused attention on the anomalies by which the constituent parts of the United Kingdom were governed'.[48]

While in opposition, the Conservatives under the leadership of Edward Heath signalled their intent in 1968 to deliver a devolved assembly for Scotland, as if fearful of being portrayed as too 'Diceyan' at this moment of constitutional speculation.[49] However, when in office, after the election of June 1970, the Heath government found its capacities stretched by the deteriorating situation in Northern Ireland, the plans for the UK's entry into the European Economic Community (EEC), and industrial relations strife. Scotland faded from the picture. Again, it is tempting to ponder a counter-factual: what if the Northern Ireland situation had not absorbed the government's attention to the detriment of the other constitutional reforms it had shown a willingness to embrace?[50] Heath was always in favour of devolution, and his evangelical fervour for Europe proved that he was not the kind of Tory leader to respond to 'Diceyan' alarm bells over matters of sovereignty.

However, the failure of the Northern Ireland government's resort to internment in 1971, to crush the terrorist campaign of the Provisional IRA that had escalated since their emergence early in December 1969, put the option of Direct Rule and the suspension of the Stormont Parliament firmly on the agenda. The events of 'Bloody Sunday' in Derry in January 1972 effectively forced Heath's hand. The British government suffered a backlash of criticism internationally and decided that it was imperative to take direct full control of security policy. The Northern Ireland government, headed by Brian Faulkner, refused to continue under such circumstances and the devolved institutions were thus prorogued in March 1972. Heath then appointed William Whitelaw as Secretary of State, with the brief of constructing a political settlement that could command support across the community divide in Northern Ireland.

The constitutional complexities involved in the imposition of Direct Rule were somewhat lost in the circumstances of the security crisis of the time. Those Ulster unionists, who were outraged at what they claimed was a breach of constitutional convention and propriety, pointed to the 1949 Ireland Act to make their point about the will of the Stormont Parliament being by-passed, albeit to no avail. In retrospect, however, this episode did raise crucial questions about the exercise of Westminster sovereignty in the context of devolution, and about the weight placed on some constitutional conventions and not others. Such matters would be debated, in particular for Scotland, in later decades. Moreover, Ulster unionist perceptions of Westminster's 'disregard for legality' contributed to the difficulties of finding a solution to satisfy both communities, with their competing identities and allegiances.[51]

It was also the case that Heath and Whitelaw favoured the restoration of devolved government in Northern Ireland with the crucial proviso that it had to be on a broader basis than the previous unionist majoritarian variant. Whitelaw's efforts in this respect were complicated by the final report of the Kilbrandon Commission. Despite the government's manoeuvres behind the scenes, designed to separate Northern Ireland from the Commission's recommendations that there should be a measure of devolution for Scotland and Wales which could be viewed as resembling that of Stormont, Kilbrandon helped to raise expectations in Scotland and give leverage to the SNP,[52] reinforce Ulster unionist arguments for the 'old' Stormont, and put the issue of Northern Ireland's representation at Westminster back on the political agenda.[53]

All of this was inherited by the Labour government that assumed power following Heath's ill-advised gamble of holding an election in early 1974. Not only did this election represent the SNP's parliamentary breakthrough – it won seven seats with 22 per cent of the Scottish vote – it also immeasurably strengthened the hand of the various Ulster unionists who had coalesced in protest over the power-sharing devolved executive for Northern Ireland that was a product of the Sunningdale talks at the close of 1973 and was established in January 1974. Within months this new Executive was brought down by the Ulster Workers' Council strike and the Northern Ireland problem again returned to demand governmental attention.[54] Labour formed a minority government until a second election was held in October 1974, which gave them a thin overall majority but also resulted in the SNP increasing its seats to eleven and its share of the vote in Scotland to 30 per cent. The Labour government now assumed it had little option but to

was intended as a forum in which all the Northern Ireland parties might reach agreement among themselves on the way forward. However, its final report bore the imprint of the unionist desire to retrieve rather than share power, and this initiative went the way of its Sunningdale predecessor.[58]

The government, led by James Callaghan from March 1976, ran into trouble with its devolution legislation in the House of Commons, where opposition was intense and involved many, mainly northern English, Labour MPs. The resort to a guillotine motion in February 1977 failed, and the Scotland and Wales Act fell. A subsequent parliamentary pact with the Liberals led to new devolution legislation, this time in the form of separate bills for Scotland and Wales. The debate was thus rejoined against a background of highly charged political theatre, in a parliament where the Labour government had to fight constantly for survival and find allies and votes where it could.[59]

Rather improbably the government was given a measure of assistance by some Ulster Unionists. The largest Unionist party, the Ulster Unionist Party (UUP), was led in the House of Commons from 1974 by James Molyneaux, who became outright leader of the party in 1979. After the October 1974 election he was supported, or perhaps directed, by Enoch Powell, who had won the seat of South Down for the UUP after controversially breaking ties with the Conservatives earlier in the year.[60] Powell and Molyneaux favoured the greater integration of Northern Ireland with the rest of the UK and sought to minimise those factors which persuaded people to regard it simply as a 'place apart'. Such factors included the way that Northern Ireland's business was conducted in parliament under Direct Rule – the 'Orders in Council' system –

and, crucially, the matter of Northern Ireland representation in the House of Commons. Powell, indeed, claimed that there was a direct connection between the latter issue and 'death on the streets'.[61] This reflected Powell's belief that only Northern Ireland being treated as an integral part of the UK with its fair share of MPs and parliamentary time would bring peace.

With the fall of Stormont in 1972 there arose the question of increasing the number of Northern Ireland MPs in line with other parts of the UK. As discussed above, the number had been kept low as a kind of trade-off for the possession of devolved institutions. When these were no longer operating, the demand for an increase by Unionists – and some Conservative allies – duly followed. Their case was strengthened by the recommendation in the Kilbrandon Report that the matter should be addressed.[62] Conscious of the delicate balancing act that dealing with Northern Ireland involved, neither the Heath nor Wilson governments between 1973 and 1976 wished to take the matter up: nationalist opinion was resolutely opposed to anything that would have the effect of 'normalising' Northern Ireland's position within the UK.

However, as the Callaghan government grew desperate, Molyneaux and Powell seized their chance. Following the defeat on the guillotine motion for the Scotland and Wales Bill, a 'no confidence' motion in the government was put before the House. Callaghan survived and he was helped by a number of Unionist abstentions after sweetening them with the promise of a Speaker's conference over the Northern Ireland representation issue, an abandonment of the government's previous position, which had been to delay such a conference until devolution had been passed for Scotland and Wales. This previous policy gestured to the need to address the question of reducing Scottish and Welsh representation in the event of devolution, a question that no Labour government could contemplate without dread. Indeed, no provision had been made by the government for such reductions in its Bill for Scotland and Wales, and the government thus put itself in an invidious position in parliament when it attempted to drag its feet on Northern Ireland representation and sought to defend the existing levels of representation for Scotland and Wales.[63]

Debates in parliament over devolution highlighted the further anomaly of whether or not members representing constituencies in parts of the UK with devolution should get to vote on issues that did not directly affect their own regions, the so-called 'West Lothian Question'. There was no definitive answer to the question, short of the break-up or formal federalising of the UK, and the messiness of the issue, as it was regularly rehashed, damaged the credibility of the government's whole devolution programme. Speculation about changes to either the number of MPs from the different parts of the UK – it was also suggested that English representation be raised to compensate – or to their voting rights, drew attention to the anomaly of the Northern Ireland case as it then stood, and the compelling arguments, logically if not always politically, for an increase in the number of MPs to which the region was entitled on the basis of direct comparison with the other parts of the UK.[64]

The Speaker's conference duly recommended that Northern Ireland's representation be increased to seventeen, and legislation was passed to this effect early in 1979. This constituted a major achievement for the integrationist variety of unionist politics epitomised by Powell and Molyneaux, and it was to shape the course of unionist politics into the 1980s and 1990s, and be an unwelcome development for future governments.[65] The government had tried to avoid upsetting the unionist–nationalist balance in the hope of eventually contriving a power-sharing settlement, but the fiasco over the devolution legislation for Scotland and Wales forced its hand. It was an episode, like many others in this hectic political period, that demonstrated the futility of attempting to compartmentalise the Northern Ireland problem and devolution more broadly. In short, the Northern Ireland question became deeply entangled in the political and parliamentary struggles over devolution, representation and constitutional change in general.

Irish echoes were also heard as the devolution saga reached its denouement in 1979. The government was forced to accept amendments to the respective Scotland and Wales Bills for referendums to be held to test popular support for the measures, and it was stipulated that, in order for the bills to pass, the vote in favour had to comprise at least 40 per cent of the total electorate. Tam Dalyell wrote in his book *Devolution: The End of Britain* that the debate in Scotland was 'haunted by the spectre of Ireland'.[66] Certainly, Irish questions and parallels infiltrated the arguments of the pro- and anti-devolution sides, although in both cases they were employed to warn voters of the dangers either of devolution being denied or delivered. On the part of pro-devolutionists there were veiled references to possible Northern Ireland-style political unrest in the event of Scotland's supposed will being thwarted. On the anti-devolution side much was made about the one-party dominance and one-issue focus of fifty years of devolution in Northern Ireland. In Scotland at this time there were communities and regions fearful of an all-powerful Labour Party, which derived its strength from the industrial west-central belt of the country. Moreover, the prospect of renewed constitutional debate around the question of whether devolution could be a terminus in itself or a mere staging-post to independence, instilled doubts among a populace wearied by a decade of squabbling over arcane issues. Warnings relating to the Northern Ireland experience, which linked the operation of local powers to discrimination and injustice, also came from academic specialists in the area at this juncture,[67] although there were those who took the view of genuine devolution enthusiasts, such as Scottish Labour MPs John Mackintosh and Donald Dewar, that positive messages and lessons could be drawn from the Northern Ireland example, and that a future devolved context in Scotland would be likely to be characterised by a greater sense of motivation to ensure that the new powers would be used more extensively and productively.[68]

Both pro- and anti-devolution camps were aware of the potential for sectarian trouble in Scotland, where there were reservoirs of support for the respective unionist and nationalist causes across the water, and many Scots were wary about the possible spill-over of violence, even if such anxieties had become less intense since the peak of the Troubles in the early 1970s. The Orange Order, a mass movement in Scotland as in Ireland, officially favoured a 'Yes' vote in the 1979 referendum on the grounds that it would hasten the return of the old Stormont, although some in its ranks feared, along with Tam Dalyell and Enoch Powell and his 'Diceyan' brand of unionism, that devolution could lead to the break-up of Britain. On the other side of the religious fence were those opposed to devolution, who tried to discourage Catholics from voting 'Yes' on the grounds that a Scottish parliament could become 'another

Stormont', with all that potentially entailed regarding the treatment of minorities.[69]

It is difficult to draw firm conclusions about the extent to which such Northern Irish factors may have influenced the outcome of the referendum. The vote was a slim one in favour of devolution, but it fell significantly short of the qualification whereby at least 40 per cent of the total electorate had to vote in favour. Matters of turnout and of voters entertaining doubts of one kind or another clearly had an influence. The Labour Party in Scotland was riven with tensions around devolution, with many of its battle-hardened 'fixer' figures aware that constitutional changes would be likely to upset the brittle alliance of Protestant and Catholic workers that it had painstakingly put together over decades. This was to be a pertinent sub-plot in the constitutional showdowns of the future, where the stakes were even higher.[70]

Thatcher's Union and Its Opponents

Following the devolution referendums for Scotland and Wales in March 1979, the Labour government lost a confidence vote in the House of Commons and the Labour cause was then decisively defeated by the Conservatives, now led by Margaret Thatcher, in the subsequent general election. Matters of constitutional reform were not on the new Prime Minister's agenda and the debate over devolution rapidly cooled as Scotland pondered its inconclusive referendum verdict, while the resounding vote against devolution in Wales seemed to leave no room for further discussion. However, there remained Northern Ireland to sustain deliberation over potential devolved schemes, electoral reform and the nature and purpose of the UK as a political project.

Thatcher's unionism has been described as 'deracinated and centralized';[71] it was certainly lacking in historical awareness and nuance, and betrayed a myopic Anglo-centric set of assumptions. The new Prime Minister was eager to roll her ideological prospectus across 'Britain' and tended to treat Northern Ireland – as many British political figures had done before her – as an inconvenient and troublesome appendix. Any hopes that Powell and Molyneaux entertained approaching the 1979 election that she would be supportive of their integrationist arguments, evaporated soon after she came to power and tasked her Secretary of State, Humphrey Atkins, with trying again to fashion an internal compromise between the Northern Ireland parties. When this brought no results, Thatcher turned to Dublin and the possibilities of Anglo-Irish co-operation, a move that was to prove fateful for unionists in the long run. The republican hunger strikes of 1980–1 ensured that the Northern Ireland problem would occupy much of Thatcher's time and profoundly shape her reputation: the relative insecurity of her domestic political position in the early years of her premiership may have inclined her to adopt a defiant and uncompromising stance. The episode certainly contributed to the strong leadership profile she was to enhance via the Falklands War in 1982. There is also little doubt that she was attracted, as so many before and since have been, by the lure of accolades in the history books regarding the solving of the Irish question.

Although Thatcher's centralising way of thinking hardly stretched to Northern Ireland, she was nonetheless aware that attempts to restore devolution as part of a settlement could refuel Scottish demands. Charles Moore, in his authorised biography, has highlighted the way that her fears in this regard lay behind her lukewarm backing for the 'Rolling Devolution' initiative pursued from 1982 by James Prior, whom she had appointed as Atkin's successor as Secretary of State.[72] In effect this was a demotion for Prior and reflected Thatcher's wish to marginalise his influence on the main parts of her policy programme. Prior's hopes were dashed in any case by the refusal of the Social Democratic and Labour Party (SDLP) to take its seats in the newly elected Assembly, which had been established as the first step towards renewed devolution under the 'Rolling Devolution' policy. This non-violent party was by now conscious of the danger posed by Sinn Féin, the political wing of a republican movement galvanised by the radicalisation of many in the minority community on account of the 1981 hunger strikes, and feared losing support if it participated in a venture most in the nationalist community considered futile.

Prior's Assembly was thus toothless and was effectively over-taken by events in late 1985, with the signing by the London and Dublin governments of the 'Anglo-Irish Agreement'. Unionist out-rage over the accord, which gave a role to Dublin in the affairs of Northern Ireland, was expressed in a storm of protests, some of which descended into violence.[73] This tended to obscure the extent to which this agreement represented another, albeit circuitous, attempt to restore devolution: the 'coercive consociationalist' fea-ture of the deal in which unionists might curtail the role of Dublin by entering a power-sharing arrangement with nationalists.[74] Such were the emotions aroused by the agreement, however, that no moves towards meaningful political dialogue could be taken until around 1990.

Nevertheless, in a decade characterised by Thatcher's 'Unitary State' approach and the containment of debates over constitutional matters, Northern Ireland kept such issues on the horizon and was something of a constitutional laboratory in this period, providing rich material for the attention of academics and think tanks. From the late 1980s, much of this was re-channelled into discussions of broad-based constitutional reform of the UK.[75] Northern Ireland provided a valuable reference point for advocates of a constitutional shake-up; they could, and did, highlight the government's willingness to consider devolution and a proportional representation (PR) electoral system for one part of the UK, while insisting on time-worn shibboleths around the 'genius' of the unwritten British constitution, the sovereignty of parliament and the 'winner takes all' election system for the other parts.[76]

Assumptions about a Unitary State also tended to gloss over the considerable extent to which Scotland remained distinctive and, indeed, autonomous.[77] If agitation for legislative devolution crumbled into internecine squabbling between pro-devolutionists and independence supporters after 1979, the key players in the administrative devolution system continued to see it as their mission to fight Scotland's corner. This they did so effectively as to receive the unintended compliment of Thatcher's resentment. In her memoirs she complained of the Scottish Office being an obstacle to her pursuit of the free-market policies she believed would benefit the whole country.[78] Her Scottish secretaries, George Younger and Malcolm Rifkind, felt they had to insist on trying to cater to Scottish national sensitivities.[79]

But the cause of a Scottish assembly or parliament was also championed in the Thatcher years by key political figures and campaigning groups. In a recent retrospective account, Tam Dalyell acknowledged that Donald Dewar, later to be the author of the legislation which actually delivered a parliament, had been key to keeping the issue alive in the Labour Party, along with other 'believers'.[80] In addition, there was the 'all party, non-party' Campaign for a Scottish Assembly (CSA), which pursued the idea of a Scottish Constitutional Convention and was to see this materialise at the end of the decade. The CSA successfully cultivated the trade unions and, as Mitchell points out, 'played a part in converting opposition to the Conservative government into support for wider constitutional change'.[81]

By the late 1980s and early 1990s it was, indeed, the Scottish question which proved to be the main catalyst for a broader debate around constitutional reform. The main political beneficiary of the anti-government mood in Scotland was the Labour Party. However, Labour was aware that opposition to Thatcher's economic policies and the run-down of key heavy industries came with a nationalistic edge. In the 1980s a striking political divergence between Scotland and England opened up in relation to voting behaviour as the Conservatives lost significant ground in Scotland in each election. Increasingly, political analysts and commentators claimed to see a serious erosion in the fabric of British political culture.[82] The idea that an elected assembly or parliament would have shielded Scotland from Thatcherism grew in the public consciousness – there was little appreciation of the way that the invisible workings of the Scottish Office's administrative machinery may be said to have done this to an extent – and the Labour Party in Scotland duly firmed up its commitment to devolution and left behind most of the doubts and counter-arguments that had caused internal divisions over the issue in the 1970s.[83] Former opponents of devolution, such as Robin Cook, became fervent advocates, arguing furthermore that the Scottish demand, if successfully pressed, might prove 'the battering ram that releases parallel claims for de-centralisation, regional autonomy and local democracy throughout Britain.'[84]

As speculation of this nature over constitutional change took hold, Northern Ireland was more often than not admitted to decentralised schemes and visions of a future UK. Those who wished to break with the 'Unitary State' model of the UK and who saw a transition to a 'Union State' as essential to a new era of progressive politics, generally found it useful to extend quasi-federal – 'Home Rule All Round' – or formal federal political thinking to the UK as a whole: the inclusion of Northern Ireland helped to fill out and substantiate further the 'Union State' case, to underscore the inherent diversity and pluri-national character of the UK, and to bolster the case for a move away from outdated notions of Westminster sovereignty being sacrosanct and maximum uniformity being a sign of strength. The distinguished political scientist, Bernard Crick, used his long scholarly engagement with the Northern Ireland problem to anchor his arguments for UK constitutional renewal and 'flexible federalism', while stressing that future arrangements should also accommodate the reality that Northern Ireland faced in two directions: to Britain and to the Republic of Ireland.[85] For Crick, engagement with Northern Ireland led to a greater questioning of what he once referred to as 'pre-suppositions about parliamentary sovereignty and the nature of power.'[86]

When he became leader of the Labour Party in 1992, John Smith, who had been the minister in charge of preparing the devolution legislation of the Callaghan government, talked of a 'decentralising mission' and an 'interlocking' set of government tiers: European,

Westminster, regional, local.[87] This, it can be argued, was reflective of a broad trend towards multi-layered governance and a new paradigm in which the nation-state counted for less than before, and traditional 'Diceyan' interpretations of sovereignty were at a discount. Old concepts of nationalism, which equated 'nation' and 'state', suddenly looked out of place. It was at this juncture that the Scottish social scientist David McCrone advanced the influential thesis that Scotland as a 'stateless nation' was well placed to take advantage of these developments and of a new climate of thinking that prioritised notions of 'subsidiarity' and the loosening of questions of identity.[88] It appeared that the late twentieth century would herald a new 'post-nationalist' era.

It was certainly a fertile period for a venture such as the Scottish Constitutional Convention, which was inaugurated in 1989 and deliberated until 1995. Although this body involved several political parties, neither the SNP nor the Conservatives took part. Both viewed it as designed to produce a blueprint for devolved government, leaving no room for serious discussion of either the independence option or retaining the constitutional status quo. Clearly, this was what the convention set out to do, and there was no doubt that it was largely driven by the Labour Party as the dominant force in the country. Nevertheless, it also brought together a range of voices from 'civic' Scotland, including the Churches and the trade unions, and Labour very quickly found that it would have to embrace causes, such as electoral reform, from which it had previously steered clear. Moreover, the founding document of the body – 'A Claim of Right' – advanced a concept of popular, as opposed to parliamentary, sovereignty, and castigated the British constitution for concentrating power in the hands of the

Executive.[89] All of this signalled the distance travelled by Labour in Scotland from the days of Willie Ross, the secretary of state who earned the soubriquet 'hammer of the Nats'.

The convention produced reports which looked forward to a Scottish parliament ushering in a new kind of politics for the impending new century: more consensual, more open and responsive to the citizens, and more oriented towards the rights and identities of minorities. The deliberations of the Constitutional Convention were also, to a significant extent, guided by the emerging thinking surrounding a 'Europe of the Regions', in which the role of nation-states and traditional concepts of sovereignty were increasingly viewed as anachronistic.[90] The models of devolution envisaged were 'maximalist' in terms of powers to be given to Scotland, including financial ones. A final report in 1995 called for PR, greater representation of women, and a limited tax-varying capacity to supplement the block grant financial settlement.[91] The blueprint formed the basis of the Scotland Act, which was eventually passed by the new Labour government following another referendum in 1997: this time Scotland voted solidly (74 per cent) in favour of a parliament, and, indeed, the taxation capacity (63 per cent).[92] Such was the Scottish question's impact in the early 1990s that Ulster unionists made notable efforts to position themselves to ensure that they would be included in any future constitutional shake-up and not treated yet again as a 'place apart'.

It was precisely this perception of Northern Ireland on the part of the Westminster political establishment that had led to the Anglo-Irish Agreement and the sense that unionists and their claims to British citizenship and belonging were expendable. Unionists thus saw an opportunity to be part of a UK debate: Molyneaux made contact with the Scottish Constitutional Convention, while the rising star of his party, David Trimble, later to replace him as leader, talked of Northern Ireland being part of a 'system of decentralisation'. The UUP justifiably called attention to their 'unrivalled experience of devolution'.[93] In this period the UUP, still the political choice of most of the pro-Union community, combined its efforts at Westminster to have Northern Ireland's business conducted along Scottish lines (with the setting up of a Northern Ireland Grand Committee), with a greater openness to constitutional reform and a willingness to look beyond traditional ideas of national identity. It seems not to have been accidental that the Ulster-Scots cultural movement was also flourishing at this point.[94]

Expectations relating to constitutional matters envisaged a change of government at the 1992 general election. However, the Conservatives, now under the leadership of John Major, were once again returned. There was, as in 1979, a sense of anti-climax around devolution for Scotland, although the convention and other forms of activity ensured that the issue did not fade from the public consciousness, and it needs to be remembered that over 75 per cent of Scottish voters had supported parties in favour of change. In addition, developments in Northern Ireland leading to paramilitary ceasefires in 1994 and the onset of what quickly became known as the 'peace process' had the effect of reinforcing demands for change elsewhere. There was a new wave of speculation about the Northern Ireland conflict being resolved within a context of a new written constitution clearly specifying citizenship rights, and of a new federalised UK.[95] As John Major's government pushed towards a settlement for Northern Ireland that involved a power-sharing devolved assembly (with a PR voting system), it exposed itself to a barrage of criticism about its inconsistency around constitutional matters. It seemed that the government was advocating legislative devolution for one part of the UK while decrying it for another; Major's 'Diceyan' arguments and warnings about devolution risking the break-up of the Union clearly did not apply to Northern Ireland.[96] In contrast to the late nineteenth- and early twentieth-century period, constitutional conservatives were now much more inclined to restrict their focus to 'Britain' rather than the UK as a whole. The Major government's last-ditch defence of 'Diceyism' – in its late twentieth-century guise – was counterposed to the Labour and Liberal parties' Gladstonian recognition of the diversity of the UK's constituent parts.[97] Such was Labour's eagerness to mine this particular seam of Conservative inflexibility and apparent refusal to acknowledge changing times that it committed itself to a programme of constitutional reform with no room to backtrack. For the leading Scottish Labour figures in this era – Donald Dewar, Robin Cook, Gordon Brown – there was simply no alternative to devolution if the Union as a whole was to survive.[98]

Thus, following its landslide election victory in 1997, Labour drew back the curtain on the UK's *fin de siècle* 'constitutional moment'. As in 1974, a Labour government faced the task of bringing peace to Northern Ireland and devolution to Scotland (and Wales) in the broader interests of the stability of the Union. Both the Northern Ireland and Scotland cases had been the causes of constitutional uncertainty since the late 1960s, with either one or the other, or both together, providing the spur to intensive political debate and manoeuvring. However, in the late 1990s the context for imaginative solutions and decisive constitutional choices was much more congenial.

New Labour and the Lost Opportunities for a New Unionism

The constitutional reform project pursued by the Labour government led by Tony Blair from 1997 amounted to a makeover for the UK as a whole.[99] The signing of the Good Friday Agreement in April 1998 effectively enabled Northern Ireland to be woven into the devolution tapestry:[100] strand one of the accord provided for a devolved Northern Ireland Assembly and power-sharing 'consociational' Executive, while strands two and three provided institutions to facilitate North–South All-Ireland, and East–West British–Irish, affairs respectively.[101] Northern Ireland was thus part of the project of disaggregation and acknowledgement of the diverse political cultures that was pursued by the Blair government. By the end of the century a politically reconfigured UK saw both Scotland and Northern Ireland in possession of devolved institutions with primary legislative powers – Wales initially possessed only the power to scrutinise Westminster legislation – and both were seemingly central to questions of the future of the restructured Union and its accompanying sense of identity.

In retrospect, the challenges involved in at once loosening and sustaining the Union had been made plain. In an illuminating exchange at Westminster shortly after the government took office, the Ulster Unionist MP for East Londonderry, William Ross, intervened in a debate on the Scottish devolution bill. Ross suggested to Scottish Secretary of State Dewar that he was being remiss in not pointing out 'the only party in the House that has direct practical experience of devolved government and its operation is the Ulster Unionist Party'. 'Is he aware', Ross continued, 'that we know that the Scottish Parliament and the Westminster Parliament must work closely together to strengthen and to maintain the Union because, inevitably, the politics of Scotland, like the politics of Northern Ireland, will be increasingly Nationalist and Unionist?' Ross went on to add: 'In these circumstances, is the Labour Party in Scotland, which will have members in a devolved institution, going to be a Unionist party?' Dewar responded that it was because he wished to avoid 'the polarisation of politics into two choices at the extreme' and to provide better government, that the government was pushing forward with devolution.[102]

Ross turned out to be much more prescient than possibly even he could have expected. Tam Dalyell, in his by now isolated role as an anti-devolution Scottish Labour MP, could not have issued warnings more salient or pertinent. Over the next twenty years Scottish politics did become increasingly nationalist and unionist, and thus closer to those of Northern Ireland than the rest of the UK.[103] Inter-governmental and inter-parliamentary relations in the new era of decentralisation were not conducted satisfactorily in the estimation of most academics, commentators and, indeed, the politicians themselves.[104] Moreover, the Labour Party in Scotland, to a significant extent, was forced to become a unionist party in the explicit sense it had never wished to be. The degree of polarisation in Scotland over the question of independence or union was deepened by the holding of a referendum on the question in 2014: despite the 55–45 per cent verdict in favour of remaining within the Union, since then the issue has only gained political traction.

Another point raised by Ross should also be noted: namely, the tendency to marginalise Northern Ireland within the broader debate about constitutional change in the UK, and to ignore lessons from Northern Ireland's prior experience of devolution. Although

...evolution for three parts of the UK by 1999 signalled
...uph of 'Union State' thinking, Unitary State assumptions
...u, to a considerable extent, guided studies of UK history and
thus contributed to the amnesia about Northern Ireland's actual
experience of devolution between 1921 and 1972, and its relationship
to the historical development of the UK state.[105] In addition, such a
Unitary State approach could obscure the significance of Scotland's
'administrative devolution' history and the extent to which the
creation of the new parliament emerged organically out of it.

There is a sense in which the Blair government did not appreciate the implications of its massive and historic reform project. Too
little thought was given to how the changes might affect the unity
of the UK and the future of the Union. From the start there was a
tendency to deal with devolved matters as they arose in an ad hoc
and short-term manner, and not in accordance with any coherent
overarching vision of how the new UK should evolve. It has been
well remarked that a 'devolve and forget' mentality seemed to
characterise successive central governments in the new devolution
times, with too little attention paid to the task of balancing the new
institutional and governmental diversity with the commonalities
underpinning notions of UK unity and solidarity.[106] Such neglect
was arguably to have far-reaching consequences in relation to
the position of Scotland within the Union, and indeed that of the
UK within the EU. The Brexit debate of recent years has thrown
into sharp relief contentious questions of sovereignty, the rights
and entitlements of the devolved institutions, and the extent to
which the UK has preserved any degree of unity.[107] As this debate
has demonstrated, old concepts and conventions regarding 'British
politics' have died hard: there has been a persistence of centralist

assumptions, with the changes brought about by devolution not properly understood, particularly in England. Again, there had been ample warning about the potential problems arising from the asymmetrical set of arrangements put in place at the end of the twentieth century: England represented a 'gaping hole' in the project and Westminster was now to be the parliament for England as well as the UK.[108]

It was in the Labour Party's interests to foster a co-operative spirit around the new project, not just between London and the respective devolved administrations, but also between those devolved governments and parliaments themselves. However, the inter-governmental arrangements – the Joint Ministerial Committees (JMCs) – were a particularly weak aspect of the new system from the beginning.[109] It has to be acknowledged that the suspensions of the workings of devolution in Northern Ireland, especially the long one covering the years 2002–7, hindered the establishment of good working relations with Scotland and Wales. Moreover, when the SNP came to power as a minority government in Scotland in 2007, it had no incentive – or at least not the incentive Labour had had – to strengthen the overall UK devolution scheme; rather, it was focused on exploiting the uncertainties and ambivalences in a UK project in transition. The SNP victory might also be said to have killed off the prospect of the formula of devolution combined with fiscal and welfare unity being given the time to bed down and become entrenched as the functioning norm. The 2007 Scottish election in effect changed the direction of the devolution project towards fiscal and welfare 'federalism'.

By the time it first tasted power, the SNP was dazzled by the economic and cultural transformation of the Republic of

Ireland; the Irish example, it was argued by SNP leader and First Minister Alex Salmond, showed what was possible. According to this narrative a 'Celtic Lion' economy would flourish in an independent Scotland and match the stunning performance of Ireland's Celtic Tiger.[110] It would not be long before the Irish economic success story was tarnished by the financial crisis of 2008–9. Nonetheless, the SNP's attraction to nationalist Ireland – Salmond was fond of comparing himself to Parnell – reflected the endurance of old-fashioned Celtic romanticism as a populist ploy. More than that, it served to divert Scottish attentions away from the part of Ireland with which Scotland had most in common. In the modern era, Scotland's experience was shared to a striking extent by Ulster–Northern Ireland, whether in terms of economic profiles and the problems and challenges of de-industrialisation, public sector reliance, ethno-religious divisions and tensions, 'National Questions' and British identity, and, not least, devolved government and the debates about how it should work.

The potential in the early twenty-first century for a closer relationship and more political interaction between the two places largely failed in its realisation, notwithstanding the flourishing of much scholarship around Irish–Scottish connections, which did involve productive deliberation on Northern Ireland's place in cultural exchanges in particular.[111] There was little consideration given during the independence referendum campaign in Scotland in 2014 to the impact of the decision – whether 'Yes' or 'No' – on Northern Ireland and the still uneasy peace which was being managed there by the two parties that had come to dominate their respective ethnic blocs, namely the Democratic Unionist Party (DUP) and Sinn Féin. In Northern Ireland, the initial strength of the more moderate 'tribal' parties, the UUP and SDLP, was quickly eroded by their more hard-line rivals, a state of affairs which many observers view as having led to power being 'shared out' rather than shared in the intended sense.[112] Devolved government in Northern Ireland was carried out for close to a decade within the constraints of rival communal pressures until suspended again in 2017.

Circumstances have thus proved unpropitious for purposeful and innovative use of devolved powers in Northern Ireland. However, despite the much more favourable political context in Scotland, the anticipated 'new politics' did not substantially materialise there. Over some twenty years, there has been little in the way of groundbreaking legislation or imaginative policy-making, while adversarial party politics have eclipsed hopes of the legislature checking the power of the executive. This has especially been the case in relation to the dominance of the SNP in the parliament since the 2011 Scottish election. Aspirations for genuine power-sharing between executive, parliament and people have still to be realised.[113]

Both Scotland and Northern Ireland continue to benefit from the block grant system of devolution financing, based as it is on the Barnett formula drawn up – as a temporary expedient – in the late 1970s as a means to calculate shares of public expenditure for the different parts of the UK. To take the example of the year 2014–15, spending per head of population in Northern Ireland came to £11,106; for Scotland £10,374; for Wales £9,904; and for England £8,638.[114] Both places thus have a vested interest in retaining this formula, even if, in the Scottish case, the increased taxation powers that have been granted by successive governments have led to adjustments in the payments.[115]

In relation to the long-running saga of what became known as the 'West Lothian Question', it should be noted that one of the most significant outcomes of the Scottish independence debate was the decision by David Cameron's government to proceed with a system of 'English Votes for English Laws' (EVEL). This measure changed voting procedures in the House of Commons, giving increased responsibility to the Speaker to determine what an 'English-only' (or 'English and Welsh-only') bill is, galvanising the SNP around a grievance, and, in the words of Nigel Dodds of the DUP, damaging the fabric of the Union by twisting the UK parliament into something it was not designed to be.[116] EVEL, in short, had not helped in the matter of providing more clarity about constitutional affairs in the UK and was quietly dropped in July 2021 by the Conservative government of Boris Johnson, secure in its eighty-seat, mostly made in England, majority.[117] The 'wicked issues' surrounding devolution continue to be troublesome.

The new devolution age, in sum, was not underpinned by, and did not cultivate, the necessary degree of consensus and agreement around common citizenship and universal benefits and entitlements. Instead, it has seen increasing fragmentation, disconnected conversations and the pursuit of divergent agendas. In retrospect, the SNP's capture of power back in 2007, albeit as a minority government, changed the direction of the debate, while the seismic impact of the Brexit referendum and its aftermath re-awakened the 'Union' or 'Unitary' State conundrum, and further complicated the question of the evolution of the UK along a federal course.[118]

CHAPTER THREE

The British Question

S cholarly concern with the idea – or ideas – of Britishness has grown considerably since the 1990s. This reflects the focus on identity as an area of public and academic enquiry as transformative developments, such as the fragmentation of the Communist Bloc in the east and debates over sovereignty in Europe, reshaped the political landscape. Against a background, at the close of last century, of escalating ethnic conflict and a reappraisal of the capacity of nation states to respond to global challenges, there was an impulse, to a great extent guided by postmodern thinking, to unpick long-established political, social and cultural constructions.

Britain and Britishness were thus subjected to a process, probably overdue, of disaggregation and re-examination. What was long implicit – that the British 'label' concealed a highly diverse set of goods – became something of a scholarly industry. Seminal studies by historians such as Hugh Kearney and Keith Robbins in the late 1980s had in effect pointed the way and posed the key questions: to what extent was there such a thing as a British nation?; what factors underpinned such a nation?; if there were forces towards

British integration on the one hand, and forces towards separatism and fragmentation on the other, how fine was the balance between them?; were we talking about four nations *or* one, or four nations *and* one?[1] Certainly, as another scholar neatly put it a few years later, Britishness was decidedly not a homogeneous concept and depended very much on context for definition.[2]

Linda Colley's game-changing work, *Britons*, appeared in 1992 and advanced the thesis that British identity was forged during the eighteenth- and early nineteenth-century period as something super-imposed on existing identities. She argued arrestingly that Britishness was a product of empire, struggles against a French 'other', and a common Protestantism.[3] Among the many virtues of Colley's scholarship was an appreciation of British identity as a capacious umbrella under which different nationalities could gather, and as an adhesive promoting sharing and co-operative endeavour. These insights for Colley's period can be applied even to the present day, notwithstanding the pressures that the Union and British identity have been put under at various junctures.

On the other hand, Colley's study raised as many questions as it answered. Her stress on Protestantism[4] glossed over very real tensions within and divisions between different denominations. This was the case particularly in Scotland, where Presbyterians were conscious of a long history of religious friction with Anglicanism and Episcopacy. As Colin Kidd has pointed out, the main fault-line of the Anglo-Scottish Union until at least the early twentieth century was religion.[5] In Scotland, in the era of empire, Presbyterianism was a creed with a pronounced missionary zeal, reflected in the popular celebration of figures such as David Livingstone and Mary Slessor.[6] Indeed, it might be said that

Britishness served Protestantism in the Scottish case rather than the other way round; it helped to provide a bigger stage for religious work and the spread of a distinctive Presbyterian outlook.

However, the most questionable aspect of Colley's thesis arose out of her omission of the Irish dimension to the phenomenon of British identity. Strictly speaking, 'Britain' did refer only to Scotland, England and Wales; nevertheless, concepts of British 'nationhood' in the modern era always had to relate to the United Kingdom state.[7] The Irish part of the UK, following the Union of 1800, was to exert a profound effect on future British developments of all kinds, and arguably had done so for a long time before this. Put simply, any study of what Britishness means is incomplete without Ireland. Despite this, the temptation to omit the Irish dimension, mainly relating to Northern Ireland after 1921 but not exclusively so, has been indulged by countless scholars of this subject area, and Colley's example was followed in the early 2000s by Gordon Brown, then Prime Minister-in-waiting, in his quest to strengthen the concept of a British identity which provided unity in diversity. Brown's omission caused particular offence to unionists in Northern Ireland and created political difficulties as a consequence; however, the broader point was that such a limited definition of who belonged was misleading and arbitrary.[8]

Ireland, Scotland and the Making of Britons

Since the political crisis over Irish Home Rule in the late nineteenth century, Britishness as a concept has been more contested in Ireland than elsewhere, and within the entity of Northern Ireland it has been central to the conflict over identity and allegiance. The idea of Britain, however, has been viewed as an essentially Scottish invention: from the Act of Union of 1707 most Scots, at least until the 1960s, conceived of the Union as a partnership and the language and symbolism of Britishness as indicative of Scotland resisting any English 'takeover'.[9] Further proof of the Union and Britishness as a joint project lay, of course, in the distinctive Scottish institutions that survived the 1707 Act and emblemised the Union as a bargain or compact: the established Presbyterian Kirk and the legal and educational systems. As the twentieth century progressed, it was political agitation either in Scotland or in Northern Ireland, or sometimes in both places simultaneously, that brought debate over British identity into the light; only the question of the UK's membership of the EEC (later the European Union) after 1973 sparked the same degree of deliberation and reappraisal, and then only near the end of the century and into the twenty-first. 'Britishness', Kidd has recently written, 'was at the very least a triangular arrangement, in which the frictions were just as much Scottish–Irish and Protestant–Catholic.'[10] As Jackson, too, has pointed out, Ireland has been crucial to the development of the Anglo-Scottish relationship since the seventeenth century: the Union of the Crowns in 1603 was followed by the Plantations in Ireland as a means of strengthening national (British) defence and security.[11] This was a key element in the historical formation of Britishness.[12]

No group of people in the UK has been asked to justify their claim to British identity as much as the pro-Union community in Northern Ireland. Historically, Ulster unionists have viewed themselves to be in an ongoing zero-sum struggle with Irish nationalism, to which the upholding of loyalty to the British Crown and to variously defined cultural markers of Britishness has been central. Such a perception of constant struggle and the need for eternal vigilance – epitomised by the enduring role played by the Orange culture in the lives of Ulster Protestants[13] – has resulted in a heightened sense of British allegiance as a defiant riposte to nationalism and republicanism in Ireland. For Ulster Protestants, Britishness could never just be taken for granted; it always had to be asserted in the face both of political pressures towards Irish unity and the reluctance of many in Britain itself to admit Ulster or Northern Ireland into the fold. In relation to the latter point, displays of British loyalty in the form of Orange marches, or when couched in religious terminology out of sync with mainstream secular British culture, could encourage outsiders to regard the pro-Union community as 'misfits' when it came to matters British.

There were, moreover, other developments which, over time, added to Ulster unionist difficulties around national identity questions. From 1921 Northern Ireland was, in effect, cut off from the mainstream of British politics, with its own party system and 'Orange and Green' political culture revolving around the single issue of Northern Ireland's position within the UK union. The presence of twelve MPs at Westminster – seventeen after 1979 – could not alter the overall impression of Northern Ireland as something of an anomalous political appendix. Consistent with government intentions in 1921-22 to remove the Irish question from British politics, none of the main British parties organised or attempted to win votes thereafter in Northern Ireland.[14] It was, indeed, in an attempt to offset such 'exclusionary' factors that successive Ulster unionist governments in Northern Ireland over the 1921-72 devolution period pursued a policy of reproducing or slightly adjusting Westminster legislation, and of keeping up 'step by step' in the matter of welfare benefits.[15]

Nevertheless, Northern Ireland's anomalous position as a devolved entity within the UK for some fifty years, followed by the 'Troubles' through to the mid-1990s, led to its marginalisation in many scholarly investigations of British identity. One such study by Christopher Bryant asserted that Northern Ireland was an 'irrelevance' when it came to the way most people in Britain understood Britishness.[16] Another, clearly anxious to 'tidy up' the debate by confining it, in the manner of Colley, to Scotland, England and Wales, simply filed Northern Ireland under 'other communities'.[17] A recent work on the Labour Party and Britishness leaves the reader guessing at several points as to whether Britain or the UK is being discussed, and as to whether Irish or Northern Irish dimensions to the subject are being given validity.[18]

Two points might be made in response to such studies. First, British identity relates to the UK state above all, whether from a political, legal or cultural perspective. In the previous chapter a number of examples are set out of Northern Ireland's importance to the politics of the UK, and to the issue of devolution and constitutional change in particular. It bears repeating that if there is an anomaly in terms of those constitutional changes at the end of the twentieth century, it is England. Also, the scholarly interventions of Hugh Kearney, Bernard Crick, Paul Ward and David Reynolds among others have amply made the case for the inclusion of Ireland – both North and South – in any proper examination of Britishness.[19]

Secondly, there are many people in Britain who value an Irish identity or are very conscious of Irish family connections. Among such people, their sense of British identity or allegiance may have been shaped significantly by their Irish background or connections: for example, it may have been weakened or compromised by pejorative perceptions of British government conduct of the Irish question and of the Northern Ireland Troubles; alternatively, it could have been affected by revulsion and shame over IRA atrocities.

Outside perceptions of Protestant Ulster as not really British, or even unBritish, could be fostered by the confrontations that occurred during the Troubles (and after) between loyalists and the security forces, and the rhetoric of defiance often used by leadership figures such as Ian Paisley.[20] There was little understanding of, or inclination to understand, the reasons for unionist and loyalist anger over British government policy at various junctures. Such perceptions might also have been fuelled by the clear message sent by Protestant Ulster that their loyalty was conditional on the state providing for their protection against being coerced into a united Ireland. This 'contractarian' relationship with the state – brilliantly and seminally explored by David Miller[21] – provides a crucial clue as to the outlook of Protestant Ulster over time, and helps explain both the intensity and the nature of its stance against Home Rule in 1912, when over 440,000 signed a covenant pledging resistance by whatever means.[22]

The 1912 Ulster Solemn League and Covenant took its inspiration from the Scottish Presbyterian covenants of 1638 and 1642, and in many ways symbolised the extent to which Ulster's cause carried a pronounced Ulster–Scottish flavour. The period of the Home Rule controversies from the 1880s had indeed seen the cultivation of what was arguably a 'fall-back' Ulster identity, heavily oriented to the province's Scottish heritage. At various points in the Troubles, such an identity again emerged to bolster communal resolve and to bring complications to the matter of Britishness.[23] However, compacts and covenants have historically been the basis of the UK Union, or series of Unions, and central to questions of British identity; as Ian Bradley has put it, Britishness is not about 'blind allegiance'.[24] Ulster was, in this sense, typical of the kind of bargaining built into the construction and reproduction of a broader shared UK and British experience. Such notions have, in effect, also defined Scotland's place in the Union, as Kidd's scholarly work has reminded us.[25] In the late 1940s, as previously discussed, the movement for Scottish Home Rule adopted the tactic of acquiring mass signatures to a covenant designed to rewrite the terms of the Union. In 1974, as the SNP threatened to disrupt British politics in similar ways to Irish nationalists almost a century before, the Scottish Labour politician and academic John P. Mackintosh wrote cogently about the 'dual' Scottish and British identity then held by most Scots. Mackintosh warned that if Scots perceived the British political system not to be working in a way that was compatible with their interests and aspirations, and if they took the view that the compact they had entered into in the cause of union and a Britain greater than the sum of its parts was being dishonoured, then they would gravitate to straightforward Scottishness and towards the political objective of independence.[26] Scottishness, for Mackintosh, was, effectively, the default setting.

There were always limits to the unitariness of the UK state, and always the potential for fragmentation. Scotland's position was as conditional as Ulster's, if in different ways. For long periods there may have been sufficient consensus to allow a 'banal' form of unionism to take hold in Scotland[27] as it never could in the perennially fraught circumstances of Northern Ireland after partition; yet, at all times in the modern era, Britishness was a complex phenomenon. The apparent confusions and contradictions around national identity in Ulster or Northern Ireland derived essentially from the mysteries and ambiguities of British identity. Ironically, Ulster was perhaps the exemplar of Colley's thesis, in as much as the defence of Protestantism and fear of the 'other' (in this case the nationalism of Catholic Ireland) continued to underpin British loyalty there, however conditional, while such factors lost their salience in other parts of the UK.

Union State Party Politics and the Detachment of Northern Ireland

Jackson has contended, in relation to post-First World War Britain, that 'class politics were unionist politics'.[28] In effect, the development of a two-party, Conservative–Labour struggle from the 1920s resulted in Scotland, England and Wales becoming oriented to the political imperatives of social class, thereby strengthening identification with a British-wide political culture. The Labour movement, in its widest political and industrial sense, was strongest in Lowland Scotland, Northern England and South Wales. Scotland supplied Labour leadership figures from Keir Hardie and Ramsay MacDonald through to John Smith and Gordon Brown.

A recent analysis of the Labour Party and British identity has advanced the idea of a 'Labour Nation', a concept the authors perceive to have been at its zenith in the post-Second World War era of the Attlee government's welfare state reforms, the establishment of the NHS and Keynesian economics.[29] This attempt to identify the idea of social citizenship with British identity and patriotism remains highly relevant to contemporary debates over the future of the UK state and Union, and was to be tellingly invoked by Gordon Brown and the anti-independence side in the Scottish independence referendum of 2014.

However, by the time Labour took power in 1997 and embarked on constitutional reform, research into questions of national identity seemed to reveal an increasingly instrumentalist form of Britishness in Scotland, which drew heavily on the perceived social and economic benefits of institutions such as the NHS.[30] For some scholars such an instrumentalist attachment was a precarious basis for the survival of the Union, especially in the light of devolution and the creation of increasingly distinctive Scottish governmental agencies and structures.[31] Furthermore, as the salience of class politics gave way to a politics shaped increasingly around matters of national and group identity in twenty-first-century Scotland, Labour lost its grip on its heartlands. With hindsight, the narrow – and disputed – SNP victory in the 2007 Scottish parliamentary election marked the end of a half century and more of Labour dominance, something with far-reaching implications for British party politics. Scotland, it seems clear in retrospect, never bought into the New Labour outlook of the Blair years, and much disillusionment was also caused by the calamities of the Iraq war. In his 1974 intervention, John Mackintosh had made the point that the dual identity held by Scots required the British part of it to appear creditable and inspiring. Blair's foreign policy turned many Scottish Labour activists towards the apparently left of centre alternative of the SNP (which was also opposed to the renewal of the Trident nuclear defence system) and added to an impression of steadily weakening identification with all things British.[32]

The dynamic in Scottish politics since the SNP came to power has been the question of the country moving towards independence or settling for enhanced powers within a practically if not formally federalised UK. Either way, the depth of feeling once stirred by a shared pride in British institutions and values, whether in relation to the monarchy, the armed forces, the BBC (especially when guided by the austere Scottish figure of John Reith) and British parliamentary democracy, appears difficult to detect. Gordon Brown, following his contribution to the pro-Union cause in 2014, both in relation to his stress on the social solidarity of 'pooling and sharing' that the Union involved and his role in the pro-Union parties' commitment to increased powers for Scotland in the event of a 'No' vote, used his valedictory address to the Westminster House of Commons in 2015 to warn of the danger of creating a UK which was about separate interests rather than the common good.[33] Brown was well aware that, notwithstanding the 'No' campaign's success in the referendum, the condition of the UK was deeply unsettled.

Hassan and Shaw have argued that the 2014 campaign was at least in part about 'two competing versions of nationalism – Scottish and British'.[34] This was very much how pro-independence activists wished to frame the issue: as a straight either/or choice. However, the 'No' side did not argue their case in British nationalist terms: overwhelmingly, the case was made for the advantages of staying in the Union while expressing a proud and strong Scottishness. It was, indeed, a case that drew on a long history of Scottish national feeling finding expression within the pluralist construct of the Union.[35] This may have been a pragmatic recognition of the degree to which British national sentiment in Scotland had waned; or it may have been an attempt to reaffirm the virtues of a Britishness that sat lightly on top of, or as complementary to, Scottish identity. Either way, the 'Indyref' episode was a reminder of the range of meanings that Britishness could have, and a caution against placing British identity on the same analytical ground as those identities formed around nationalisms in which ideas of nation, state, history and culture fused more easily.[36]

In Northern Ireland, just as in other parts of the UK, social class has always mattered. Northern Ireland shared in the post-Second World War 'New Jerusalem' reforms of the Labour government, measures from which the Catholic minority – a predominantly working-class community – benefited significantly.[37] Indeed, pragmatic recognition of the advantages of UK citizenship in such respects has been the basis for a section of those from a nationalist background, consistently shown in surveys to be between 20 and 30 per cent, opting for the constitutional status quo. Whether recent controversies over Brexit and the Irish border produce long-term changes in such an outlook remains to be seen. Certainly, there can be some similarities detected in attitudes towards the Union and Britishness in a notable section of Catholics in Northern Ireland and those of Catholics in Scotland – also mainly working class – into the early twenty-first century.[38]

Labour politics in Scotland flourished from the 1920s, while Labour politics in Northern Ireland always struggled to find room within the sectarian 'zero-sum' dominance of unionist and nationalist appeals. Nevertheless, trade unionism was relatively strong in Northern Ireland's heavy industries and the vast majority of workers belonged to British-based unions. The Northern Ireland Labour Party (NILP), which modelled itself on the British

Labour Party at least from the 1930s, actually achieved more than a superficial reading of the region's electoral politics may reveal, and the party's presence in the early years of the Troubles arguably prevented sectarian violence from being even worse than it was. The Labour experience in Northern Ireland is an example of an east–west connection linking the working class with their counterparts in Britain – perhaps especially west-central Scotland – which is often overlooked.[39]

As conflict raged in Northern Ireland after 1969, the pro-Union community sought security and a reaffirmation of their place in the UK above all else. Politically, they were divided as to whether such a goal could best be achieved by the restoration of devolved government following its suspension in 1972, or further integration into the UK state; some even felt driven to advocate a 'Dominion Status' form of independence if the British government appeared unwilling to treat them as full British citizens.[40] But in all cases, the Ulster Unionists felt marginalised in relation to debates about the nature and future of the wider UK. A kind of 'hyper Britishness', expressed by many Ulster unionists and manifest at various critical points in the Troubles, seemed to hanker after a form of British identity which was rapidly slipping into the past. The endurance of an ethnic and Protestant religious component to this identity, promoted by the Orange Order, invited such labels as 'last-gasp Britons'. In a survey carried out in 2003, in a Northern Ireland beyond conflict, some two-thirds of Protestants declared themselves 'British', the highest percentage out of any other ethnic group in the UK.[41]

Yet it might be contended that there has never been one British norm against which all else should be measured, and that the historical consciousness of an organisation like the Orange Order and the dilemmas that a multi-cultural Britishness presents were and are crucial aspects of a debate from which no one in 'these islands' should be excluded. To revert to Scotland, there were those for whom the passing of more traditional forms of Britishness was also a matter of regret,[42] and even a spur towards a more exclusively Scottish set of allegiances. To paraphrase John Mackintosh, if Britain was no longer to be 'Great', and if Britishness was to be reduced to a civic or legalistic form of identity, then Scotland would have the primary claim on loyalty.

Above all, however, the outside perception of Northern Ireland as an anomalous part of the UK, and of the ideological make-up of Ulster unionism as incoherent, derived from the region's long-established political marginalisation within the UK. Had Northern Ireland been represented in the party system in the manner of the other parts of the UK, where the Labour, Liberal and Conservative parties represented 'multi-national coalitions',[43] the overall balance in the UK political world would have tilted further to the 'periphery' and Northern Ireland would have fully participated in the constantly evolving politics of negotiation, balancing and compromise integral to a genuine 'Union State'.

This politics of continuous negotiation, the creative tension of the British party system for so long, may provide a clue as to the fundamental unionism of those notable Scottish political figures in the Labour, Liberal and Conservative parties. Such figures include those passionately in favour of devolution and the Union State, such as Mackintosh, Donald Dewar, John Smith, and Gordon Brown for Labour; Jo Grimond, David Steel and Ming Campbell for the Liberals; and Malcolm Rifkind and Alick

Buchanan-Smith for the Conservatives. Such Scottish politicians relished the task of making the multi-national UK Union work, thereby bringing credit to a joint 'British' enterprise. They were fascinated by the challenge of accommodating difference and diversity, and managing asymmetries and anomalies.[44] Northern Ireland politicians were never truly part of this project and their expressions of unionism and Britishness could never be as subtle, despite the emergence of a significant strain of civic or liberal unionism with the leadership of David Trimble.[45] Indeed, it was arguably the desire of Trimble to integrate Ulster unionism into this broader UK tapestry which proved crucial in the signing of the Good Friday Agreement. It was Trimble and Ulster unionism's tragedy that the hesitant steps towards finding a role in UK-wide conversations were, in effect, halted by the eclipse of the UUP by the DUP in the early years of the twenty-first century. The dominance of the DUP's brand of socially conservative unionism and unreflective Britishness – evident around Brexit[46] – has stymied the engagement of Ulster unionism with the challenges of the Union State and reinforced many pejorative perceptions of Northern Ireland in Britain.

Radio On: A Road Movie Through the British Question

Subtle explorations of Britishness in the creative arts have been rare. However, a much-neglected British Film Institute film made in 1979, *Radio On*, written and directed by Chris Petit, rewards investigation.[47] This road movie, structured around a journey from London to Bristol taken by the main character to retrieve the body of his dead brother, goes to the heart of what might be called the 'British Question', and it does so with particular insight into the Northern Irish and Scottish dimensions of that question. The film now also seems highly prescient in its concern with the UK's relationship with Europe, and the choice to be made of strengthening that relationship politically and culturally, or retreating to a detached, self-referencing position. In effect, Petit anticipates the late twentieth-century out-workings of internal British tensions and divisions over nationality, class and ethnicity, and the confrontations over EU membership which came to a head in 2016; and he does so just at the point of the advent of the Thatcher era, which remains central to the explanation of these political and cultural showdowns.

Early in the film, as the central character, a male in his thirties whose name, Robert B., we gather in passing, goes through the motions of his daily routines, the radio – an important character in the film in its own right – broadcasts news about the latest violence in Northern Ireland and the latest civilians and soldiers to perish in the Troubles. It is clear that Petit's protagonist is paying no attention to it and is blissfully detached from a crisis deeply rooted in British history which is playing out in the background of his existence. He could, in this respect, represent the indifference that Bryant, as noted above, has claimed to be typical of people in Britain as a whole regarding Northern Ireland. However, he is clearly portrayed as someone moulded by a Home Counties or 'middle England' environment; self-absorbed and rather bland, if civil and dutiful, he drifts almost anonymously through the film.

A key scene in the film involves Robert B. stopping his car to pick up a hitchhiker, who turns out to be a Scottish squaddie who has deserted from army duty in Northern Ireland. Deeply troubled, he relates some of the horrors he has experienced, only for Robert

B. to respond airily that he had 'never been able to understand what it's all about'. This provokes an incendiary outburst from the hitchhiker, whose accent denotes an upbringing in the west of Scotland, the region where sectarian tensions echo those in nearby Ulster. This outburst conveys resentment towards the powers that be who have placed him in this situation, and frustration over the lack of concern and knowledge of so many in England about the Northern Ireland problem. However, it also carries wrath towards those – the Provisional IRA and other republican paramilitaries – who have murdered his comrades.

The scene highlights much about contemporary Scottish perspectives on the Troubles in Ulster: it points to the instinctive understanding that Scots, in general, possessed relative to other British people regarding both the IRA's war against the British state and the loyalists' 'No Surrender' stance against their perceived tribal enemies. Both perspectives existed in the social and cultural world of parts of the country. The weight of the Irish Troubles rested more heavily in Scotland, and blended with attitudes to England that could range from mild irritation over 'England' being confused with 'Britain' through to outright antagonism and blame for all manner of ills and disadvantages. There were, in fact, genuine fears in Scotland in the early years of the Troubles that there could be a spill-over of communal divisions and violence. When three young Scottish squaddies, all of whom came from the west of the country, were murdered by the IRA in 1971 while off duty, such anxieties produced a concerted civic effort involving politicians, Church leaders and trade unionists to ensure that emotions were contained. In retrospect, this seems to have been a turning point: Scotland then proceeded to watch the grim saga across the narrow sea unfold with only fringe loyalist and republican elements offering sporadic suggestions of disorder.

Radio On clearly indicts an inward-looking Englishness inclined to nostalgic wallowings and lacking in awareness of the cultural complexity of the UK as an entity and 'these islands' as a site of historic interaction. This kind of complacency and failure to show empathy are seen as contributing to the problem of a UK, or Britain, facing an uncertain future and leaving behind the heavy industrial economy and memories of the shared sacrifices of the Second World War that had provided the societal adhesive for some decades. The film, in this respect, seems to give expression to the political thinking of scholars like Bernard Crick, who wrote piercingly about the lack of English engagement with wider concepts of British/UK and European identity, and warned that such an absence could result in the UK losing its sense of purpose and overall commonality.[48] Indeed, there appears to be a kind of 'endism' implicit in *Radio On* in the way it highlights failures of communication and English indifference to the 'periphery', and sounds a note of surprise that the UK is still in existence and a degree of puzzlement as to what still sustains it.[49]

Yet, although Petit's sceptical perspective on Britishness is unmistakeable, his film also provides, perhaps unwittingly, clues as to its longevity. There is, for example, the referencing of cultural 'solids', such as the reading of the football results as a Saturday ritual, the weather, the dinginess of much of the surroundings, the traditional pubs. All of this is handled affectionately, as if Petit was aware that the endurance of institutions and habits in itself gave them a significance that could not be conjured away. Maybe, too, it could be said that there is some, albeit reluctant, recognition that apparent indifference and phlegmatism could underpin qualities such as tolerance, pragmatism and even-temperedness.[50] To push the point further, was the stoicism of the majority of English people in the face of a vicious IRA bombing campaign in the early to mid-1970s an important factor in ensuring that matters did not get much worse and that the essential unity of the UK was not more endangered by the Irish Troubles?[51] Was English 'indifference' central to the 'banal unionism' of everyday shared experiences? Should we view matters in terms of English complacency and presumptuousness being at the root of the UK's crisis, or in terms of English equanimity providing necessary ballast within a finely tuned and balanced whole? The Scottish army deserter in the movie intrudes furiously into the central character's buffered world, but rather than confront his provocations and challenges, Robert B. takes evasive action, drives swiftly off while the deserter is relieving himself, and restores stability. This may, at one and the same time, be seen as cowardly, myopic, sensible and self-preserving.

Petit, who would go on to write a novel about the Northern Ireland conflict, *The Psalm Killer*, is clearly troubled by the ignorance of fellow English people about British and Irish history, and the distancing strategy adopted in the face of a home-grown political crisis. He is alert to the internal diversity of Britain; although the squaddie is Scottish, resentments around social disadvantage and cultural remoteness from the metropolitan centre would have made Robert B. just as uncomfortable had the deserter been a Scouser or a Geordie. The movie is concerned with 'Border Zones',[52] both the internal ones within the UK, as well as those between the UK and other countries. There is a sense of frustration in the film around perceived English insularity, yet there is also a celebration of British creativity as evidenced in the film's rock music soundtrack, with David Bowie positioned as a kind of cultural ambassador.[53]

In short, *Radio On* encourages us to think about the nature of Britishness and its many ambiguities, both in relation to the pivotal late 1970s period of the film's creation and the eventful years since. Much can be gleaned from it to explain why the UK as a political entity has found itself under threat and why British identity has been viewed as so problematic or, indeed, assumed to be in terminal decline. Yet there is also much in the film to help us assess why the break-up of the UK has not yet happened, and why Britishness and different interpretations of it remain live topics of discussion. Moreover, the film does a signal service in bringing Irish matters in from the margins, demanding to be addressed in a way that too many scholars and commentators, in the manner of the central character of the movie, shrink from doing.

Britishness and the End of the Post-nationalist Moment

The 'post-nationalist' climate of the late twentieth century significantly affected deliberations on the 'British Question': the question of whether constitutional reform was required to hold the Union together. On the surface this was an era in which the interrogation of the nation-state idea and its future appeared to betoken a loosening up of matters of identity and allegiance, as well as an impulse towards a more pluralist and 'pick and mix' approach to political life. In relation to Northern Ireland, the Good Friday Agreement of 1998 might be viewed as emblematic of this post-nationalist turn. In its open-endedness about the constitutional future, its alternative to the 'endgame' of a victory for one or other nation-states, its accommodation of both British and Irish identities and aspirations, its confederal features, and its fidelity to the European project, the Agreement spoke of a future of overlapping identities and of multi-layered governance removed from nationalist shibboleths. It was eminently of its broader intellectual time, as well as its more parochial imperatives.

The peace process and the Good Friday Agreement were viewed positively by constitutional nationalists in Northern Ireland, whose Europeanness grew noticeable in the 1990s.[54] They undoubtedly also viewed developments in terms of the loosening of the British governmental grip on Northern Ireland and the involvement of the Republic of Ireland in the Agreement's architecture. Unionists were seriously split over the deal, and Paisley's DUP was soon to exploit wider community concern over the issues of decommissioning, reform of policing and release of paramilitary prisoners. However, it is important to remember that the UUP, steered by Trimble, had come to see the value in arrangements that seemed to leave the traditional thirty-two-county Irish sovereign state ideal in an historical cul-de-sac. A Trimble ally, Michael McGimpsey, put the point in the following way in 1994: 'Unionism as a philosophy remains strong and in its refusal to countenance the heresy of Nationalism, is remarkably in harmony with the spirit of the new Europe.'[55]

Sinn Féin's acceptance of the Good Friday Agreement was predicated on the belief that it could provide a basis for the wearing down of unionism and the 'de-Britishing' of Northern Ireland. Indeed, the republicans at this juncture were Eurosceptic, did not favour the dilution of sovereignty the EU entailed and never bought into the post-nationalist idea. They sensed the likelihood of using the political energies into which they had so successfully tapped to achieve substantial gains in the 'culture wars' that replaced the guns,[56] and they knew they could grow as a political force in both parts of Ireland by putting the stress on themes such as equality and social justice. Their effectiveness in such areas following the Agreement spooked those unionists and loyalists who were easily distracted from appreciating the constitutional and security gains they had made.[57] Tribal imperatives reasserted themselves as Sinn Féin and the DUP pulverised their more moderate rivals in both Northern Ireland and UK elections from 2003.

Adapting to a post-nationalist perspective was never going to be straightforward for Ulster unionists, given their history of gearing themselves constantly to resist Irish nationalism, and their tendency to assume a robust and defensive Britishness in such a process. The limits of the civic variant of unionism and the more flexible and receptive responses to the new political realities of the Good Friday Agreement and UK devolution were plain to see by the time of the Brexit debates; moreover, Ulster unionists had been driven back to fundamentals shortly before when Scotland threatened to vote itself out of the UK Union.

The belief that devolution and remaining in the UK was 'the settled will'[58] of the Scottish people came to look decidedly questionable as the Scottish Parliament found its feet after a shaky start and disillusionment grew with the Blair Labour government and its involvement in America's 'war on terror'. As argued in the previous chapter, there were also serious deficiencies in the management of the devolution project by the centre, a failure to strike a healthy balance between diversity and pan-UK solidarity,[59] and a failure to read the signs of Scottish distinctiveness assuming a virtual 'post-unionist' dynamic. Almost imperceptibly an increasing number of Scots were coming to regard the Union and the wider British framework as confining rather than enabling, and, conversely, viewing in independence the possibilities of the expansion of Scottish horizons and influence.[60] Such outlooks may well have been shaped by the cultural vitality in the country from the 1980s and 1990s, a development which suggested comparisons with the Irish experience of the late nineteenth and early twentieth centuries when cultural nationalism fuelled political change. In the early years of devolution some in the SNP, including party leader Alex Salmond, turned to such Irish parallels; Salmond was particularly fond of quoting Charles Stewart Parnell's injunction that no man had the right to fix the boundary of 'the march of the nation'. The quote was duly to adorn the frontispiece to the SNP's *National Conversation* document published on its ascent to power in 2007.[61] For nationalists, dabbling in Irish precedents had the effect of fortifying a teleological reading of history that conceived of independence as the nation's 'natural' destiny. If only from the point of view of convincing more and more Scots that independence was 'inevitable', and that whatever their doubts they could not stand in the way of history, this was perhaps a shrewd tactic.[62]

The SNP from the 1990s onwards cast off its previous opposition to the European project and seemed to indicate that it was comfortable with the post-nationalist and regionalist turn in international affairs. It looked as if it was adapting to new times, paying more attention to convincing voters of its left-of-centre character on social and economic questions; it probably perceived the critical interrogation of the role of the nation-state as essentially an opportunity for small nations, even if stateless, to exert more influence. The SNP, moreover, placed itself firmly in the 'civic' column of nationalism, and repudiated, in a context of bloodletting in the Balkans, any notion of 'ethnic' nationalism.

Nevertheless, the SNP's stunning victory in the 2011 Scottish parliamentary election, at which it achieved an overall majority, and the subsequent pursuit of an independence referendum, had the effect of pushing matters of national identity back into the either/or and binary framework redolent of traditional nationalism. At the same time, the crisis, if such it had been, of the nation-state largely passed; narrow notions of sovereignty, and chauvinistic populism, became a feature of the European political landscape once more. Nationalism was again the driver of political change as the new century gathered pace.[63]

Thus, Scots were forced to make a choice in the referendum in 2014. The question – 'Should Scotland be an independent Country?' – encouraged at least some 'Yes' campaigners to foment anti-Britishness, with rhetoric about 'obeying London masters' and being kept subservient. The 'No' side in the campaign complained bitterly of intimidation and having to endure slurs about being 'traitors' and 'quislings'.[64] Although the campaign was fought in a healthy spirit in many parts of the country, deep divisions emerged that would not fade in the aftermath. Indeed, the 'No' side's eventual victory produced a seemingly entrenched strain of anti-British feeling among many supporters of independence, who took up the demand for another referendum.

The official 'No' campaign, 'Better Together', made it clear that it did not welcome the participation of the Orange Order or the assistance of Ulster unionists. The much-publicised loyalist flag protests of 2013 in Northern Ireland represented precisely the 'uber-Britishness' from which they wanted to distance themselves. Understandably, they were fearful of sectarianism being stirred up,[65] but there was also the sense in which support for the Union in Scotland was essentially 'civic' rather than 'ethnic'. Scottish unionism had become largely a matter of the workings of the Union and how to improve them, while Ulster unionism still related more obviously to a 'comfort blanket' sense of Britishness and the quest for emotional reassurance. Scottish unionists, for the most part, had adapted to the new devolved order and had accepted more readily than their Ulster counterparts the lowering of the temperature around Britishness. It might be noted that in 1976, during the controversy over devolution in that decade, a 'Scotland is British' pressure group was set up to play on people's fears about identity issues and encourage them to assert a British allegiance.[66] No such campaign, drawn up explicitly around identity labels, appeared during the 1997 devolution referendum campaign, and nothing of the kind either in 2014.

There were thus strong reasons for the pro-Union side in 2014 not to encourage discussion of how Northern Ireland related to the Scottish independence question. Nevertheless, this should not obscure appreciation of Northern Ireland's relevance as a variable in the development of the 'Scottish Question': it is no coincidence that the onset of the peace process resulted in a more expansive public discussion of Scotland's constitutional options, as well as her own sectarian divisions. It was a matter of great importance to Scotland, as she negotiated profound governmental and cultural changes into the new century, that nearby Northern Ireland, with all its historic ties, should be at peace.

More consideration, therefore, might have been given in Scotland during 'Indyref' to the effects of the vote on Northern Ireland.[67] Politically, a 'Yes' vote would have been likely to destabilise the region; although the devolved institutions were functioning in 2014, there was still the sense of an uneasy peace and an absence of trust between the dominant DUP and Sinn Féin parties. Culturally and socially, much of the Ulster unionists' sense of belonging and sense of who they were was bound up with Scotland; an Ulster-Scots identity had become recognised as part of the complex tapestry of Northern Ireland and central to the ongoing 'culture war'. A 'Yes' vote would have deprived unionists of much of the cultural capital that Ulster-Scots affords – it would have been awkward for unionists to celebrate the cultural bonds in the context of a political rupture to the Union – and left them over-reliant on symbols of what remained of Britishness, such as the monarchy. A truncated UK of England, Wales and Northern Ireland would not have had the same emotional resonance for unionists. Some unionist politicians, despite the cold shoulder from 'Better Together' in Scotland, made pleas to Scots not to break the ties of kith and kin, an anguished echo of similar urgings made at the height of the Irish Home Rule crisis a century before. Alex Salmond, at the time of 'Indyref', attempted to assuage the anxieties of some Scots about leaving the UK by talking positively about the 'social union' comprising deep and extensive ties between the peoples of the different parts of the British Isles. He argued that independence would not attenuate such bonds.[68] However, Salmond's arguments were clearly made with Anglo-Scottish relations chiefly in mind, and they did little to ease the Ulster unionist sense of vulnerability.

Even the 'No' vote that eventually transpired brought important consequences for the rest of the UK, including Northern Ireland. The additional fiscal powers given to Scotland following the referendum, in accordance with 'The Vow' made by the pro-Union parties, complicated the devolutionary financial arrangements more broadly, and there was also the question of 'English votes for English laws' and the changes to parliamentary procedure this entailed. On top of all this, as the 2015 general election demonstrated, the 'Scottish Question' simply rose to a different level of national soul-searching, and the future of the Union and Britishness continued to be in jeopardy. In relation specifically to Northern Ireland, the lack of consideration given in 'Indyref' to how it might be affected seemed to suggest that any future independent Scotland is just as likely to try to evade the task of helping to maintain and build peace, and of fashioning policies that acknowledged the Scottish dimensions to Northern Ireland's difficult history, as it had been during the Troubles. Equally, in an SNP-dominated Scotland, there has been the same reluctance to address the question of how Northern Ireland affects Scotland. In ways that may not be obvious, the capacity of the UK – at least until very recently – to accommodate a plethora of national, regional, ethnic and cultural identities, and to absorb conflict and tensions, is relevant to the divisions in Northern Ireland and the containment of their effects in culturally contiguous areas such as the west of Scotland.[69]

In both Scotland and Northern Ireland, those wishing to see the break-up of the UK state have been on the front foot in recent years. From the pluralistic context of the close of last century, with the more labile and fluid concepts of identity that then prevailed, there has re-emerged a political landscape of sharp, binary choices – exemplified in both the Scottish and Brexit referendums – and a reassertion of the supposed virtues of 'oneness' and an atmosphere of impending ruptures and endings. The grievances expressed through the identity politics of the new century have proved to be territory congenial to nationalists in both places. The Union, unionism and unionists have been portrayed by Scottish and Irish nationalists and republicans as on the 'wrong side of history'. Such are the many varieties of unionism, and such have been the justifiable grounds for critiques of recent British governments in their handling of domestic constitutional issues and the European challenge, that an effective response to this kind of nationalist prophesying has as yet been elusive. It is nonetheless always a risky business to assume that history is on your side. The Union and Britishness contain a lot of history that will not easily fade away.

Perhaps, amidst the contemporary clamour of identity politics and thirst for clear-cut choices and clean breaks with the past, a remnant of those very different times at the close of the twentieth century might come to assume a constructive role in the management of change and the resetting of relationships, in whatever political direction they may happen to be steered. The third strand of the Good Friday Agreement included a British–Irish Council (BIC), an intergovernmental body spanning all the governments of these islands including the Isle of Man and the Channel Isles. This body – designed to reassure unionists that east–west relations were being treated as seriously as north–south – was colloquially known at the time as 'The Council of the Isles' and seemed to hold out much potential in relation to new policy initiatives and relationships.[70] This potential has largely gone untapped; the BIC has achieved little in the way of innovation and its profile has been much lower than the North–South Council. The BIC, indeed, lacked a proper secretariat until 2008, when one was established in Edinburgh. This might have given the Scottish government the incentive to put the body firmly on the political map, but the SNP clearly saw no great benefit in doing so.

However, there remains the possibility that the BIC could be put to work if there was the will on all sides to construct functional models of governance and the sharing of ideas, policy initiatives and responsibilities for the future. In relation specifically to Northern Ireland, the economics scholar Paul Teague has recently suggested that, within a revived Strand Three scheme, governing Northern Ireland could be 'something akin to the novel post-nationalist framework that some envisaged the agreement to be when it was first signed in 1998'.[71]

Such a development, and a revitalising of the 'post-nationalist' framework, would be eminently in the spirit of the 'Interrelations' ideas of Bernard Crick, who himself was greatly influenced by the work of historians such as Hugh Kearney.[72] A new architecture of cross-national policy networks and arrangements could well meet the realities of the co-existence and interactions of the peoples of these islands, and mitigate the divisiveness and recriminations that have resulted from the continuing difficulties in Northern Ireland, the 'Scottish Question' and Brexit. The writer and broadcaster Andrew Marr was perhaps on to something back in 2000 when he wondered if some kind of British political identity could be preserved through a 'Union of Island Peoples'.[73]

CHAPTER FOUR

The Ulsterisation
of Scottish Politics

Religious divisions underpinned politics in Northern Ireland in obvious ways from the time it became a devolved entity within the UK in 1921. The Unionist-Protestant–Nationalist-Catholic polarisation fed off baleful perceptions of 'the other' and the ritualistic rehearsal of communal grievances and national allegiances. There was little room within this sectarian 'zero-sum' culture for an alternative politics of social class interests, as demonstrated in the lack of electoral success, if not the heroic efforts, on the part of the NILP, even if class still clearly mattered in the life of both communities.

Scotland's political development was noticeably different, especially in relation to the factor of class consciousness, and this was reflected in the Labour Party's dominance in the late twentieth century. Nevertheless, religion was an important cleavage in Scottish politics for the greater part of that century, and it remained a relevant variable in those matters of identity underpinning political behaviour into the ostensibly secularist new era of devolution.[1]

Indeed, as the constitutional question has come to overshadow all else in contemporary Scotland, a line of argument has been advanced to the effect that Scotland's politics have become 'Ulsterised'. Certainly, it is important to explore the extent to which the new politics and political culture of twenty-first-century Scotland have revealed evidence of Irish or Ulster influences and similarities, and upset previous assumptions about Scotland's distinctiveness as the struggle over its future, in or out of the UK Union, has taken controversial twists and turns.

A Regretful Silence? Scotland and Twentieth-century Irish Questions

The Labour Party in effect inherited Catholic support in Scotland (and that of Irish Catholic communities in England) in the context of the divisions in the Liberal Party and the political realignments of post-First World War Britain. Labour had an obvious appeal to a relatively poor community on the grounds of social and economic policies; however, the party's ability to satisfy the Catholic Church on its opposition to communism and its willingness to defend the 1918 Education Act, also helped considerably. The Education Act brought Catholic schools into the state system with full funding, but effective control was left in the hands of the Church. This was a highly symbolic measure, later hailed as central to the integration of Catholics into Scottish society.[2] It was also to assume the character of a pillar of Catholic community identity and something to be defended against those who not only considered it divisive and discriminatory, but felt that the provision of separate schools was too much of a strain on the public purse. Education, in short, was a matter that could be said to have facilitated the immigrant Irish

Catholic community's identification with Scotland on the one hand, and contributed to the maintenance of a defiant tribalism on the other. Controversies surrounding the 1918 Act have outlived its own centenary.

Labour in Scotland, and indeed in urban centres in the rest of Britain, benefited, too, from the removal of the Irish question from British politics in the early 1920s. While the fact of partition offended the nationalist outlook of the Irish communities – and it should be remembered that Irish Protestants in Scotland had their own grievances over the settlement of the question – the way was clearer for political energies to focus on social class. Key figures in marshalling the Catholic vote, following the franchise extensions of 1918, were John Wheatley, a minister in the first Labour government in 1923–24, and Patrick Dollan, who became Glasgow's first Catholic Lord Provost (First Citizen) in 1938. Dollan's political prominence, in particular, reflected the way that the Labour movement in its widest sense could offer a vehicle for Catholic participation and advancement in public life.[3]

As the Labour–Catholic alliance firmed up in Scotland, there was a corresponding correlation between Protestants and the Conservative Party. However, in the case of working-class Protestants at least, this was more about popular unionism than conservatism as such, and, as has been noted, the political label used in Scotland for that party until the mid-1960s was indeed 'Unionists'.[4] Furthermore, Protestant electoral choices were much more widely spread over the various Scottish parties – Labour, Unionist, Liberal and SNP (after 1934) – than the Catholic vote, and appeals to class interest came increasingly to trump religious concerns as the twentieth century progressed.

Irish and Ulster reverberations were nonetheless still felt in the politics of certain parts of Scotland even beyond the Second World War. On the one hand, the Labour Party continued to be regarded by Catholics as sympathetic to Irish nationalist goals, and there were Labour MPs, such as Neil MacLean, who offered public support to anti-partition campaigns in the post-Second World War period. On the other, the Orange Order provided crucial working-class support for the Unionists in certain constituencies in the west of Scotland, including that of Secretary of State for Scotland Walter Elliot, during the 1930s. Overall, however, the broader British political context served to defuse the capacity of sectarian issues to polarise communities in the manner of Northern Ireland. Members of the Labour and Unionist parties in Scotland, for example, were part of broader British parties and movements that did not wish to be hamstrung by sectarian labels or characterisations.

The embedding of the post-war welfare settlement and the consolidation of the Labour–Conservative class-based politics seemed to stabilise the Union in Scotland as never before. Then, in the late 1960s, serious challenges to that stability arrived in the form of an electoral breakthrough for the SNP and the eruption of the Troubles in Northern Ireland. Support for the Conservatives (who ditched the 'Unionist' name in 1965) remained predominantly Protestant but decidedly less popularly based.[5] Dissatisfaction with the two main parties over the failure to revitalise Scotland's economic base resulted in the SNP becoming a serious player, as was evidenced in the turbulent world of British politics in the 1970s.[6] The rapid growth of secular trends in the culturally dynamic 1960s affected the Protestant Churches in Scotland most deeply, and triggered a loosening of the country's association with a distinctive history of Presbyterian struggle, schism and cultural shaping. The SNP's support in the 1960s and 1970s was notably Protestant,[7] suggesting defections in many cases from the Conservatives; it seems also to have been the case that many from a Protestant upbringing who no longer adhered to the Kirk or other denominations broke politically from Conservatism and Unionism.

The effect of the Northern Ireland situation on Scotland was ambiguous, reflecting perhaps the fluid nature of the times politically and culturally. There was certainly sympathy in certain communities for one side or the other in the conflict, and small numbers of activists engaged in fundraising for paramilitaries and even crossed the North Channel to offer their help.[8] Ulster's agony may have reinforced 'Orange and Green' identities and rivalries in the west of Scotland, although the nature of how the Troubles were experienced in Scotland was largely vicarious, with songs and chants in support of loyalists and republicans at football matches involving Rangers and Celtic, or at Orange and republican parades.[9]

The early years of the conflict probably posed the most serious challenge in terms of the possibility of the spill-over of violence and disorder. In this respect the murder of the three young Scottish soldiers in 1971 was a significant turning point. Crucial interventions on the part of civic leaders, political and clerical figures, and, indeed, army spokesmen who stressed the mixed religious character of the Scottish regiments in Ulster, served to maintain overall calm and restrain inflamed passions.[10] Thereafter, it might be said that leadership figures in Scotland went to great lengths to keep discussion of the Northern Ireland problem away from the mainstream of Scottish public life, and this was very much the case in the political sphere: no party or even individual politician attempted to exploit the situation for partisan purposes until at least the late 1980s.

These unofficial, though well understood, conventions were justifiable and may have saved Scotland much grief. Conversely, they also effectively curtailed the possibility of influential Scots in public life contributing constructively to debates about Northern Ireland and its future. Scotland in a sense 'opted out' of this debate, even though it was the part of Britain most intimately related to Ulster in a cultural sense and a place where distinct echoes of the Troubles were routinely heard. A rare parliamentary intervention at the time of the Anglo-Irish Agreement by a Scottish MP at Westminster, Labour's Hugh Brown, acknowledged that Scottish 'voices' had been absent in deliberations on Northern Ireland; this, he said, was regrettable given that 'in Glasgow and West of Scotland we understand what a Billy and Dan situation is'.[11]

Certainly, the political parties had worked hard in the 1970s to keep discussion of the Scottish devolution question from colliding with the Northern Ireland problem, even if this resulted in obvious connections being overlooked or downplayed. Fears about Ulster-style discord affecting Scotland did, however, play some part in the devolution referendum campaign in 1979. The arch-opponent of a Scottish assembly, Tam Dalyell, warned that the kind of sectarian problems so evident in Northern Ireland would be much more likely to grow in what he called 'a small, inward-looking governmental set-up' in contrast to the more capacious context of British politics centred at Westminster. It was these fears that also led some anti-devolution campaigners to attempt to scare Catholic voters with the argument that a Scottish assembly would be a facsimile of Stormont.[12]

The Anglo-Irish Agreement of 1985 provoked loud loyalist protests in Scotland and even led to political machinations conducted by the Orange Order there to weaken Conservative support. There is some evidence, indeed, that this intervention helped to cause the Conservative losses to Labour in the 1987 general election.[13] Labour's nominal 'united Ireland by consent' policy discomfited those most sympathetic to Ulster unionism, but by and large Labour prospered in Scotland as opinion hardened against the Thatcher government. Labour's ability to craft a working-class support base across sectarian lines reached its apogee in these years. Notwithstanding sensitivities around Northern Ireland, and its own internal tensions over Scottish devolution, Labour's careful handling of Orange and Green factions, and its success in putting issues of jobs, health and housing at the front of the political agenda, kept Scotland swimming with the current of British politics. Moreover, as Scotland remained relatively unscathed by the nearby Troubles, it became clear that factors distinguishing the country from its neighbour were of crucial importance: as well as the greater degree of class solidarity, there was also the relative lack of residential and workplace segregation, and the way that 'mixed marriages' had become commonplace in Scotland while remaining exceptional in Northern Ireland.[14]

However, the 1990s would see a greater degree of convergence between the respective Scottish and Northern Irish questions as constitutional reform pushed its way back onto the political agenda once more. The 'peace process' in Northern Ireland opened up more space for tentative explorations of Ulster-Scottish, and wider Irish–Scottish, links. Such initiatives and ventures fed off the political developments around devolution and the Good Friday Agreement, and the reconfiguration of relationships across the British Isles that they heralded. Donald Dewar, Scotland's first First Minister, remarked in a landmark speech in Dublin in 2000 that these developments were already leading to a greater understanding and appreciation of the Irish connection, acknowledging at the same time that there had been a wish 'to avoid discussion about the Troubles' in the past.[15] This trend would continue into the twenty-first century, which was to see Scottish political life increasingly influenced by preoccupations of a distinctly Northern Ireland kind.

Sectarianism and the Search for a New Scotland

Two factors underpinned the emergence of high-profile concern over the issue of sectarianism in Scotland in the new era of UK decentralisation. One was devolution itself: the creation of a Scottish parliament provided a forum for the examination of matters that were regarded as having received insufficient attention up until then. The members of the new parliament were anxious to demonstrate that devolution could make a difference: a topic such as sectarianism and how to remove it fitted the job description very persuasively. Secondly, the peace process in Northern Ireland allowed many in Scotland to take the view that discussion of such a controversial and sensitive subject could now take place with much less risk to the stability of Scottish society and to the chances of Scottish developments exacerbating the situation across the water.

Sectarianism had provoked an outbreak of public concern before the devolved institutions were in place, although that discussion was, in effect, confined to the media. In 1993 allegations of sectarian discrimination were made against Monklands District Council in the Lanarkshire Labour heartland. The entirely Catholic Labour Party in the council was accused of favouring its co-religionists in relation to matters of public spending and the awarding of jobs and contracts. This was, on the face of it, a grubby local government scandal familiar in the world of local politics and the dispensing of patronage. However, in this case the matter took on the character of a sectarian grievance reminiscent of the local authority malpractice that was one of the main causes of the civil rights campaign of 1960s Northern Ireland. In the Monklands case, contrary to the most glaring examples in Ulster, those said to be unfairly treated were local Protestants in towns such as Airdrie. Interest in the affair was also intensified on account of Monklands being part of the parliamentary constituency of the national Labour Party leader of the opposition, John Smith.[16]

An independent inquiry later dismissed the 'nepotism' charges, but at the same time criticised the way local councillors had exercised power. However, by then there had been a by-election in the area following the sudden death of Smith in 1994. It was to prove a bitter contest, one in which sectarian passions ran high and long-held and deeply rooted resentments and grievances were fully aired. The safe Labour seat – Smith had enjoyed a majority of almost 16,000 – was put in jeopardy as Protestants, alienated by what they termed a 'Catholic Mafia' in the council, set out to punish Labour by rallying behind its most credible opponent, in this case the SNP. Labour later alleged that the SNP had played 'the Orange Card' and threatened to close Catholic schools, charges the latter party vigorously denied. In the event, Labour held the seat with a majority of only 1,640, and a poll taken at the time of the election reported that 80 per cent of Catholics voted Labour and 65 per cent of Protestants SNP.[17]

In retrospect the Monklands affair stands out as somewhat anomalous given the subsequent development of the sectarianism debate, focused as that debate largely became on claims of anti-Catholicism. Moreover, the affair looks odd in the light of the seismic transfer of support on the part of the Catholic community from Labour to the SNP by around 2010, and the media's preoccupation in the immediate aftermath with the subject of segregated schooling.[18] In the 2000s, as the debate widened in many respects, the matter of fully state-funded Catholic schools was effectively discounted, by both media and politicians, as an instrumental factor in the problem.

The intervention in 1999 of the classical musician and composer James MacMillan goes some way to explaining the changes in the trajectory of the debate. MacMillan, a widely admired and highly regarded cultural figure, used an Edinburgh Festival address to claim that anti-Catholicism was 'endemic' in Scotland, and to make what many regarded as disparaging comments on the Reformation and Scotland's Protestant history.[19] The timing of MacMillan's speech was highly significant: it came just as the Scottish Parliament was about to open. The effect of it was to encourage the new batch of politicians to address the issue as something deeply rooted in Scotland's history. In addition, Mac-Millan's framing of the issue steered it away from consideration of separate schooling: indeed, it may have been a coded warning to the new devolved Scotland to leave Catholic schools alone and not, in effect, blame the 'problem' on the 'victim'. Concurrent with the way MacMillan attempted to direct the debate, the Catholic Church quickly established an effective lobbying apparatus in relation to the new structures of government, with defence of its schools the top priority.[20] The intention, it seemed, was to put the issue of the schools off-limits in respect of public concern over sectarianism. The Catholic Church at the time of the Scottish Parliament's inception was headed by Cardinal Thomas Winning, a formidable figure adept at applying political pressure, as was shown in the early years of the Parliament when he orchestrated a populist campaign against a measure proposing the repeal of the 'Section 28' legislation prohibiting discussion of homosexuality in schools. Although ultimately unsuccessful, this flexing of the Catholic Church's political muscles in these early devolution days put down an important marker for the future.[21]

The effect of both Monklands and, in particular, the MacMillan intervention was to jolt Scotland out of the sense of complacency over the salience of religious tensions that had led, for example, to a media assumption at the time of the 1992 general election that religious affiliations played no significant part in politics any more.[22] The way that the issue was taken up in the new devolved Scotland suggested there was now an eagerness to make up for lost time in scrutinising the subject, time that had been lost largely on account of fears of contagion from the Northern Ireland tragedy.

However, Scotland was a very different place in 2000 than it had been back in the 1960s, when such scrutiny might have been given to the issue in the absence of the 'war next door'. By the close of the century there was much more emphasis on ethnicity and identity politics rather than social class, and much more doubt about the future of the UK and the Union. The problems of deindustrialisation, the rise of a more service-based economy and the impact of new technology on work and leisure complicated traditional concepts of religious and community identity. Religious identity, it might even be contended, had become detached from religion itself; attendance at church, across the faiths, continued to decline. Much of the commentary on sectarianism that was unleashed in the early 2000s drew on subjective and inevitably partial recollections – expressed often in the form of unverifiable anecdotes – of a world that had either gone or been substantially altered, or was based on interpretations of that world and its legacy that were shaped by decidedly current preoccupations and values. From another angle, and in relation specifically to the Irish or Ulster dimension, it may have been the case that anger or outrage about the Troubles, whether in relation to paramilitary terrorism or the state's handling of the crisis, found an outlet in the new climate of openness around sectarianism after being suppressed or internalised while the killings continued in Northern Ireland.

However, it has to be noted that explicit references to the Northern Ireland situation proved to be few and far between as the controversy over sectarianism developed. Neither the politicians who sank their teeth into the issue, nor the media seemed inclined to incorporate the legacy of the Troubles into their contributions to the debate; moreover, opportunities to draw lessons from the Northern Ireland conflict were largely passed over. Thus, the first Labour–Liberal Democrat coalition government in Scotland pursued the matter along the lines of the approach of Nil By Mouth (NBM), an anti-sectarian pressure group set up in 2000 as a response to the tragic murder of a Celtic fan in 1995 while walking through a largely Rangers-supporting neighbourhood.

NBM's focus was on the bitter Rangers–Celtic 'Old Firm' football rivalry and the history of sectarian strife between the supporters of those teams. The group produced a 'Charter for Change' that included a proposal for law reform. That the Scottish government took its cue from NBM was reflected, firstly, in a change in the law to make sectarian behaviour (where it could be proved as such) an aggravation of a criminal offence (effected in 2003), secondly, in the inclusion of NBM's charter as an annex to the 2002 report of a parliamentary working group into 'religious hatred' and, thirdly, in government funding to this group and, subsequently, to several others that clearly scented the opportunity for influence.[23] In effect, an 'industry' around sectarianism materialised, despite the fact that none of these groups provided particular expertise in the area, and in spite of the sceptical views of some academics about the extent and nature of the problem.[24]

The line advanced by NBM and others took little notice of the separate schools question and instead laid emphasis on crude sectarian language, football songs and chants, and the allegedly harmful 'banter' around the subject. This diagnosis lent support to the MacMillan thesis and appeared to put the blame on time-worn anti-Catholic prejudice in Scottish society. In 2002 Archbishop Mario Conti, effectively the successor as leader of Scotland's Catholics to Cardinal Winning, stated that calls for the abolition, or even the amalgamation, of Catholic schools were 'tantamount to asking for the repatriation of the Irish, and just as offensive'.[25] Conti was no doubt aware of the significance of the repatriation charge, echoing as it did the campaign in the Church of Scotland in the 1920s against Irish Catholic immigration, for which the Kirk had publicly apologised in 2001.

On becoming First Minister in 2002, Labour's Jack McConnell decided to make a 'crusade' against sectarianism a priority. High-profile government 'summits' followed, involving Church and football club representatives and other civic society leaders. The campaign effectively adopted a 'hate crime' discourse influential in analyses of racial and ethnic discord in England and elsewhere, and promoted re-education programmes that largely avoided discussion of the root causes of the phenomenon. A consensus that sectarianism was 'Scotland's Shame' was advanced with little in the way of a clear definition of the problem or an examination of its history, a history which involved Irish immigration into Scotland and subsequent Scottish–Irish interactions of a social, cultural and political kind. McConnell's campaign was, in this sense, a cosmetic exercise. Moreover, the First Minister himself was in the awkward position of having built his career from a power base in Lanarkshire that was deeply compromised by sectarianism and carried the stigma of the Monklands affair. In 2001 the local Labour organisation, of which McConnell was a leading light, had caused embarrassment to the then First Minister Henry McLeish by sabotaging a proposed visit by the Irish Taoiseach Bertie Ahern to the region on the dubious pretext of security concerns around an Old Firm fixture on the same day. McLeish was later to refer scathingly in his memoirs to a 'clique which seemed to think it had some hereditary right to control Scottish Labour' and to the sectarianism which often scarred local politics.[26]

Such was the eagerness of politicians and pundits to argue that Scotland was in the grip of religious strife, that any news story regarding sectarianism, however trivial, was given prominence, while academic research that challenged the narrative was ignored.[27] Investigations, such as the one conducted by Glasgow City Council in 2003, were left undiscussed: the findings, while attesting to 'social anxiety' around sectarianism, revealed that only a small minority had actually experienced it.[28] What fuelled the popular anxieties and media interest around the subject was not the prevalence of animosities to the extent claimed; rather, it was the way the matter related to the new political dynamics of Scotland under devolution, in particular the struggle between the country's two largest parties, Labour and the SNP. It was clear to both parties that the Catholic vote in West-Central Scotland – which had long assumed the character of a 'block vote' – was essential to the achievement of power. Labour's hold over this vote had been one of the signal features of the Scottish political landscape for decades and had resulted in a string of Westminster seats that were vital to the party.

The SNP, under the leadership of Alex Salmond, was determined to eat into Labour's electoral heartland. If Monklands, rightly or wrongly, had cast the party in an unfavourable light with some Catholic voters, then the party's subsequent efforts to repair the damage were striking in their purposefulness. These included the SNP declaring its support for the scrapping of the Act of Settlement, which forbade a Catholic from becoming monarch, and Salmond cultivating Cardinal Winning and the Catholic Church with assurances about the high value the SNP placed on Catholic schooling.[29] In the light of the fact that both Labour and the SNP were left-of-centre parties, there was a great incentive for both to appeal to Catholics on the alternative grounds of ethnic or tribal identity. In this, the SNP can be said to have achieved partial success by 2007 – aided undoubtedly by the unpopularity of Labour's stance on the Iraq war – when it emerged as the largest party in the Scottish parliamentary election and became a minority government; and then reaped the full reward in 2011 when the Labour vote collapsed so spectacularly as to enable the SNP to win an outright majority. This 2011 victory proved to be of profound significance, not just for Scotland but for the UK as a whole, paving the way as it did for the independence referendum of 2014 and the intensification of the debate over the future of the Union.

The public concern over sectarianism that was such a feature of the first decade of Scottish devolution was bound to make an impact on community relations, to blend with wider social and cultural trends and to shape political behaviour. It is not easy to say precisely what impact it has had, but it is possible to advance some suggestions.

First, developments around the issue of sectarianism, such as McConnell's summits, the emergence of pressure groups like NBM, claims regarding the extent of the problem, relentless media coverage of even the most tangential instances, and the new legislation passed by the Scottish Parliament, all fed the growth of another form of identity politics within which class concerns and loyalties have been challenged for primacy as never before.[30]

Second, Catholics moved away from seeing the Labour Party as their protector in a society many felt was hostile to them. By the early years of the new century many Catholics came to feel that their opposition to aspects of the Labour Party under Tony Blair overrode ancestral loyalty; yet perhaps even more transformative was their willingness to identify with, and indeed shape, a Scottish national(ist) cause. The highlighting of the sectarianism question, however dubiously it may have been conducted, seems to have convinced many Catholics that Scotland was taking responsibility for past discrimination, although at the same time it might be observed that Catholics have become more inclined to perceive anti-Catholic biases and prejudices still lurking in Scotland. One of the research findings of the Advisory Group later tasked by the SNP government to report on how to tackle sectarianism was that there 'remained acute sensitivity in the West of Scotland Catholic community'.[31] The climate of identity politics, in short, has arguably heightened the Catholic communal antennae; Catholics have viewed the new politics positively in the light of old injustices. Even if by the early 2000s many in this community could be more accurately described as 'cultural Catholics' rather than devout adherents – and it has to be noted that many were disillusioned by the sexual abuse scandals which rocked the Church – there was still a strong atavistic sense of seeking 'payback' for the past.

Third, the sectarianism debate has revealed a 'liberal' or 'moderate' slice of Protestant opinion that is willing to accept, as per MacMillan, a definition of sectarianism as essentially an anti-Catholic phenomenon. This group feel that there is an unedifying past to live down or own up to and, in this respect, the Church of Scotland's apology in 2001 for the anti-Irish Catholic rhetoric and stances of some of its leadership figures during the inter-war period is germane. This was undoubtedly an attempt to heal past divisions and defuse tensions, but the 'politics of the apology' are seldom straightforward. In this case what may have occurred was a deepening of the divisions between this group of Protestants and another group to be discussed below.

Fourth, there is now a large number of Scots from a Protestant (mainly Presbyterian) background who claim to have 'No Religion' and seem inclined towards independence and leftist politics. This mirrors the trend in certain other European countries.[32] This group sees sectarianism as 'Scotland's Shame' – in the terms routinely used by the media in the wake of the MacMillan speech – and, like the previous group of liberal Protestants, tends to view bigotry as a largely Protestant problem. In their case this outlook is probably shaped by a wish to throw off the religious associations of their past. They may, in theory, support the idea of integrated schooling, but their sensitivity about being 'implicated' in past wrongs generally prevents them from lining up with the few militant secularists who have challenged the Catholic Church in demanding an end to state-funded faith schools, which, in the Scottish case as well as, significantly, that of Northern Ireland, means Catholic schools.[33]

Fifthly, there might be said to be the remaining part of the Protestant 'block' or 'community', which contains those other believers or those from a Protestant background for whom Protestantism still matters as an important aspect of their identity. The report of the SNP's Advisory Group noted the emergence of a 'Loyalist' working class 'more distinct from the secular and Protestant mainstream of Scottish society than Catholics'.[34] These people – much in the way of their counterparts in Northern Ireland – are resentful of the way the sectarianism debate has developed publicly; they feel scapegoated and believe that Catholic intolerance or inflexibility has been overlooked, while instances of Protestant sectarianism have been magnified. They often feel bitterness towards the Church of Scotland for effectively 'disowning' them, and they have watched as the Labour Party and the SNP have prioritised the courting of the Catholic vote. They are baffled by

Catholic perceptions of 'Protestant Scotland' as a single community of interest when they feel it to be fractured and lacking in communal togetherness. They are resentful that factors such as the Catholic Church's historically hard-line stance on mixed marriages and how children should be raised in them have received little attention in analyses of how discord and distrust have been fomented over time. Above all, they argue that separate schooling ought to be seen as the root cause of sectarianism, and they complain that this question has in effect been ruled out of bounds in the public conversation.[35] In this view they are aligned with those secularists who otherwise would have little in common with them. An interim report by the Advisory Group indeed simply stated that it did not believe sectarianism stemmed from denominational schools, and neither offered any evidence to support this contention, nor provided any serious consideration of the opposite viewpoint.[36]

The sidelining of the schools question has meant, among other things, that Scotland has not seriously explored the merits of integrated schools and has not considered the evidence that now exists in Northern Ireland, where there has been a successful, if small, state-funded integrated schooling sector since the 1980s and where there is evidence of greater mixing in the state sector.[37] Indeed, Scotland could certainly have benefited, in its concern over sectarianism, from the Northern Ireland experience more broadly: for example, there may have been an opportunity to learn from academic and inter-faith studies of the issue in order to define the problem more clearly and draw informed comparisons.[38] Furthermore, a plethora of cross-community initiatives have taken place in Northern Ireland – some, post-conflict, involving former paramilitaries – which might have provided guidance to those groups in Scotland which ostensibly wished to tackle the issue at grass-roots level. None of these connections and opportunities were taken up. It appeared all too often that Scotland was content to caricature the problem and steer clear of any Irish dimension that might lure the country to a place that its politicians and media had no desire to go. Yet the evidence of these Irish influences in Scotland has been plain to see for many years, in the form of controversial marches, graffiti, the flying of flags, and football songs and chants. Moreover, the sectarianism question, as it has actually been highlighted in Scotland, has run the risk of adversely affecting social cohesion in certain parts of the country. There have long been 'Orange and Green' tensions in West-Central Scotland, but the way a 'sectarianism industry' has emerged has done little to diminish them. Indeed, as will be discussed below, the Scottish independence question has in some ways intensified them and produced an 'Ulsterisation' effect on Scottish political life.

In relation specifically to the Labour Party and the loss of its political grip in Scotland, the sectarianism issue is pertinent as part of a wider trend. That trend is the eclipse of class politics by those of identity. In respect of religious tribalism, the Labour Party has played into the SNP's hands by encouraging the identity politics that were always likely to flow from any public inquisition trumpeted as a 'crusade' and ill-defined and couched in terms of a 'blame game'. Greater care should have been taken about how Labour led such an initiative, and more appreciation shown of the role of religion in Scottish history and society. McConnell embarked on his campaign to end what he was happy to assume was 'Scotland's Shame' as a way of accumulating political capital and demonstrating that positive change could come through devolution. The issue, however, could be said to have backfired. In uncritically endorsing the idea of sectarianism as 'Scotland's Shame', McConnell in effect made it impossible for the Labour Party to highlight its own achievements in appealing across the religious divide, and to reaffirm the primacy of class-based politics.

In 2016 the former Scottish Labour MP and government minister Brian Wilson expressed the view that the Labour Party in Scotland was inept at reminding people of its achievements, and was so remiss in this respect that it left nationalists a clear path to rewrite history in their interests.[39] A glaring example of Labour in Scotland failing to do justice to its own record is precisely the subject of sectarianism and the successful effort to make Protestant and Catholic workers join together in common cause around matters of socio-economic interest, no mean feat against a background of severe religious discord in the inter-war years and the risk posed to the improvements in community relations by the Northern Ireland Troubles. McConnell, albeit unwittingly, threw all this away.

In the early years of the Scottish Parliament, it became clear that the Labour Party in Scotland could not manage the issue of sectarianism with the skill and dexterity that it had displayed pre-devolution, or at least pre-Monklands. McConnell's handling of the matter brought him some media plaudits but no electoral pay-off. The relentless focus on sectarianism, along with other issues, disrupted established patterns of Scottish politics. Much that was positive about Catholic–Protestant interactions in the late twentieth century was forgotten as the tensions which had endured were remorselessly highlighted and represented as a chronic societal disease.[40] Feverish claims of endemic prejudice and anti-Catholicism being hard-wired into the national psyche were met with counterclaims of victimhood wallowing and special pleading. Hard as the opinion-formers tried to avoid saying it, Scotland was looking and sounding increasingly like Northern Ireland.

The Old Firm in the SNP's Scotland

Once in government, the SNP found itself under attack for allegedly soft-pedalling efforts to combat sectarianism. Following their outright victory in the 2011 election, which allowed it to govern without the caution forced upon it in the minority government years, the SNP took up the matter with the kind of zeal shown previously by McConnell's administration. However, just as that government had blundered into controversy, so the SNP brought trouble on its head by ploughing a bill through Holyrood to curb what was called 'offensive' sectarian behaviour at football matches.[41] The legislation became law early in 2012 but was repealed in 2019.

Focusing on football again played to the gallery of the media's fixation with the troubled history of the Old Firm rivalry, and a kind of 'middle Scotland' abhorrence of the hooliganism that often accompanied the fixture. In his epic novel of post-Second World War Scotland, published in 2010, James Robertson – an enthusiastic supporter of independence – has a key character attend two Old Firm matches as a neutral spectator, one at Celtic Park and the other at Ibrox, home of Rangers. The character, who is from a small-town background in the east of the country, recoils from the raw passions he cannot comprehend, exasperated by a feature of industrial working-class Scotland that jars with the image of the country he holds and would like to see fulfilled: 'He was not of their kind and he realised he never would be.'[42]

This piece of fiction is actually very revealing of the cultural dissonance long produced by a football rivalry that has drawn its bitterness from essentially Irish political divisions between Protestant Rangers and Catholic Celtic. Such Irish influences indeed produced the very songs and chants heard from the fans of both clubs that were the target of the SNP's legislation. Despite this, there was little acknowledgement by the government of the way identities and allegiances around the Irish conflict were woven into the everyday life and popular culture of West-Central Scotland. No serious attention was given to the submission by the Association of Chief Police Officers to the Parliament's Justice committee in advance of the legislation being put forward that 'the greater driver' of sectarian behaviour in Scotland was 'Irish loyalist/republican *political* prejudice'.[43] The protests from fans, particularly those of Celtic, who wished to be free to pay tribute to Irish 'freedom fighters', were couched in terms of expressions of political viewpoints being curbed. Celtic-supporting Labour politicians, such as James Kelly and Jim Murphy, attempted to exploit such grievances to turn the tables on the SNP,[44] notwithstanding the growing number of leading SNP figures who were Celtic fans in that party.[45]

These counter-manoeuvres by Labour may have gained traction were it not for the issue being overshadowed in 2012 by the prospect of a referendum on independence. Coincidentally, the arrangements for the referendum, to take place in 2014, were put in place just as Rangers underwent a financial implosion, which led to them being put into administration and then demoted to the lowest level of the professional game in Scotland. The historic Old Firm fixture thus went into cold storage for the next five years, notwithstanding two cup ties during this period, and traditional antagonisms were left to find an outlet, at least to some extent, through the game-changing developments in the world of contemporary Scottish politics.

The binary choice of 'Yes' or 'No' to independence put before Scots in 2014 belied a history of fluid, tangled and pluralist concepts of national identity and belonging. Had there been a third option on the ballot paper – a stronger devolution scheme – the subsequent debate may not have been so polarising. As it was, the campaign, while clearly conducted civilly and constructively in many parts of the country, took on a 'tribal' aspect in other parts, with ancestral loyalties relating to Ireland and Ulster coming into play. In those areas it was a proxy for an Old Firm game, with Rangers fans – sticking with their club in remarkable numbers through the lower leagues – ramping up vocal expressions of Britishness and ultra-loyalism, and Celtic fans displaying 'Yes' banners at matches. As will be discussed below, the extent to which elements in the Celtic fan-base, such as the 'Green Brigade' ultras, politicised support for the club in these years, resulted in the language and sentiments of the Irish 'struggle' against the British state being transposed to Scotland.[46] On the other side of the divide, although there were Rangers fans who were pro-independence and those who may have felt that peace in Northern Ireland released them from the obligation of giving more moral support to Ulster unionists, the most vocal were those whose displays of British loyalty became all the more defiant for the sense in which they perceived themselves to have been marginalised and discounted in the Scotland of the twenty-first century. Times had changed starkly from the days when the club's proud assertion of a Scottishness combined with Britishness chimed with the country more widely.[47] Clashes between Rangers and Celtic fans occurred in the latter stages of the 'Indyref' campaign in the centre of Glasgow, and there were further outbursts of trouble following the vote.[48] These examples of disorder on the streets were reminiscent of Northern Ireland and were a foretaste of others to come.

Post-referendum Scotland: New Politics and Old Divisions

The religious breakdown of those in favour of independence in the 2014 referendum was one of the most striking, if under-discussed, stories of the whole affair. Some 57 per cent of Catholics voted 'Yes' compared to 41 per cent of those identifying as Protestants. Around 56 per cent of those who claimed to have 'No Religion', the majority without doubt from a Protestant background, voted 'Yes'. Clearly a majority of Catholics had decisively overcome their historic doubts about their place in an independent Scotland.[49] A corollary of this was the association of support for the continuation of the Union predominantly with Protestants, and the consequential danger of the independence question becoming increasingly 'sectarianised'.

Those of a pro-Union cast of mind had fondly imagined a 'No' vote laying the constitutional question to rest in Scotland, at least for a generation. In fact, the opposite happened: the campaigning energies of the 'Yes' side flowed into strengthening the SNP in the aftermath of the vote, and the Labour Party was made to pay a heavy price in its electoral heartlands in the UK general election of

May 2015, when the SNP scooped fifty-six out of fifty-nine Scottish seats and Labour was reduced to a solitary one. The political journalist Iain Macwhirter remarked of the SNP 'tsunami' that it signalled the replacement of class by nationalism as 'the driving force' in Scottish politics, and 'drew a line under a century of working-class industrial politics in Scotland'.[50] Another journalist, Alex Massie, commented that 'Nationalism is our new secular religion', and that 'identity politics defeats all comers'.[51]

In the light of such developments some commentators began to refer to Scottish politics as having been 'Ulsterised'.[52] This contention met with fierce rebuttals from academics and other opinion-formers. Gerry Hassan, a prolific author and essayist on Scottish politics, claimed that such terminology 'doesn't help anyone'. He went on: 'It doesn't assist us in opening up or understanding anything about ourselves.'[53] The country's leading historian, Tom Devine, labelled the 'Ulsterisation' term 'vacuous'.[54] The emphatic, not to say dogmatic, nature of these responses suggested that raw nerves had been touched. There was also a tendency for those outraged by the use of the term to take it literally, to ask where in Scotland was the evidence of the death, destruction and civil strife that marked the Troubles in Northern Ireland.

This kind of response missed the essential point of the 'Ulsterisation' line of argument, perhaps deliberately. This related to the way that the political dynamics in Scotland had changed in fundamental ways. As a nationalist blogger, Jamie Maxwell, put it at the time: 'Almost every issue in Scottish politics is filtered through the national question.'[55] That, it might be said, is as good a definition of an 'Ulsterisation' effect as could be imagined.

Moreover, the shrill dismissals of 'Ulsterisation' could be

said to have echoed the refusal on the part of successive Scottish governments, pressure groups with a vested interest in presenting the matter in certain ways, and the bulk of the contributors to the sectarianism debate of the previous fifteen to twenty years, to consider the extent of the Irish influences in Scottish life, their persistence and their role in sectarian behaviour. Of course, Scotland was not Northern Ireland: the two places had very different political histories. However, the main difference revolved around the dominance of class politics in Scotland and its relative weakness in Northern Ireland. By the time of 'Indyref' and its aftermath, that model in relation to Scotland had undergone significant change. Class still mattered, but then it had always mattered in Northern Ireland too. By 2015, in Scotland as well as in Northern Ireland, the national question complicated the political expression of class interests.

Sectarianism in Scotland has certainly not been the same phenomenon in kind and in scale to that in Northern Ireland. Factors such as intermarriage and the absence of residential segregation in Scotland ensured this. Yet there have remained enough similarities to make serious comparative analysis viable and potentially beneficial. This, however, has been eschewed by those tasked with addressing the issue in Scotland. Among the many Scotlands in existence, there has been a reluctance to acknowledge that in some of them there are affinities with Northern Ireland that can influence political behaviour.

One such common theme between the two places is education and the matter of religiously divided schooling. Again, those who repudiate the 'Ulsterisation' concept have been disinclined to address the similarities in a situation where, unlike England

and many other societies, those 'faith schools' which are publicly funded are, in effect, Catholic schools.[56] In both Scotland and Northern Ireland there is a similar narrative on the part of the Catholic Church about the defence of the schools they control. In both places Catholic schools are distinguished by the Church's ability to provide religious instruction and effectively decide appointments and promotions of staff.[57] In both places, educational institutions appear as central to the perpetuation of identities rooted in religion and are vigilant regarding perceived threats to the culture around them.[58] In 2015, in relation to proposals to merge teacher training colleges in Northern Ireland, Jim Gibney of Sinn Féin, a party ostensibly in favour of socialist ideals, celebrated the 'dynamic campaign' which united 'the Catholic Church, Sinn Féin, the SDLP, the GAA [Gaelic Athletic Association], and INTO [Irish National Teachers' Organisation] – a rare and vital achievement to see off this latest and most potent threat to St Mary's and Stranmillis University Colleges'.[59] Critical comments made by President Barack Obama about segregated schools on a visit to Northern Ireland duly brought down a wave of condemnation orchestrated by the Catholic Church and the nationalist political parties.[60]

In Scotland, jaundiced perceptions of sectarianism being generated through separate schools have fed off cases such as that of a Catholic teacher in 2016 tweeting about 'Orange xxxxx' and 'the 'Ra', and asking: 'Before we address the so-called problem of refugees, what's being done about Protestants?'[61] When political figures in Scotland in recent years, such as Stewart MacDonald of the SNP, have expressed criticism of Catholic schooling from personal experience, the backlash has been fierce and has usually resulted in a climbdown on the part of the critic.[62] A 2019 study which revealed that boys in Catholic secondary schools in Scotland 'cling to sectarian views' was immediately called into question by the Church.[63] In covering the story *The Herald* (Glasgow) commented: 'Experts say the results are indicative of growing extremist views held by teenagers on both sides of the sectarian divide.'[64]

'Ulsterisation' critics also have nothing to say about the way the language of politics in Scotland has come to resemble that in Northern Ireland. By the time of 'Indyref', the term 'Unionists' had become ubiquitous in political discourse, after a fifty-year absence, reflective of the way that those seeking independence wished to lump together all the parties which did not share their view.[65] They may also have been cognizant of the way the term carried uncongenial echoes of Northern Irish politics and the long years of unionist domination and Catholic nationalist powerlessness. Certainly, Jim Murphy, in his brief spell as Scottish Labour leader following the referendum, took care to disown the label in as much as it made someone with his Irish Catholic background uncomfortable; he tried to distinguish between what he called a 'Conservative and Unionist' political tradition, and the trades unionism and 'socialist solidarity tradition' of the Labour Party.[66] It was all to no avail, judging by the results of the 2015 UK election and subsequent elections in Scotland and the UK since. Indeed, as Ulster Unionist MP William Ross had predicted, in his exchange with Donald Dewar back in 1997, the politics of Scotland, like those of Northern Ireland, had become polarised around the national question.[67]

Ulster Reverberations: The Politics of Commemoration, the Street and the Tweet

By the time of the referendum in 2014 most Catholics in Scotland seemed to have left behind fears of being a disadvantaged minority in an independent country and developed trust in the SNP over Labour to defend their interests. It looked as if the SNP had finally triumphed in the long struggle to win the vital Catholic vote in the industrial and post-industrial areas of West-Central Scotland. However, the challenge remained for the nationalists to maintain this trust and support. Since 2014, there has been a significant tendency on the part of SNP elected representatives and activists to meet this challenge by voyaging into the choppy waters of the Irish question, territory the party had always been careful to navigate around during the period of the Troubles. In this respect, the relative peace achieved in Northern Ireland proved to be an important variable in the SNP feeling freer to explore Irish connections and parallels, and, indeed, sending reassuring signals of solidarity to a community which had never forgotten its Irish forebears and whose sense of Irishness had, in many ways, been revitalised in the context of contemporary cultural preoccupations with identity and the recognition of past wrongs on account of those Irish roots.[68]

Thus, over the past five or so years, there have been controversies over Irish matters in Scotland that have made considerable political waves and lend support to the 'Ulsterisation' thesis. In 2017 there was the case of the SNP candidate for South Ayrshire Council, Chris Cullen, who was accused of posting a message about 'the Ra on tour'. The candidate, who was from Northern Ireland, claimed he was the victim of sectarian and 'anti-Irish' attacks when the story broke.[69] Then, also in 2017, an SNP aide, Allan Casey, who was reported to have written 'Up the Provos' and praised former IRA members on his Facebook account, was passed by the SNP to stand for a council seat in Glasgow.[70] He was subsequently elected. Similar controversies concerning pro-Irish republican social media activity have surrounded Chris McEleny, who is an outspoken advocate of holding a second independence referendum without agreement being reached between Holyrood and Westminster, and the SNP MSP for Argyll, Brendan O'Hara.

In the book *Why Not?: Scotland, Labour and Independence*, published just prior to the 2014 referendum as a pro-independence intervention in the campaign, the Irish historian Owen Dudley Edwards contended that Scottish nationalism had firmly rejected the bloodshed to which Irish nationalism in the twentieth century 'so foolishly succumbed'.[71] Since then, some in the SNP have threatened to make a mockery of this historically accurate observation. In 2017 there was a major political row over SNP MSP for Glasgow Shettleston John Mason's tweet about IRA 'freedom fighters' in response to a request for support for a fresh inquiry into the murder of the three Scottish soldiers in 1971, the killings which had tested the nation's resolve not to travel down the road of political violence.[72] This episode, which needed First Minister Nicola Sturgeon's personal intervention to pressure a reluctant Mason into an apology, demonstrated that there was scant appreciation in the Scotland of 2017 of either the sensitivities that linger on from the Northern Ireland Troubles, or the complex legacy issues that remain to be resolved before Northern Ireland can truly put the conflict in the past. As the commentator Alasdair McKillop put it, the eventual SNP apology over Mason's tweet was 'simply a gesture learned from a public relations textbook' to limit the damage to the party.[73] Mason was merely reprimanded and since this affair, has continued to rile working-class unionists with other interventions over Orange marches.[74] Whatever way this affair is looked at, it is clear that for many on the nationalist side of the argument, indulging in support for the Provisional IRA should not be considered part of the sectarianism discussion.

In any event, the Mason affair reflected the SNP's recent willingness to side openly with the cause of Irish unity, and in the case of some prominent members, with physical force Irish republicanism. Even ex-Justice Minister Kenny MacAskill could be found saluting the rebels of 1916 on the centenary of the Rising, something the party would not have risked in the past.[75] Moves, indeed, were made by some local councils to commemorate the Rising, but these were met with objections and threats to mobilise protestors on the streets.[76] These tensions had followed on from the 'sectarianising' of the commemorations of the fallen in the two World Wars and of the wearing of the poppy. In September 2016 IRA graffiti was daubed on a Great War cenotaph in Coatbridge.[77] Hitherto such divisions had only been apparent in Northern Ireland.

Controversies over Orange marches, with the SNP-controlled Glasgow Council attempting to restrict the number of them, likewise echo Northern Ireland. In 2019 the Orange Order attempted to stage a protest in Glasgow's George Square regarding the curtailment of some marches. The Grand Master, Jim McHarg, who clashed bitterly with SNP government minister Humza Yousaf over the issue, referred to 'a narrow-minded band of anti-

Unionist Nationalist councillors' introducing measures against the Order while doing nothing about 'Irish republican supporting groups' causing 'fear and alarm' to the 'Protestant communities of Glasgow'.[78] As the rhetoric was pumped up around such matters as marches, the football fans' forums reflected the extent of growing political tensions. On the Rangers' fans 'Follow Follow' site, many claimed the SNP was turning the west of Scotland into a 'mini-Ulster'. 'The SNP knew,' wrote one contributor, 'that the only way to political power in Glasgow was to target the Labour vote and play the sectarian green card. Those SNP photo-ops in bigot pubs and elsewhere were beyond cynical.'[79]

In May 2017 commentator Ronnie Smith referred to the 'apparent weaponising of current Scottish political debate through the quite public introduction of religious sectarianism'. 'The cause of independence,' Smith went on, 'is becoming, in some parts, associated with Irish republicanism and the wish to stay in the UK is again being identified with good old-fashioned loyalist Protestantism.'[80] Former Labour government minister Brian Wilson – a Celtic FC director it should be noted – spoke out, also in 2017, claiming that the SNP was engaged in a 'deliberate attempt to sectarianise Scottish politics'.[81] The tensions that had been building since the referendum finally exploded in street violence in Govan in Glasgow at the end of 2019, when loyalists staged a protest against an Irish republican rally in support of the dissident groups currently operating in Northern Ireland. The shooting dead of journalist Lyra McKee in 2018 has been attributed to one of those groups – all in favour of physical force methods – for which the Govan rally was a show of support.[82]

Further street clashes of this kind took place following the

Govan trouble. In January 2020 clashes broke out during a loyalist counter-demonstration at the 'All Under One Banner' pro-independence march, demonstrating the way the Irish and Scottish questions have become intertwined, at least at the level of street politics. However, even at the level of high politics, the links are now clear: the SNP and Sinn Féin held meetings in January 2020 to discuss Brexit, language rights and campaigns for referendums on Irish unity and Scottish independence.[83] In the same month protestors disrupted the proceedings of the Scottish Parliament with shouts about the SNP government containing 'supporters of the IRA'.[84] In April 2020 the academic and commentator Tom Gallagher, in a piece concerning a Westminster SNP MP, Steven Bonnar, alleged that Nicola Sturgeon had gone to 'considerable lengths to cultivate Sinn Féin'. Bonnar had made the news by hanging a Celtic FC flag outside his house in a mixed estate in Lanarkshire and was subsequently embroiled in a public confrontation about it with a neighbour. Gallagher accused Bonnar of 'pouring petrol on the flames of simmering disputes over religion, Ireland, football or obscure local quarrels in a part of Scotland long known for its communal tensions' and contrasted his behaviour unfavourably with that of a previous Labour representative for the area, Michael McMahon, also a Celtic supporter but someone who 'worked with all sides to strengthen community cohesion'.[85]

This affair, it might be said, was indicative of the way football could be a trigger of a broader problem and could be made to serve political ends. Once again, in the eyes of those most opposed to independence and the SNP, the governing party gave the appearance of indulging in populist gestures around symbols of Catholic identity in Scotland in order to solidify political allegiance.

The trouble in Govan and elsewhere produced some belated recognition among Scottish media commentators that Ulster-style tensions and antagonisms have deep roots in Scotland and the potential to flare up into serious disorder. Northern Ireland-born journalist on *The Herald*, Neil McKay, wrote of his fears that extremists on both sides of the Irish question would try to make Scotland 'fertile ground for themselves'.[86] The indignation surrounding the application of the term 'Ulsterisation' to Scottish developments showed signs of giving way to an acknowledgement of the extent to which Irish and Ulster loyalties and allegiances now complicate Scottish politics on account of the dominance of the independence question. The potential for the 'Scottish Question' to become 'sectarianised' that was clear in the respective Protestant and Catholic proportions in favour of independence in the referendum of 2014 looked as if it was firming up (and may have been given a further twist by Brexit).[87]

While parts of Scottish civic society might be said to have woken up to these potential dangers, it is another matter to make firm assessments of their electoral impact. Has the pro-Irish unity, pro-IRA activity of some SNP figures damaged the party? The answer at present is apparently not, if recent election results at local and Westminster level are any guide. The SNP's success in the 2019 UK and 2021 Scottish Parliament elections would suggest that it has suffered no significant harm; most voters have apparently been prepared to ignore it if indeed it has not simply passed them by. It could be hazarded that it gave a slight boost to the Conservatives – at least if reference is made to the local election results of 2017, which, incidentally, saw a Tory councillor returned for Glasgow Shettleston for the first time in many years. But any such boost for the Conservatives has been at the expense of Labour, with some former Labour voters more inclined to turn to the Tories on account of the 'national question' and their more robust unionism.[88] The SNP also continues to benefit from the way the category of voters saying they have 'No Religion' has increased. Indeed, recent statistics show that, in 2018, a majority of people in Scotland, some 59 per cent, claimed to be non-religious.[89] It can be conjectured that many of these voters, determined to downgrade anything linked to religion and sectarianism, have simply blanked out controversial interventions about the Irish Troubles.

However, there is perhaps another way to look at the question. The growing association of Irish republican and Sinn Féin political goals, and strident anti-Britishness, with the SNP and the independence movement more broadly, has probably alienated still further the anti-independence, Orange-influenced, working class and maybe also some people beyond this group who are emotionally British and would have regarded the IRA campaign during the Northern Ireland Troubles with abhorrence. Furthermore, it might suggest that an 'Indyref2' in the near future will be very different from 2014. It could be much more divisive and bitter, with the potential for violent disorder.[90] The anti-independence core will have been reinforced in their view of independence as a project with no place for them or indeed for anything British. They may refer to the Northern Ireland situation and argue that, like the unionists and loyalists there, their identity and culture is at stake. The parallels with Ireland in the late nineteenth and early twentieth century are tempting to draw: those opposed to independence may start to feel uncomfortable with their Scottishness; they may increasingly regard Scottish identity as being appropriated by supporters of independence and effectively ring-fenced. Certainly today, in contrast to the late twentieth century, Scottish identity is being defined by supporters of independence as an identity that requires no supplement – any kind of British 'add-on' is repudiated in the manner of Irish republicans.[91] Those who wish to uphold a dual Scottish/British identity are decidedly on the back foot.

Perhaps, too, those who feel alienated by the independence movement will read into the SNP's apparent tolerance for IRA tributes and so on, the message that the party is no longer as impeccably constitutionalist in its approach as, historically, it has been. It is not a big leap from demonstrations and counter-demonstrations and accompanying disorder on the streets over the Irish question to the same over the Scottish one. In a tense 'Indyref' campaign of the future, these set pieces will have the potential to get nasty. The evidence provided above has contributed to an intolerant political culture and discourse around the independence question.

Few analysts of the Scottish question today have acknowledged that the substantial support the Conservatives received in Scotland until the late twentieth century was a vote for unionism rather than conservativism ideologically, the Union being the Irish and not the Scottish one. This has left a legacy. It has conditioned responses in a significant number of cases to the Scottish question in the contemporary period. This is the kind of point – linking Scotland and Northern Ireland – which is routinely ignored by those who analyse and comment on Scottish politics. Moreover, it needs to be acknowledged that Catholics in Scotland of Irish descent have been encouraged in recent years – particularly the last twenty – to prioritise their Irishness and Irish roots, and to be more aware of how this was held against them in the past along with their religion. They have been encouraged by 'pop-up' pressure groups, such as 'Call it Out', to swap the politics of class interest and commonalities with other non-Catholic Scots for the identity politics that marks them out as a distinctive group with their own agenda. In 2019 'Call it Out' issued a statement concerning the health and poverty of 'our community', that is Catholics, not working-class people in general.[92] The more this community comes to stress its Irishness, the more they are encouraged to sympathise with the nationalist 'struggle' of the land of their ancestors. This helps contemporary Scottish nationalism in the sense of encouraging them to break with all things British, a case in point being the Labour movement to which they contributed so much over generations.[93]

Irish Allegiances and the Identity Politics of Modern Scotland

'Identity', wrote the late Tony Judt, historian of modern Europe, 'is a dangerous word.' He pointed to examples of countries in Europe in the early twenty-first century where it was used politically to inflame anti-immigrant sentiment. He also contended that the word's impact on academic life had encouraged minorities to study themselves, 'thereby simultaneously negating the goals of a liberal education and reinforcing the sectarian and ghetto mentalities they purport to undermine'. Referring to 'a generation of boastful victimhood', Judt 'called out' those who 'wear what little they do know as a proud badge of identity'.[94]

This bracing critique can be applied to contemporary Scotland as it catches up with the identity politics Northern Ireland has long pursued. The 'Call It Out' pressure group discussed above is a fitting example of what alarmed Judt; however, the broader point of significance is the way that the preoccupations of such groups have been hoovered up and put to work by the SNP for their separatist ends. The SNP has not been slow in recent years to adopt the political language and tactics of Sinn Féin in Northern Ireland around the reduction of British or pro-Union cultural signifiers to 'imperialism', and the fashionable academic discourse around the 'decolonisation' of studies of the past and of state institutions.

Identity politics, as many scholars and commentators have argued, is geared narrowly to group grievances and the assertion of personal and group agendas rather than any concept of citizenship or broader societal good.[95] They encourage a 'race to victimhood' and they resort to simplistic takes on complex historical phenomena, such as, pertinently in the history of these islands, imperialism. It matters little to those in Scotland prepared to fuse their 'identity' agendas with that of the independence objective that Scotland's role in the Empire helped to define the shape of the modern nation it has become.

The American writer and scholar Anne Applebaum has written of the 'authoritarian predispositions' of those whose politics conforms to this new identitarian style, and whose use of social media powers such politics without the need for old-style persuasion and the painstaking building of a movement. Such people, Applebaum contends, 'are bothered by complexity' and 'seek solutions in a new political language that makes them feel safer and more secure'.[96] For nationalist-aligned pressure groups like 'Call It Out' in Scotland, what many would see as the positive features of the UK – pluralism, complexity, flexibility – are dismissed as colonial conceits designed to hoodwink the supposedly culturally oppressed.

'Call It Out' has embarked on a mission to change the language of the sectarianism debate in contemporary Scotland. It is set on scrapping the word 'sectarian' itself and replacing it with 'anti-Irish Catholic racism'. In this quest it has received support from prominent SNP MSPs such as James Dornan, who has been untiring in his efforts to find examples of this form of 'racism', even going as far as to claim that industrial action called by Edinburgh bus drivers over anti-social behaviour was somehow an instance of discrimination against Catholics of Irish background celebrating St Patrick's Day.[97]

In the world of political activists like Dornan, sectarianism is thus something only done to Catholics of Irish descent in Scotland. Anti-Protestantism cannot exist because, in effect, there is no language to describe it. This is very similar to the way Sinn Féin has attempted to redefine sectarianism as essentially an anti-Catholic phenomenon and a tool used malignantly by the British state to 'divide and rule'. In addition, it is clear that those pushing for such linguistic and category changes wish to claim the highest moral ground in the contemporary culture wars, namely that of race and the cause of 'anti-racism'.[98] The aim here seems to be to establish a new orthodoxy of public discourse which conforms to a particular definition of sectarianism, notwithstanding this orthodoxy's ahistorical nature and the way it is impervious to empirical evidence to the contrary.[99] The aim might also be said to be the foreclosing of discussion, or at least to ensure that it proceeds along carefully drawn ideological tramlines. If ultimately successful, such a drive towards new rules of engagement will have profound significance for Scottish–Irish relations and Scottish–Irish studies. It could also have the effect, it can be argued, of removing any sense of agency from minority groups such as those of Irish descent in Scotland and rendering them fixed categories to be used instrumentally in the struggle for Scotland's future.[100] Such is the SNP's grip on contemporary Scotland that counterblasts around cultural issues tend to come from independent commentators rather than from academia or the mainstream media.[101]

The sectarianism debate in Scotland of the early twenty-first century has been pushed into the arena of culture wars. It has been instrumentalised by those wishing to break up the UK and who take inspiration from the apparent likelihood of Northern Ireland being subsumed into an all-Ireland state when, in classic sectarian head-counting fashion, demographic trends produce a Catholic majority. Following another victory in the Scottish Parliamentary elections of 2021, the SNP, now in formal coalition with the pro-independence Green Party, reasserted its wish for a second independence referendum. Anticipating this, an Orange Order spokesman in Scotland warned that this could 'reignite hatred'.[102] Even the pro-independence – and Ulster-born and raised – Neil MacKay, editor of *The Herald* in Glasgow, conceded that the way Irish issues had entered Scottish politics was 'toxic' and 'ugly'.[103] Following a warning to Scots from Northern Ireland Alliance Party leader Naomi Long of the dangers of the constitutional issue dominating politics and creating cleavages in society,[104] a high-profile Scottish commentator took up the theme of 'Ulsterisation'; he was forced to conclude that 'the idea of a society divided into two camps is much more familiar to Scots than it would have been twenty years ago'.[105]

CHAPTER FIVE

Leaving, Remaining and Remaking

The 5 May 2016 elections to the Northern Ireland Assembly saw the DUP under new leader Arlene Foster solidify its place as the Assembly's largest party and uncontested leader of unionism. The first woman leader of a major party in Northern Ireland, Foster was in the midst of a honeymoon period and her background as a Church of Ireland-attending former Ulster Unionist lawyer symbolised the DUP's moves away from its Paisleyite origins as a party of protest outside the establishment institutions of unionist and Protestant life.[1] The broader political context looked secure for unionism, with one 'senior unionist' telling the historian Paul Bew: 'There are calm seas ahead for Northern Ireland as far as anyone can see.'[2] The one-hundredth anniversary of the Easter Rising had long been earmarked by Martin McGuinness and Gerry Adams as the year their united Ireland would be realised,[3] but by 2016 Northern nationalist momentum was difficult to locate beyond old hopes placed on changing sectarian demography and birth-rates. Commemorations of the Easter Rising were marked by conciliatory public commentary on the island and in Great Britain, reflecting the continuation of unprecedented harmony in British–Irish intergovernmental relations since the Good Friday Agreement.

In May 2016 discussion of borders within these islands focused on Scotland. A third victory in elections to the Scottish Parliament confirmed the SNP's dominance, despite their loss of six seats, and the resurgence of the Conservatives suggested that a Scottish variant of the unionist–nationalist binary was the new normal for Scottish politics.[4] The weakest spot in the Union appeared, therefore, to be Scottish not Northern Irish. Nearly ten years of relatively stable devolved government in Stormont between 2007 and 2017 withstood serious political and legal challenges, in large part because of the DUP's commitment to the power-sharing institutions. It withstood widespread unionist street protests in 2012–13 following the reduced flying of the Union flag at Belfast City Hall; and more tellingly withstood, or some would suggest ignored, a 2015 Belfast murder judged by the Police Service of Northern Ireland (PSNI) to have been 'carried out with the involvement of the Provisional IRA'.[5] The proverbial dogs on the street knew the implications of this murder, but, after some careful political choreography, the DUP, then led by Peter Robinson, stayed in government with Sinn Féin – in return receiving little recognition or political leverage in London or Dublin, or from international opinion.

This relative stability led to a tentative political and cultural confidence in Northern Ireland, and much hopeful discussion re-garding the potential of an emerging civic Northern Irish identity.[6] Against this backdrop came the Northern Ireland football team's success qualifying for the finals of the European Championships in France, where the team had success on the pitch and supporters were celebrated for the positive image they presented to Europe. But even before the football in France was over, within seven weeks of the Stormont elections, the European political question fundamentally destabilised Northern Ireland and the wider UK. Against the surreal backdrop of the collapse of the shambolic Renewable Heat Incentive (RHI), which saw Sinn Féin collapse power-sharing in protest at alleged DUP mismanagement of the scheme,[7] Brexit suddenly raised fundamental questions about the sustainability of the political settlement in Northern Ireland and the durability of the Union; furthermore, the borders, economics and governance of Northern Ireland became a political football across the spectrum of British, Scottish, Irish and EU politics. The ball is still in the air.

A History of European Integration and British and Irish National Questions

The political potency of the EU Referendum of 2016, and its protracted aftermath, has been its place right on the fault-lines of competing conceptions of sovereignty, identity and democratic consent across the devolved, and increasingly fragmented, United Kingdom. These competing conceptions have fed off other divisions common across the liberal democratic world – primarily attitudes to migration, the economic discontents of globalisation and the deepening political alienation of many citizens. In Scotland and Northern Ireland these dividing lines predictably became enveloped within constitutional questions, but an examination of the history of how Scotland, Northern Ireland, the UK and Ireland as a whole have engaged with questions of European integration highlights that there have never been simple ideological divides regarding the European question. Instead, the positions of many political factions have evolved, and often flipped, unpredictably. The long view of British and Irish attitudes towards European integration, with a particular focus on referendum debates of the 1970s, can help us understand why Brexit has had such a profound impact and how it interacts in often surprising ways with the UK's national questions.

It was the 1951 Coal and Steel Community which signalled the beginnings of European economic integration as part of rebuilding a continent shattered by war.[8] The six members – France, West Germany, Italy, Belgium, the Netherlands and Luxembourg – deepened their relationship in 1957 with the foundation of the EEC, the Common Market. The UK and Ireland, at this stage, had no desire to join the club. Post-war British policy encouraged European integration but wanted to stay separate, or semi-detached, from the process. However, gradually a new British elite consensus developed, which saw integration with European markets as a necessary response to relative economic decline in comparison with the extraordinary growth of the Common Market Six.[9] It was 1961 before the government of Harold Macmillan applied for Common Market membership – accompanied by an application from the Republic of Ireland – but Macmillan and subsequently, in 1967, Harold Wilson were to see successive UK applications vetoed by General de Gaulle, who feared the impact of the UK on EEC cohesion.

The speed with which the original Common Market Six had economically caught up with the UK and in some important measures, such as productivity and wages, overtaken them,[10] set the scene for British European debates in the 1960s and 1970s.[11]

The importance of downward economic trends in changing British elite and public opinions on Europe does not mean that questions of sovereignty were absent from these debates. The now widely accepted British Eurosceptic myth that took root in the late 1980s – that British voters were sold a simple economic project with no political implications – is not supported by the historical record. The political implications of pooling sovereignty and restraining both Westminster and state economic intervention were regularly foregrounded in the British debates of the 1970s.[12]

Throughout the British–French veto dramas, Ireland was treated by the EEC as, at best, co-dependent on the UK's application, or often as an appendix of the UK.[13] Stated bluntly, the depth of the Republic of Ireland's trade, economic and monetary links with the UK ensured that its place in the new Europe was de facto dependent upon the UK's direction of travel. Then, as now, one of the key misunderstandings in British attitudes – including those of many Ulster unionists – towards Ireland has been a failure to recognise how, for successive Irish governments, the European project has been a vehicle for increased independence from the UK, by decreasing Irish dependence on the British market. In this regard, for Ireland, the pooling of sovereignty within the EU has been a clear and demonstrative success.

The Irish state's decision to apply for membership of the EEC in 1961 represented a shift away from de Valera's protectionist vision of Irish independence, and represented a pro-European consensus across Fianna Fáil and Fine Gael. However, from the 1960s to the referendum of 1972 that confirmed Irish membership, Irish pro-EEC voices had to address concerns about what membership of the EEC would mean for traditional conservative values and for Irish republican aspirations. For example, in 1962 Charles Haughey, as Minister for Justice, affirmed: 'There is a distinctive European tradition founded on a long history of Christianity which is common to the Six. This we also share ... I do not therefore fear we are relaxing our spiritual values and accepting a purely materialistic outlook in joining the Common Market.'[14] While partition was a secondary issue during Irish considerations of EEC entry, the opinion that the Common Market would in the long term help to dissolve the border was widely held within the Department of Foreign Affairs and much of nationalist Ireland. Garret FitzGerald agreed, arguing that, although it would be wrong to look to Europe as 'a panacea for the Irish problem ... such influence as membership will have is likely to be uniformly directed towards a path to a United Ireland'.[15]

As throughout the UK, the Irish Labour movement was split on the issue, but the leadership of the Irish Congress of Trade Unions (ICTU) and Labour campaigned for a 'No' vote – as did future president Michael D. Higgins. The republican movement, unsurprisingly, focused on the sovereignty issue and the impact of membership on Irish neutrality. Provisional Sinn Féin campaigned for a 'No' vote for referendums in the Republic in 1972 and Northern Ireland in 1975; they saw the EEC as opening up the possibility that 'foreigners will be able, without restrictions, to buy Irish land', and argued that it would cripple small farmers and damage Irish language and culture. Although still a political operation in its infancy, the Provisionals also used their prisoners to advocate a 'No' vote.[16] Despite this opposition, Irish EEC membership received an overwhelming mandate, with an 83.1 per cent 'Yes' vote. It is important to note that the Republic achieved EEC membership without having to alter its neutrality or its territorial claim over Northern Ireland – now a part of another EEC member state. The continuation of this territorial claim proved to be extremely important in the North after the Sunningdale Agreement and beyond.

The UK's entry into the EEC was ratified by the constitutional innovation of a UK-wide referendum in 1975 – the 1973 Border Poll in Northern Ireland had been the first such poll in any part of the UK. For a Labour government badly divided on Europe, the device of a referendum was, as Jim Callaghan famously predicted, a 'little rubber life raft into which the whole party may one day have to climb' – echoes of 1975 were heard when David Cameron agreed to a referendum to manage his party's divisions.[17] The coalition of forces brought together in the 1975 versions of 'Remain' and 'Leave' were eccentric and noticeably different from the 2016 incarnations. While Labour was split – with the Labour left of Tony Benn, Michael Foot, Peter Shore and Barbara Castle convinced opponents of the Common Market – a comfortable majority of Conservative MPs were pro-EEC, as were the Liberals, almost all of the print press and all leading business groups. The pro-EEC campaign was fronted by Ted Heath, Roy Jenkins and Jeremy Thorpe. The 'No' campaign was mocked by an effective *Evening Standard* cartoon of a 'Get Britain Out' march, which featured the Labour left alongside Enoch Powell, the SNP, Plaid Cymru, the National Front, the Communist Party, the IRA and the Orange Order – with the caption 'Join the Professionals'.[18]

The SNP's opposition to European integration, at its peak in the mid-1970s, was sustained until 1988, when, under the leadership of Alex Salmond, it moved towards its current 'Independence

in Europe' policy.[19] Emerging oil revenues from the North Sea –
coined 'Scotland's Oil' by successful SNP campaigns[20] – formed
the backdrop to leading SNP figures viewing the EEC as a threat
to Scottish self-determination and sovereignty, and a vehicle for
larger nations to dominate smaller ones.[21] Donald Stewart MP, the
SNP's then leader at Westminster, said the EEC 'represents everything our party has fought against: centralisation, undemocratic
procedures, power politics, and a fetish for abolishing cultural differences'.[22] The SNP position was also influenced by the desire to
promote political and cultural differences from England, where
pro-EEC sentiment had a clearer majority.

A combination of the SNP's nationalistic concerns and the left
critique of the EEC, which was popular across Britain but had a
particular base within the Scottish labour movement, led to much
speculation in 1975 as to what the impact on the Union would be
if England voted 'Yes' to Europe and Scotland voted 'No'. Indeed,
the opposition of the SNP, Plaid Cymru and Provisional Sinn Féin
to EEC membership in 1975, contrasted with the support of all
three for EU membership in 2016 and shows how these distinct
secessionist movements within the UK have been on a similar
journey in their analyses of the EEC/EU as a vehicle for expressing
nationalist interests and dissatisfaction within the UK. In 1975
concerns regarding the implications of nationalist Euro-scepticism
were held by the head of the official Britain in Europe campaign,
Con O'Neill, the son of former Ulster Unionist MP Hugh O'Neill
and himself a staunch Ulster unionist. As a high-ranking career
diplomat in the Foreign Office and UK Ambassador to the EEC,
O'Neill had led the UK's negotiations for entry into the Common
Market, the proudest achievement of his career and one he saw

as vital for the future of the Union where his roots lay, in Ulster.[23]

How did Ulster unionism view the EEC through the turmoil of these years and how did the European debate interact with a divided society in crisis and conflict? When EEC membership first appeared on the agenda, successive Unionist prime ministers actively supported the UK's applications to join.[24] Brooke expressed disappointment at the de Gaulle veto and also hoped that the Republic would soon gain entry.[25] For Terence O'Neill, European integration was a plank of his modernisation agenda. O'Neill's speeches on the subject, speaking from the perspective of someone who lost his father to the First World War and two brothers to the Second, focused on the role the ECC could play in promoting peace. Speaking in West Germany in 1967, he stated that: 'I speak for Northern Ireland, the most westerly Atlantic bastion of the United Kingdom, and I tell you tonight that we are Europeans with a European destiny.'[26] O'Neill's approval of European integration was allied with his advocacy of regionalism and devolution throughout the UK. This integration of Europe into a new multi-layered model of governance for Northern Ireland was to be a theme that some unionists, who otherwise opposed O'Neill, were to return to in the decades to come, until Brexit narrowed this conception of unionism by again hardening borders and culturally encouraging binary options of identity. During the negotiations that finally saw UK entry secured, the Unionist governments of James Chichester-Clark and Brian Faulkner again emphasised the potential benefits of the Common Market.

By the time the UK and the Republic joined the EEC on 1 January 1973, the violence and division of the Troubles had transformed the politics of the island of Ireland, and the Euro-enthusiasm of

Con O'Neill and the pragmatic positivity of Brian Faulkner were soon a minority view among elected unionist representatives. One aspect of this transformation was a retreat from front-line unionist politics of the old paternalist Ulster gentry and much of the business and professional classes, who were replaced by representatives less inclined to be swayed by the broad support for Europe in the business community and wider civil society.[27] Furthermore, the core nature of Ulster unionism's defence of British sovereignty at the height of the Troubles convinced a new generation of unionist leaders to view the EEC as a threat to this sovereignty – echoing how much of 'Celtic nationalism' within the UK then viewed the EEC as a threat to Welsh, Scottish and Irish sovereignty. Concerns regarding trade, unemployment, wages and inflation were central to the 1975 referendum debate in Northern Ireland, but questions of sovereignty, national identity and 'our place in the world' had more immediacy and deadly potential in Belfast and Derry than in places like Birmingham or Dundee. Possible interpretations of the EEC were clearly not a priority in 1975 Northern Ireland, but in an era of constitutional uncertainty and repeated attempts at novel political solutions to contested sovereignty,[28] reimagining a new European settlement allowed people across the full spectrum of politics to advance ideas regarding softer borders, devolution, regionalism, federalism, parliamentary sovereignty and the state's role in the economy.

In 1975 the executive of the UUP confirmed its opposition to EEC membership, in line with the views of the new UUP MP for South Down, Enoch Powell, but the party leadership made no contribution to the campaign and gave no clear advice to voters. This silence reflected an awareness of divergent opinions held by the community's grass roots, evident for example in the Ulster Farmers' Union strong pro-EEC position, but it also highlighted the party's safety-first, minimalist approach to constitutional change. Such ambiguities were absent from the DUP's campaign. Ian Paisley echoed Garret FitzGerald's thesis that European integration would shorten the journey to a united Ireland, and he saw disastrous consequences for local farmers, but it was religion that he moved centre stage. To him the EEC was 'a Catholic super-state', and 'the Pope had announced the Virgin Mary to be the Madonna of the Common Market'.[29] It is difficult to tell how many people took this sort of rhetoric seriously, but anti-Catholicism of course had the power to energise some unionist voters or raise doubts in others about the 'cultural differences' with the Common Market Six.

The most interesting unionist perspective on European inte-gration came from Ulster Vanguard. The party formed by Bill Craig more than any other represented the anger and disempowerment felt by unionism following the introduction of Direct Rule. In co-operation with loyalist paramilitaries and trade unionists, Vanguard was the pivotal political force behind the loyalist strike of 1974 that brought down the Sunningdale Agreement, but Vanguard also possessed an openness to new ideas not overly evident elsewhere in local politics. Initially the party turned towards a reconception of Ulster identity and Northern Irish independence, but soon members such as the academic Anthony Alcock advanced ideas of a federal settlement for the British Isles.[30] A majority of Vanguard's activists appear to have been anti-EEC, or were simply disengaged from the debate, but Craig and the majority of the leadership and his young advisors, such as Alcock and David Trimble, were convinced pro-marketers.[31] There is a personal element to this story – Craig was married to a German academic – but it was the Vanguard leadership's conception of devolution and a 'Europe of the regions' that led them to support the EEC. Alcock, a lecturer in Western European Studies at the University of Ulster, was perhaps the most articulate voice in favour of the EEC heard during the campaign in Northern Ireland.[32] In a speech entitled 'Britain, Europe and a changing world', he argued that the UK had to accept that strong relations with the Commonwealth and America were insufficient to provide the living standards and the social protections provided on the continent.[33]

Within Northern nationalism, the SDLP argued for a 'Yes' vote, while the various wings of armed republicanism – the Provisionals, the Officials and the INLA – all argued for a 'No'. The SDLP's pro-European agenda was heavily influenced by the consensus in Fianna Fáil and Fine Gael, with whom the new party had established deep relationships in the years of intense talks leading up to the 1974 Sunningdale Agreement. The new constitutional realities and possibilities opened up by the 1973 entry of the Republic of Ireland into the EEC, and the strength of the pro-EEC consensus in Irish opinion, were ones that John Hume grasped and welcomed as part of his all-Ireland framework. In the midst of the horrors suffered by Northern nationalist communities in the early 1970s, there was also a certain political confidence, evident in Hume and others, that the collapse of the old Stormont, disarray within unionism, and serious question marks over the commitment of successive UK governments to staying the course in Northern Ireland all pointed towards a new constitutional settlement where European integration would play its part in moving Northern

Ireland towards Irish integration. Hume embraced the rhetoric of the EEC transforming the island and making the border irrelevant in the longer term. He also saw the Common Market as especially important for economic investment in his native Derry and on both sides of the border in the north-west.

The republican argument that the EEC compromised Irish sovereignty and therefore republicans should vote 'No' in the Northern Ireland referendum was a hard sell in 1975 when Irish membership had been confirmed. This was especially the case in border areas and the north-west, where a Northern Ireland outside the Common Market would be on the other side of a new European trade and labour border. Responding to the republican 'No' campaigns, the *Derry Journal* said of the position of the Provisionals and the Officials that: 'both Sinn Féins are plainly arguing for another partition from the rest of the nation and all in the name of a national objective'.[34]

UK Party Politics and the Nation in the European Union

The result of the 1975 Referendum was a decisive two-thirds majority for the pro-EEC side. Unexpectedly Northern Ireland and Scotland both voted 'Yes', Northern Ireland by 52 per cent, Scotland by 58 per cent. With Northern Irish ballots all counted together, the only polling districts that returned anti-EEC majorities were those of Shetland and the Western Isles, but the Scottish and Northern Irish results and the slight decline in the size of 'Yes' majorities the further north you travelled in Great Britain did speak to some of the regional differences that some feared could fragment the Union. However, this was an overwhelming and ultimately united UK vote, unlike in 2016. The 1975 vote in Northern Ireland was

LEAVING, REMAINING AND REMAKING

a striking and isolated example of the electorate there having the opportunity to engage with an issue that cut across clear Orange and Green narratives, and ignoring much of the fearful rhetoric from communal leaders.

We can now also see that confirmation of EEC membership led to a wider challenge to British constitutional conservativism, and a reappraisal of issues such as devolution and multi-layered government within the UK. The unlikely, and uneasy, alliance between confirmed ideological enemies on the 'No' side in 1975 concealed many shared assumptions and priorities around democracy and Britishness. Consistent in the analysis of Enoch Powell, Michael Foot and Tony Benn was a constitutional conservativism holding in reproach dilution of Westminster's sovereignty and scornful of the democratic potential of any European transnational structure. Expressed by the troika of Westminster's finest orators, this analysis almost resembled a deification of the (uncodified) United Kingdom constitution and an ode to Britain's, or perhaps more coherently England's, democratic heritage and established norms. Many of these themes struck a chord with a disorientated Ulster unionism and ironically had parallels with how much of Scottish nationalism and militant Irish republicanism saw their desired unitary states and political economies.

Incorporated into Powell's vision was a brew of patriotism and British nationalism that was positive about the UK's potential outside of the EEC and only saw domestic treachery and direct foreign intervention behind the European project.[35] For Powell the EEC referendum and Northern Ireland were bound together in a broader narrative that questioned the sustainability of the UK. Increasingly throughout 1974 and 1975, the recently elected MP for

South Down saw support for Northern Ireland's place in a union with Great Britain as the key weathervane for whether the British state was up to the challenges of maintaining nationhood and sovereignty – Northern Ireland was 'the test of Britain's national will to live'.[36] As Paul Corthorn has demonstrated, alongside Irish republican violence, Powell saw Scottish and Welsh nationalism and increasing demands for devolution, American influence on foreign policy, and the Common Market as overlapping challenges to British national dignity.[37] This world view signalled a post-imperial British nationalism, with Powell defending and defining the boundaries of the UK state – a siege mentality with clear commonalities with an Ulster unionist experience.[38] Rather than nostalgia for the British Empire, as writers such as Fintan O'Toole have argued,[39] much of the energy underpinning the 2016 'Vote Leave' campaign was nostalgia for an imagined version of the clearly defined and separate UK which Powell imagined in 1975. This nostalgia ignored the fact that the UK as a nation(s)-state without empire had only existed in the decade that preceded the UK's membership of the EEC – a decade of relative decline in a western European context. Indeed, as historian Timothy Snyder argues, the European Union more broadly can perhaps best be viewed as a transnational refuge for European former imperial powers, which, because of their empires, had either briefly or never been independent nation-states in the true sense of the term.[40]

The anti-EEC British left sought to maintain an internationalist message, but their political economy had developed along the lines of a siege economy to sit alongside Powellite and unionist siege mentalities. By 1975 Tony Benn was advocating a radical Alternative

Economic Strategy,[41] which he summarised as: 'import control, control of the banks and insurance companies, control of export, of capital, higher taxation of the rich, and Britain leaving the Common Market'.[42] Although rejected by all of the other members of the Labour cabinet, important elements of this strategy remained the basis for the British left's platform until the late 1980s, and required the preservation of an economically interventionist and strongly centralised nation-state – in other words, a variation of British Labour's long-standing scepticism towards devolution for Wales or Scotland, and its constitutional conservativism.

As with the SNP, the turning point for British Labour and Conservative attitudes towards Europe came in 1988. Jacques Delors' speech to the Trade Union Congress that year, advocating a 'social dimension' of collective bargaining and stronger workers' rights in a social Europe, caught the mood of a labour movement re-evaluating its own core principles and desperate for any break on Thatcherism. In response Thatcher, one of the architects of the Single Market, rejected the vision of Delors in her iconic Bruges speech, where she argued this agenda would 'introduce collectivism and corporatism' and 'concentrate power at the centre of a European conglomerate'.[43] The stage was set for both a Conservative Euro-sceptic shift and the era of Blair–Brown pro-EU Labourism. Whereas in 1975 the EEC was seen by most Conservatives as central to a more open and modernising free-market economy, moving away from what it viewed as a statist post-war British consensus, by 2016 most Conservatives and the conservative press saw the EU through the prism of regulation and restraints on sovereignty. In the New Labour years, a party constructing constitutional reform with devolution for Wales and Scotland, as well as the profound constitutional implications for the whole of the UK flowing from the Good Friday Agreement, saw the EU dimension of multi-layered British governance as allied with both Blairite economics and a liberal multicultural and multinational conception of British identity and Union.

This conception of the Union was either dramatically narrowed, or perhaps closed, by the victory for 'Leave' in 2016. The alliances of 1975 had dramatically changed by the Brexit referendum, and the interaction between Europe and competing nationalisms within the UK now pointed in a new direction – most notably with regard to the Europhile position of the twenty-first-century SNP. Sinn Féin's position on Europe was, by 2016, still distinctly Euro-sceptic; they were vocal critics of successive EU treaties in Irish referendums, and in the Northern Brexit referendum although officially supporting 'Remain' in a lukewarm way, they spent £0 on the campaign, despite the party's healthy bank balance.[44] It is worthwhile noting that turnout in the referendum was noticeably lower in predominately republican and nationalist areas. Post-referendum, however, the constitutional and political implications of Brexit saw Sinn Féin move more firmly into the Remainer camp.

The shock 52 per cent UK vote for 'Leave' collided with a 38 per cent vote in Scotland and 44 per cent in Northern Ireland. The lack of Scottish and Northern Irish consent for such a profound change as leaving the European Union not only caused multiple political crises, but also raised structural and systemic questions about the diverging visions and political ecosystems within the UK, the relationship between the devolved jurisdictions and central government, and the medium-term survival of the Union.

A Spirit of Disagreement: Post-Brexit Politics and Northern Ireland

Several months before the Brexit referendum of June 2016, Paul Gillespie, one of the few Southern Irish commentators knowledgeable about Scottish affairs, speculated on the possibility of a 'Leave' vote breaking up the UK.[45] He argued that recent developments had brought 'a greater convergence and a rediscovery of common interests and identities' between Ireland and Scotland, and observed that it was 'strange' to see the DUP supporting a Brexit vote 'that could trigger Scottish Independence'. 'Where', he went on to enquire, 'would they then be in a diminished UK minus their Scottish historical inheritance and which is less willing to support a weak periphery?' Gillespie added that such a decision could also undermine the power-sharing arrangement in Northern Ireland and disrupt cross-border relations, putting Irish unification on the political agenda.

Gillespie proved, to a great extent, to be prescient, and there were a number of other voices making similar predictions. The DUP had ample warning about the likely impact of a 'Leave' vote on the stability of the UK Union and the Northern Ireland arrangements, yet, in the manner of their hard Brexit Tory allies, they ploughed on, pushing the envelope of a 'take back control' and 'restore our sovereignty' narrative. Gillespie was also correct about the anger in Scotland among many Remain voters, who had also voted to remain in the UK union in 2014, although after this initial anger the extent to which minds have been changed permanently on the Union is as yet uncertain. What is not in doubt is that Northern Ireland has witnessed a return to a politics of seeking victory over the 'other side',[46] and that while the Brexit vote has been the main catalyst of such a development, the Scottish question is very much part of the mix. Another informed commentator, Paul Nolan, ventured the view in 2021 that Scotland voting for independence would be 'the biggest challenge to relationships within Ireland'.[47] Neither should it be forgotten how the Northern Ireland situation can affect life in Scotland, as discussed in the previous chapter.

Brexit threw into relief, and accentuated, the different conceptions of sovereignty, state and nation across the UK; and it put the UK and Ireland on 'different trajectories'. As a recent academic study in relation to the Northern Ireland problem pointed out: 'dualities and complexities are harder to accommodate' with Northern Ireland out of the EU.[48] Brexit could be said to have scuppered the ease with which so many people were willing to take practical advantage of the right to be both British and Irish.

If pursuing a hard Brexit provided satisfaction for those in the DUP who were never comfortable with the compromises reached in 1998 and in subsequent agreements, then it could only have done so as an exercise in nostalgia. Moreover, it could only be done by disregarding those delicate balancing acts which had historically held the Union together. The lack of awareness on the part of the Brexiteers for the way the vote undermined the notion of the UK Union as a covenant or contract between partners, was striking. They were either ignorant of, or indifferent to, the long history of the UK as an interaction between its component parts, interactions, in the view of the eminent historian J.G.A. Pocock, which 'modify the conditions of one another's existence'.[49] If the English nationalism at the heart of the hard Brexit project helps explain the motivations of those in the Tory party who thwarted attempts at compromise, it is much harder to find excuses for the DUP, notwithstanding its concern not to upset Protestant working-class voters who saw voting for Brexit as an opportunity to express long stored-up grievances about the outworking of the 'peace process'.

Historically, there was a blurring of the borders between unionism and nationalism in Scotland that spoke to the nature of the Union settlement of 1707 and the space it left for the preservation of distinctively Scottish institutions and national pride.[50] This stood in contrast to the more sharply drawn divisions between unionism and nationalism in Ireland after the Act of Union of 1800. However, the impact of the referendums of 2014 and 2016 on Scotland in this respect has been to push unionism and nationalism apart, thus bringing the country closer, in relation to questions of national identity, constitutional stability and political temper, to contemporary Northern Ireland. Both referendums brought politics into a frame of binary choices and either/or decisions, and supplanted the pluralism and 'multipleness' of the post-nationalist moment of the previous century's end. Moreover, Brexit threatened fatally to narrow ideas of the meaning of Britishness.

Although the UK entered a new era of devolution and de-centralisation after 1999, it was slow to develop a political culture to match. Old centralist assumptions in British politics died hard, and the meaning and purpose of devolution and constitutional reform were never adequately communicated to the public, particularly in England, where a strand of opinion which viewed the new arrangements as being at their expense was allowed to take firm root in a damaging way. This was particularly the case in relation to perceptions of Scotland on the part of many English voters, and such sentiments contributed to the backlash that the

Brexit vote has been characterised as.[51] In addition, the persistence of Unitary State assumptions among so many in the British political class resulted in the marginalisation of Northern Ireland and the failure to give enough attention to – and thus to anticipate – the problematic relationship of Northern Ireland to anything but the softest of Brexits.[52] The irony here, as Michael Keating has pointed out, is that the UK resembles more the multi-national EU than it does a conventional nation-state.[53]

Brexit, and its fall-out in relation to Northern Ireland and UK–Ireland relations, has weakened the east–west dimension integral to the 1998 Good Friday Agreement. The north–south dimension has dominated post-Brexit politicking. In this respect it is instructive to return to the words of the late Seamus Mallon, the SDLP deputy First Minister in the first Northern Ireland executive set up following the Agreement. Mallon, incidentally, also made an important intervention before he died to warn that a 50 per cent plus one vote in favour of Irish unity at any forthcoming border poll would not be a satisfactory or acceptable outcome from the point of view of building a new harmonious society.[54] In January 2000 at Stormont, Mallon stated that the 'ultimate benefit' of the BIC was 'the co-operation with the other Administrations and Governments'. He went on to say:

> We live cheek by jowl with all of those involved in the British–Irish Council – even though in some cases there is a sea or a border between us. However, in reality there is no border because the days of borders in international business and national life are gone. We will benefit by learning from the experience in other areas, by dealing with those experiences

in a collective way and by producing, in conjunction with each member of the Council, policy positions from which we can all benefit, individually and collectively.[55]

Mallon's visionary sentiments have been mocked by recent history. We live now in an age when borders have come back to pose major political challenges. Nevertheless, there may still be something relating to the original purpose of the BIC – and the way east–west relations were conceived of – that could help defuse tensions and rebuild co-operation. As the historian David Reynolds has written, a looser UK Union – 'stripped of "central imperial condescension", suited to an age of devolution and taking modern Ireland seriously' – would seem essential to the task of rekindling the optimism of the apparently transformative turn-of-last-century moment.[56] Paradoxically, the more upfront and resounding the expressions of Britishness are in the contemporary Brexit-shaped context, the less secure is the Union.

The myriad ways in which Brexit changed and destabilised UK politics was, therefore, remarkable but not always unpredictable. In the case of Northern Ireland, many of the challenges of Brexit were foreseeable and indeed foreseen. In a pre-referendum June 2016 visit to Londonderry, former prime ministers John Major and Tony Blair set out some of the unanswered questions on customs and trade borders that were to dominate the next few years of UK–EU negotiations; more broadly they warned that Brexit would be a 'historic mistake' and mean 'throwing all of the pieces of the constitutional jigsaw into the air'.[57] Major predicted that Brexit would make a second Scottish independence referendum 'politically irresistible',[58] and in the short term, Brexit undoubtedly added further fuel to SNP grievances around English dominance of the UK and a democratic deficit for Scots. A majority of English and – it is often forgotten – Welsh voters dragging Scotland out of the EU against the will of 62 per cent of Scots seemed tailor-made to move Middle Scotland and lukewarm unionists into the nationalist camp.

Beyond the short-term politics of Brexit and the dismay felt by a majority of Scots, Brexit, however, raises serious economic and strategic questions for Scottish nationalism. Setting new customs and single market borders was always going to have implications for the political border in Ireland, but it also dramatically exemplifies the challenges any future independent Scotland within the EU would face with English neighbours outside the EU. As commentator Alex Massie states:

> Brexit may simplify the political argument for Scottish independence but it also complicates the reality of independence as a practical matter. The SNP argues that putting up barriers against your largest trading partner is a disaster for the UK vis-à-vis the EU, but, on the other hand, an urgent necessity for Scotland with regard to the rest of the UK.[59]

Putting these profound trade and economic questions aside, much of the political complexity of Brexit revolves around the difficulties of clearly defining consent and democratic authority within the fragmented UK. These questions in turn raise the more fundamental question of nationhood and where consent should lie. In both Scotland and Northern Ireland Brexit happened without the consent of the people in these devolved jurisdictions. Cross-community consent is of course additionally complex to achieve in Northern Ireland, and the Northern Ireland Protocol has been imposed without the consent of any elected Unionist representative at local council, Stormont or Westminster levels. This is a profound challenge to the devolved architecture of Northern Ireland still, shakily, built upon consociationalist principles.

With no functioning Stormont Executive from January 2017, the intractable Brexit negotiations were a factor in Stormont not returning until January 2020 (just in time for a global pandemic). During these three years of rule by civil servants and 'Indirect Rule' from London on some issues, the Northern Irish political parties' European policies moved further apart. In the aftermath of the shock referendum result, Arlene Foster and Martin McGuinness had jointly written to new Prime Minister Theresa May in August 2016 setting out their joint objectives and concerns – by the start of 2017 it already read like a letter from a previous consensual era.[60] In that letter Foster and McGuinness asserted their 'determination the [Irish] border will not become an impediment to the movement of people, goods and services', adding that it was 'equally important that the border does not create an incentive for those who would wish to undermine the peace process'. After detailing specific concerns regarding agri-food and other sectors of the economy, the First and deputy First Ministers stated: 'We therefore need to retain as far as possible the ease with which we currently trade with EU member states and also importantly retain access to labour.' These objectives were general and occasionally vague but signalled towards a 'soft Brexit' of continuing close alignment between the UK and EU; quickly, however, they met the reality of Theresa May's 'red-lines' of ending freedom of movement and leaving the EU single market and customs union.[61] Foster and McGuinness' happiness in August 2016 that they were 'reassured by your commitment that we will be fully involved and represented in the negotiations' was rendered redundant when an ailing McGuinness resigned and brought down devolution on 9 January 2017, ensuring there was no Northern Ireland Executive for May to consult with.[62]

From the high watermark of the Foster–McGuinness letter, unionist and nationalist visions of what a post-Brexit Northern Ireland should look like quickly headed in different directions. The DUP supported, or in some cases merely acquiesced with, UK government red-lines in negotiations with the EU, and nationalist Ireland moved to seeing additional barriers to trade on the island – especially any physical infrastructure – as an unacceptable threat to peace. This unity of purpose and analysis across almost the full spectrum of nationalist Ireland received widespread support in Brussels, Capitol Hill and the White House, exposing Northern Ireland unionism's isolation beyond its unreliable friends in power in London. The potency and success of an Irish nationalist framing of the Brexit problem was utilised by EU negotiators politically to close off possible technical measures to soften the choices flowing from Northern Ireland's unique position. These possible mitigations will not in and of themselves enable all the tough choices of customs and market borders to go away, but in the different international context of early 2022, many measures initially dismissed by the EU – such as wider exemptions from checks for goods from Great Britain staying in Northern Ireland – were quietly being accepted as negotiable. The small size of

Northern Ireland in the context of protecting the single market, and the realpolitik of the UK's close security alliances with EU members, has the potential to make solutions deemed impossible in 2017–19 suddenly possible.

Within the politics of Northern Ireland not only was there a failure to build a cross-community compromise on Brexit, there was a lack of will by most political tendencies to try. This failure was most evident with the hubris of the DUP, who from 2017–19 held the balance of power at Westminster but consistently refused to challenge the drift of the Conservatives towards a form of Brexit that placed Northern Ireland in the middle of pronounced customs and economic borders. The DUP's support of the Tory right's hard Brexit in the context of a majority Remain vote in Northern Ireland and no functioning devolution at Stormont again felt tailor-made to alienate Remainers – including 40 per cent of those from a Protestant background[63] – who are the core of the growing Middle Northern Ireland 'Other' community. The DUP strategy also angered and energised nationalism. However, the DUP's retreat from the political realities of a divided society during the Brexit wars was in many ways replicated by others. The strong 'Remain' stance of the liberal Alliance party saw them move away from their traditional role as a consensual force in a deeply divided society to being firmly on one side of the new entrenched Brexit divide. This has proved to be part of a successful electoral strategy, with an increased vote for Alliance at successive elections, but not conducive to building common ground. Bridge-building and respecting both unionist and nationalist sensibilities, and ultimate mutual vetoes on power-sharing, became unfashionable. Instead, Brexit became a new forum for the traditional sports of whataboutery and politicians condemning others for raising the spectre of violence in the political process while also noting, with sadness, that violence from extremists within their own community might be inevitable unless their concerns over potential Irish land or sea borders were addressed.

The chasm between the parties and their missteps are exemplified by two set-piece events. Firstly, in November 2018 the DUP cheered the warm words and false promises of Boris Johnson, then a backbencher, when he told their party conference of his absolute opposition to an Irish Sea Border: 'We would be damaging the fabric of the Union with regulatory checks and even customs controls between Great Britain and Northern Ireland', adding: 'I have to tell you that no British Conservative government could or should sign up to any such arrangement.'[64] Within less than a year Prime Minister Johnson agreed to the Protocol.[65] Responding to unionist rage at this clear, if predictable, betrayal, and the continuing double-speak of Johnson's government on an agreement he signed but refused to accept responsibility for, the majority of previously pro-'Remain' parties increasingly defended the Protocol in absolute and moral terms. As a result, in September 2020 Alliance joined with the Greens, SDLP and Sinn Féin in demanding 'the rigorous implementation of the Northern Ireland Protocol'.[66] Where were the voices calling for reform, compromise and a genuine 'best of both worlds' option for the North? Arguably the Ulster Unionists are the one party who, despite inconsistencies and occasional abrupt shifts in tone, have come closest to consistently pursuing compromise – accepting the need for special arrangements for NI, but aiming to keep internal UK trade much more open than the Protocol envisages.[67] All the Northern

Ireland parties who demanded 'rigorous implementation' have subsequently quietly retreated from this demand and welcomed the piecemeal reduction in the Protocol and the grace periods granted by the EU.

At the heart of much of the bad faith rhetoric using Northern Ireland as a Brexit football has been the conjuring of the 'spirit' of the Good Friday Agreement into disputes unforeseen in 1998. The Agreement was constructed with continuing Irish and British EU membership taken for granted, and as a forum for inter-governmental meetings, co-operation and shared interests, the EU was significant in long-term improvements in British–Irish relations and with regard to peace funding and other structural funds,[68] but Brexit did not directly violate the Agreement and nor will potential economic barriers within these islands – wherever they may end up. Legitimate fears for long-term stability and serious questions regarding how the dynamics of Brexit interact with cross-community consent and other principles of the Agreement morphed into an alliance of EU negotiators, prominent British Remainers, much of nationalist Ireland and Joe Biden's American administration presenting the full implementation of the Northern Ireland Protocol as essential to protect the Good Friday Agreement. On the other side of the fence, after Boris Johnson's signature dried on the Protocol, DUP personalities who had supported Brexit without much concern for Northern Ireland's consent, and who had opposed the actual 1998 Agreement, found themselves arguing against the Protocol for violating the Good Friday Agreement's consent mechanisms.

It is, however, important to recognise that, well outside the circles of the DUP and committed Brexiteers, many unionists have increasingly begun to question the implications of how the peace settlement is now commonly interpreted in the new Brexit era. The role of the Irish government, in particular that of Leo Varadkar, in affirming a narrative which blends the Agreement and the Irish Sea Border together is only one of multiple shifts in nationalist Ireland's understanding of the North that antagonises a wide spectrum of unionists. A more assertive nationalist culture in Ireland in recent years has been evident not only in popular culture and the toxicity of social media, but also in relation to the decade of commemorations. Especially notable was President Higgins' refusal to accept an invitation from the Churches to an ecumenical 'service of Reflection and Hope, to mark the Centenary of the partition of Ireland and the formation of Northern Ireland' in Armagh.[69] The overwhelming public support in the Republic for the President's absence from this most benign of ecumenical commemorations was telling – one poll finding that 81 per cent of voters answered 'No' when asked if Higgins should have accepted the invitation.[70] And in the background to all these concerns is the spectre of Sinn Féin's surge in popularity, consistently making them now the most popular party in the state in opinion polls – comfortably more popular in the twenty-six counties in percentage terms than in the six counties.

Informed unionists recognise that this popularity may be driven primarily by Sinn Féin's positions on housing and other social challenges facing the Republic, but a by-product of their growing leverage is the pressure for all Southern parties to lobby for a border poll, and a growing mainstreaming of Provisional Sinn Féin narratives of the Troubles. When many unionists consider the trends of Irish political culture and the Brexit negotiations together, it can appear to them that a new consensus is forming around them, one which asserts that nationalist Ireland's consent to any Brexit solution is sacrosanct but unionist dissent can be treated as a sideshow; that the Irish state should aggressively now 'Think 32' but the UK state should, at best, be neutral on the Union; that the IRA campaign is either something worthy of justification or a legacy issue irrelevant to Sinn Féin's rise, or perhaps both; and that north–south dimensions of the peace settlement are non-negotiable but the east–west relationship should be viewed as purely technical. If this consensus is widely accepted, it is tailor-made to alienate unionists from any political process, never mind wishful thinking about a new inclusive nationalism and a 'Shared Ireland'.

Referendum Politics and the Future of the Union

The failure of successive Conservative governments and Westminster parliaments to build a cross-party compromise following the 2016 referendum set the tone and wider context for this failure of politics in Northern Ireland. At Westminster the referendum ended the premiership of David Cameron, and the failure of Theresa May to gain parliament's consent for her Brexit deal led to the fall of yet another Tory prime minister due to Europe. The rise of Boris Johnson to power brought disputes between the UK government, the courts and parliament to a crescendo, before he eventually 'Got Brexit Done' by imposing an economic border down the Irish Sea.

The multi-dimensional institutional and constitutional crises in British politics during these years are in some ways best exhibited by the Labour opposition party. From 2015–19 Labour was led by Jeremy Corbyn, who held a record of Eurosceptic views while leading an increasingly Europhile party,[71] held historical views sympathising with Irish republicanism which were well outside the mainstream of British politics,[72] and who many Scottish unionists suspected was, at best, indifferent regarding Scottish independence.[73] In the weeks following the 2016 Brexit vote, MPs in the Parliamentary Labour Party expressed no confidence in him by 172 votes to 40 but, following the letter, if not the spirit, of his party's rules, Corbyn simply refused to go and remained leader until electoral defeat in 2019. In these different ways the politics of Scotland, Northern Ireland, the Conservatives, Labour, Britain's weak political parties and weak parliamentary democracy, and the constitutional future of the Union were entwined and thrown into collective flux.

Negotiations between the UK government and the EU following the referendum have been a labyrinthine loop of missed deadlines, fraying alliances, the UK reneging on agreements, and ongoing re-negotiations – and all with Northern Ireland at the heart of the contention and Scottish grievances stirring in the wings. While, as we have seen, historically the North of Ireland has been a bridge connecting Britain and Ireland, now it is also the interface where the European Union and the United Kingdom meet. The Protocol, as it currently stands, places Northern Ireland within the EU customs territory and the EU single market for goods but not services, while Great Britain stands outside of them all. This weakening of the UK internal market was powerfully symbolised by the banning of plants with Great British soil from 'import' to Northern Ireland – a case perfectly scripted to antagonise unionists.[74] This ban and many other aspects of the Protocol were subsequently softened by a combination of 'grace periods' agreed between the UK and EU and some unilateral decisions by the UK not to implement the deal fully, which merely pushed the problem down the road.

The Brexit paradox May and Johnson found themselves in was simultaneously to promise they would take the UK out of EU customs and single market arrangements but also not implement 'a hard border' on the island of Ireland. What constitutes a hard border was open to interpretation, but early in negotiations the interpretation advocated by the Irish government and the EU and accepted by the British government, to the surprise of at least one leading Irish diplomat,[75] was that of any checks or controls on goods moving between the Republic and Northern Ireland equating to a hard border. Alongside this stringent definition, a hard border was also explicitly associated with a return to conflict – most clearly in October 2018 when *The Irish Times* reported that 'Taoiseach Leo Varadkar has given European leaders his clearest warning yet that a return to a hard border would threaten a return to violence in Northern Ireland.'[76] Theresa May's 'backstop' solution to this bind temporarily offered continuing close UK–EU alignment as a solution, but this was unacceptable to many Tory MPs, who asked what was the point of Brexit if the UK remained tied to EU rules? The DUP rejected May's deal in large part because of their desire to see 'a clean hard Brexit' for the whole UK, but also because they doubted the value and lifespan of the promises of a weak Tory Prime Minister not to exclude Northern Ireland from the brave new world. Without a dramatic softening of the EU's position, or a longer-term close alignment between the UK and the EU, a sea border similar to that subsequently accepted by Johnson was a possible, perhaps likely, long-term outcome of May's strategy.

The economic and political impact of the Protocol remains contested and difficult to judge – not least because grace periods and disagreements have ensured that the Protocol has yet to be implemented, and the difficulty of disentangling it from Covid and other economic factors. Many Northern nationalists feel justifiable anger at the outcome of this chaotic process, not just because of the loss of EU political membership, but also with regard to sectors such as banking and financial services experiencing something equating to a hard border on the island. Despite these concerns, however, a nationalist consensus supporting the Protocol has formed due to its protection of the open Irish border and the potential it offers for growth of the all-island economy. For unionism the outworkings of Brexit and the Protocol mark a profound political defeat; disagreements within unionism are restricted to differing assessments of the potential longer-term implications for the foundations of the Union. There is uncertainty regarding the economic position in which the Protocol places the North; continuing open access to the EU single market has clear potential advantages for many businesses, but the burdensome and uncertain bureaucracy added to trade with the larger Great British market may cancel out these economic positives for other sectors and for consumers.

Former DUP advisor Lee Reynolds argues that the outcome of the Protocol is: 'half membership of the UK goods market; only part inclusion in UK trade deals; out of the UK state aid regime; in the EU goods single market; excluded from EU trade deals'.[77] A scenario closer to the much heralded 'best of both worlds', with Northern Ireland receiving much fuller access to both British and EU markets, would have the potential to transform both the socio-economics and politics of the region. For some unionists this would remain a dilution of the Union, confirming Northern Ireland as a place apart, but for others it would herald the potential appeal to the middle ground of Northern Irish society of a stronger economy. If the long-term Brexit solution for Northern Ireland offers unique economic advantages why, therefore, not maintain Northern Ireland? Such a scenario would require a much less rigid approach from the EU regarding protections for its single market, but if – and it is a big if – this special status for Northern Ireland ever transpires it, in turn, raises questions for Scotland.

During the Brexit turmoil of the 2017–19 Westminster parliament, the SNP's rejection of Brexit and support for a second EU referendum across the UK was front and centre in their European policy, but the special status granted Northern Ireland in first the backstop and then the Protocol also influenced the party's analysis.[78] The SNP accepted the unique challenges Northern Ireland faces as a post-conflict society, and supported the analysis that a 'hard border' in Ireland threatened the peace process, but they also saw Northern Ireland as a possible template for Scotland to follow in order to maintain EU single market membership. When responding to Theresa May's backstop, Nicola Sturgeon argued that:

> While I welcome the proposed commitment for Ireland and Northern Ireland – and while the particular circumstances in Scotland are distinct and separate from those in Ireland – today's developments show very clearly that if one part of [the] UK can retain regulatory alignment with the EU and effectively stay in the single market, there is no good practical

reason why others cannot do the same. Indeed, any special status for Northern Ireland would make a similar solution for Scotland even more vital. For Scotland to find itself outside the single market, while Northern Ireland effectively stays in would place us at a double disadvantage when it comes to jobs and investment.[79]

There is more than a whiff of political opportunism in Sturgeon's stance – her party joined in the chorus accusing the UK government of threatening peace by not accepting the need for a unique solution for Northern Ireland, but then when a unique Brexit settlement for Northern Ireland arrived, it was seen as unfair on Scotland. However, this argument does point to another strain on the Union that flows from divergent forms of Brexit happening within the UK, namely that perceived advantage for one part of the UK creates grievances in another.

Question marks over the economic and political sustainability of the Protocol have ensured that envious looks from the SNP across the Irish Sea have become less frequent, but in April 2021 Sturgeon observed that a successful Northern Ireland Protocol could instead offer a template for an independent Scotland, easing border pressures between a Scotland in the EU and an England outside it. She stated: 'The Northern Ireland protocol, if there are easements there, yes, I think that does offer some template, but we work in a proper planned way to make sure that any rules that have to be applied are applied in a way that absolutely minimises any practical difficulties for businesses trading across the England–Scotland border.'[80] Whatever the merits of the Protocol as a template for a soft border in a future partitioned Britain, this is unsafe territory for the SNP and highlights the tough choices Brexit creates for those arguing for independence. The Scottish nationalist narrative of 2014 that nothing would change with regards to the 'social union' of Britain post-independence now has to address similar hard choices daily highlighted by the Northern Irish Brexit experience. Just as the UK cannot in the long-term hide from the consequences of divergence from the EU, Scottish nationalism needs answers on borders and alignment between a potential separate Scotland and the rest of the UK.

While the constitutional future of Scotland and Northern Ireland will in large part be decided by the success the UK makes of Brexit and the Protocol, it will also be won and lost in the context of quickly changing and volatile electorates. The twin forces of unionist–nationalist divides and Brexit have reinforced existing trends in both jurisdictions and opened up new electoral cleavages. In the midst of this complex fragmentation we can, however, make out the broad parameters of a Middle Scotland and a Middle Ulster who could prove amenable to constitutional change, and therefore could decide any potential second independence referendum or Irish border poll. These 'persuadable' voters are key to the survival of the Union.

In Northern Ireland declining vote shares for traditional unionist *and* nationalist parties and a corresponding rise in support for 'others' – primarily Alliance but also the Green Party – means that a traditional 'two communities' conception of Northern Ireland is increasingly out of date. Traditional unionism, meaning those who vote for capital-U Unionist parties and identify as Protestant, is now a minority of the population – those from a Catholic background now outnumber 'Protestants'.[81] A younger

Catholic–nationalist population is undoubtedly a significant part of the changing picture, and Brexit's main impact on the constitutional question so far has been to make the Union less attractive to the significant minority of Catholic voters who were comfortable with the Union pre-2016. Also key to understanding contemporary Northern Ireland is the changing profile and values of those from a Protestant–unionist background. As in Scotland, those from a nominally Protestant background have secularised earlier and in larger numbers than those from a Catholic background, and these 'nominal Prods' and a wider cross-section of Protestant Ulster increasingly have values at odds with the dominant DUP strand of unionism. As successive University of Liverpool electoral and social surveys have detailed,[82] the most liberal section of Northern Irish society – with regard to attitudes towards issues such as sexuality, women's reproductive rights and integrated education – is consistently among younger voters from a Protestant background. In parallel with these social trends, in 2017 it was surveyed that while support among Protestants aged under forty for the Union remained high, at 82 per cent, only a minority of this demographic voted in elections for the Assembly or Westminster.[83]

The brutal electoral process in Northern Ireland may continue to push Northern Ireland unionist parties towards their traditional bases of older more socially conservative voters, but the longer-term future of the Union is dependent on securing the support, or at least a lack of opposition, of these new 'others'. Brexit has undoubtedly made this task more difficult, combining, as it has across the UK, with other liberal values to alienate many key younger demographics from Brexiteer parties. The decision of Doug Beattie as leader of the UUP to appeal directly to liberal unionist opinion may alienate core sections of the UUP's current support, and could result in short- to medium-term electoral losses – few unionist leaders have advanced their careers by taking such a direction – but offering a liberal alternative to a growing, and pivotal, section of the population is surely in the best interests of those seeking to broaden the appeal of unionism. The imperatives of party politics in a deeply divided society often run counter to the imperatives of building a wider coalition in support of the Union.

In Scotland the twin referendums of 2014 and 2016 have fractured the electorate in fascinating ways, most clearly by hamstringing Scottish Labour, but also by producing other often underappreciated political minorities in Scotland.[84] As Sobolewska and Ford detail in their epoch-defining book *Brexitland*, Scotland now has four referendum tribes: by 2017, 31 per cent of the electorate supported 'Yes' to independence and 'Remain' in the EU; 20 per cent supported 'No' and 'Leave'; 15 per cent 'Yes' and 'Leave'; and 34 per cent 'No' and 'Remain'.[85] Subsequently some of these 'No but Remain' voters have shifted towards support for independence, and the 'No' voter disenchanted by Brexit is now established as the key demographic for Scotland's future – the embodiment of persuadable Middle Scotland. But another underappreciated slice of the electorate is those who previously supported Scottish independence but have been alienated from that cause by their support for 'Leave' – it is often forgotten that an estimated 32 per cent of SNP voters in 2016 voted 'Leave'.[86] In the shifting sands of this four-way constitutional split, opinion polls on the independence question have been remarkably stable and Scotland is stuck split almost precisely down the middle on its future. For all the obvious tensions and the continuing SNP domination, what many Scottish unionists feared was the perfect storm of Brexit combined with a Boris Johnson premiership has not, as of yet, shifted the Scottish national question definitively.

The 'Yes and Leave' demographic of Scotland also points to a broader conclusion that Sobolewska and Ford reach, namely that levels of ethnocentrism are 'comparable in Scotland and England, and ethnocentric voters in both contexts tend to view larger political unions with more suspicion'.[87] Rather than accept the often repeated assertion that Scots are definitively more progressive than the rest of the UK, it is the common trends and instincts of the identity politics of Brexiteer England (and Wales) and contemporary Scotland that stand out: 'Both Scottish independence and Brexit won their strongest early support from identity conservative voters wishing to "take back control".'[88] In this regard the Scottish independence fault-line obscures many fears and divisions common across the whole of the UK. How unionist and nationalist political forces succeed in constructing alliances across these different post-referendum political tribes will decide the future of the Union.

The Choices Ahead

A growing section of unionist opinion has responded to the fragility of the Union by questioning the devolution project – and indeed blaming it for the disuniting of the Kingdom. 'Muscular Unionists'[89] have noted how increasing the powers and scope of devolution has failed to stem the tide of separatism, especially in Scotland, and argue for either scrapping devolution or reconfiguring a greatly enhanced role for central government post-Brexit. Anti-devolution sentiment appeared to find support in Downing Street when, in an unguarded comment over Zoom with Conservative colleagues, Boris Johnson was reported as saying 'devolution has been a disaster north of the border' and was 'Tony Blair's biggest mistake'.[90] But while muscular unionism can offer a valuable critique of New Labour and Cameron-era devolution, proponents who take this analysis to the conclusion of abolishing Holyrood, the Welsh Senedd and Stormont fail to confront either contemporary political realities in these constituent parts of the UK, or the compromise, asymmetry and partnership central to the Union's history. Despite the less than impressive performance of the devolved administrations in many aspects of public policy, devolution is popular in Scotland, Wales and Northern Ireland.[91] Ending devolution would be perfectly engineered to alienate Middle Scotland and Middle Ulster from the Union. Electorally and politically devolution is the only game in town for any form of unionism that wants to maintain the consent of the Scottish people and a stable Northern Ireland.

Any anti-devolution unionism that extends to Northern Ireland and which sincerely wishes to integrate Northern Ireland more firmly into the Union fails adequately to address the sheer infeasibility of imposing de facto Direct Rule as a long-term settlement. A variation of devolution – and reforms are undoubtedly needed – is the only gateway to maintaining the Union in Northern Ireland. Furthermore, for Northern Ireland not to be a place apart constitutionally, devolution across the UK is the only form of constitutional integration. When the power-sharing institutions at Stormont collapsed in 2017–20, it was the absence of devolution that made Northern Ireland a place apart, with the North unrepresented in UK forums. The history of the Union in Northern Ireland is largely a history of devolution or efforts to restore devolution, and the constituency in Northern Ireland open to old integrationist arguments is – for better or worse – decreasing. If, as most candid unionists surely would accept, devolution is the least-worst realistic option for Northern Ireland, then accepting devolution in Northern Ireland but supporting a type of Unitary State in Great Britain would exclude Northern Ireland all over again. Ciaran Martin has pointed to the broader danger of the anti-devolutionary turn in unionism: 'The practical reality of this philosophy is that the terms of Union are set on the terms of an English majority in a unitary state. And if you don't like that, then don't forget who is paying for all this.'[92] Martin defines this as 'know-your-place unionism'.

Rather than chase historical what-ifs about the pre-devolution era – counterfactuals that in themselves are not convincing explanations of the historical nature of the Union in Scotland or Northern Ireland, or of the reasons why devolution emerged – unionists across the UK should engage with contemporary political and constitutional realities, while seeking solutions to the undeniable failures of the devolution era: the weakening sense of shared citizenship across the UK; poor policy outcomes for devolved executives and central government; the ill-defined relationship between central government and devolved powers; and the lack of common unionist endeavours across the UK. The historic malleability of the uncodified British constitution and pragmatism of unionism should be utilised anew to find a new path, a constitutional third way perhaps, towards a more successful set of devolved institutions, stronger east–west institutions as one forum for much improved intergovernmental UK relations, and a more coherent and defined role for central government across the UK. Rather than a top-down imposition of British nationalism, a wider comfort within the UK for its citizens in devolved jurisdictions requires both respect for national and regional identities, and a shared British sense of purpose.

The Covid pandemic revealed the extent to which devolution has transformed the architecture of UK government, and how poorly understood it is by citizens.[93] Johnson addressing 'the nation' to reveal emergency measures for workplaces, schools and health that in many cases only applied to England – and which were frequently significantly different in Scotland, Wales and Northern Ireland – exemplified the UK's constitutional incoherence and imbalance. Yet the successful pooling of UK resources for the equitable distribution of furlough funds and vaccines across the nations and regions also highlighted the continuing essential importance of central government and the security an economy the size of the UK can still provide. Despite differing public perceptions, and much political grandstanding, regarding how governments in London, Cardiff, Belfast and Edinburgh performed during the pandemic, there was, as Stuart McIntyre and Graeme Roy note, 'limited variation in public health and economic outcomes' across the UK.[94]

Two interventions from the Labour Mayor of Greater Manchester, Andy Burnham, during the pandemic captured both the complexities and the potential of the devolved Union. When Burnham attacked central government for pandemic funding decisions allocated to his region, and for a lack of consultation, he highlighted that for a growing patchwork of England devolution is creating new political dynamics, grievances and regional advocates with a voice on the national stage.[95] Burnham's second major intervention came when he criticised another leader for a lack of respect and consultation when imposing a travel ban on his region; this time the target was Nicola Sturgeon.[96] A northern English Labour leader attacking an SNP government pointed to a potential future for a devolved UK where Scottish nationalists have to contend with a variety of English political leaders who can't be dismissed as 'Westminster' or 'Tory', which is often polite SNP code for 'English'. As well as making it more difficult for nationalists to 'other' or caricature England – by far the most multicultural and diverse UK nation – if the north of England can find a renewed political voice it could begin to recreate a version of its historic role as a cultural and economic link and mediator between the constituent parts of the UK. New meaning needs to be given to the strong cultural and socio-economic commonalities shared between, for example, post-industrial Belfast, Glasgow and Liverpool.

Burnham's anger towards central UK government also highlighted the weak powers and wildly uneven nature of UK devolution. Among the key unanswered questions of UK devolution are what financial settlement and powers regional English leaders should accrue, and what happens with regard to the 59 per cent of the English population who live in regions currently without mayors or local government with significant power – over transport and economic policy for example – devolved to them by central government?[97] The famously tricky 'English Question' is in fact two questions, as Robert Hazell describes:

If the aim is to give England a separate political voice, to rebalance the louder political voices now accorded to Scotland, Wales and Northern Ireland, then solutions are English votes on English laws, or an English Parliament. But if the aim is devolution *within* England, breaking the excessive domination of the central government in London, then the solutions include elected regional assemblies, city regions, stronger local government, elected mayors.[98]

Devolution decisions face the English in a context where, perhaps surprisingly, resentment towards the current constitutional imbalance remains incoherent as an English political force. Arthur Aughey describes the resulting system as one of 'subsidised self-determination', where 'the Scots, Welsh and Northern Irish get the self-determination and the English do the subsidising'.[99] The size and power of England within the UK may mean some imbalance of this type is a necessary condition of the Union, but the attitudes of English voters towards these imbalances, and the future path English devolution follows, will do much to influence the direction of Scotland and Northern Ireland.

Related to the English Question is the question of how better to represent the nations and regions within pan-UK forums. As discussed, there is a need for much stronger inter-governmental relations which could build upon the east–west dimensions of the Good Friday Agreement, and other forums could also be strengthened and made inclusive of regional English representatives, but there is also the potential for other radical reforms. For example, as Douglas Dowell asks: 'Why, unlike almost any other state with a territorial challenge, don't we even discuss some extra seats for the smaller nations in a reformed Lords?"[100] A new second chamber – with disproportionately loud scrutinising voices from Northern Ireland, Scotland and Wales – would also tackle the absurdity of the overcrowded and anarchistic patronage of the Lords.

Former Prime Minister Gordon Brown is a powerful advocate for a new Union with such a new second Chamber – a 'Senate for the Nations and Regions' – alongside an intergovernmental 'Council of the Regions and Nations', a new Barnett formula with a fairer funding model for English regions, and an ambitious new UK constitution.[101] These are huge undertakings with profound constitutional implications, even without the political difficulties that flow from the current holders of office in Downing Street and Holyrood, but if an alternative to both nationalist separatism and an unrealistic and unwanted Unitary State is to be found, these ideas need to be engaged with.

The role of the central state across the UK is the great unanswered question for any remaking of the Union. After a journey across Britain and Ireland in 2021, Tom McTague noted the almost entire absence of the UK state, British institutions and symbolism from the day-to-day lives of most Scottish citizens:

> Visiting Scotland today is to very obviously visit a land from which the British state has all but withdrawn. The national industries and national institutions that once existed have gone. By the time we arrived in Glasgow, we'd passed an abandoned British nuclear-research facility and an abandoned British military base. The only signs of the British state were the partially privatized post office, the pound, and the monarchy. Is this really enough?[102]

When, as McTague observes, 'no other major power on Earth stands quite as close to its own dissolution', can the UK survive in the long-term without developing a shared sense of purpose and belonging? And is it possible for these to develop without visible British institutions positively impacting the lives of Scottish, Welsh and Northern Irish citizens?

One possible way to begin answering such profound questions is to frame the role of the central UK state around the key challenges facing its citizens: equitable redistribution of resources tackling regional inequalities; energy insecurity and climate; food insecurity; infrastructure connecting the regions and nations; and defence and national security in an unstable world of pandemics and war in Europe. Each of these issues either requires or would greatly benefit from central government resources and reach, and, if successfully addressed, each has the potential to grow a shared sense of citizenship. These are all huge challenges, not least because of the impact the Protocol could have on any coherent UK-wide energy or agriculture market, or state aid policy, and then the politics of impinging on policy areas currently devolved to Edinburgh, Cardiff and Belfast. A battle over where power lies with regard to energy, agriculture and tax powers appears to be inevitable, but even if the UK moves towards a more quasi-federal system, central government needs to play a coherent and visible role throughout the quasi-federation – and not just through the redistribution of money carried out opaquely and received without much recognition. Outside of the European Union it is legitimate both for the central government to take on some of the powers that lay with the EU and, ironically, for the EU to be a model when implementing structural funds and investment.

Towering over any potential reforms are doubts as to the UK's very survival in the medium-term. The consistent support of 45–48 per cent of Scots for independence and the prospect of a Sinn Féin first minister in Northern Ireland raises immediate political challenges for the Union that have to influence any longer-term constitutional reform. A Sinn Féin first minister does not in and of itself signal the inevitability of either a border poll or the end of Northern Ireland, and indeed the stasis in the overall nationalist vote highlights how the blurring of traditional loyalties in Northern Ireland is also a profound challenge for nationalism; neither the DUP nor Sinn Féin are designed to win many converts to their constitutional position. There is, as yet, little evidence of Brexit resulting in a significant increase in support for taking Northern Ireland out of the UK.[103] However, a Sinn Féin first minister and the uncertainties of Brexit do symbolise the failures of the recent DUP project – a new unionism is needed for the Union to prosper in Northern Ireland. In Scotland, too, 'border polls' have stubbornly not moved in the expected nationalist direction, and the SNP government's poor record with regard to educational attainment, health outcomes, the tragedy of its drugs crisis, shipbuilding and many other issues is increasingly difficult to spin. Furthermore, unlike in Protocol Northern Ireland, Brexit complicates the nuts and bolts of Scottish separation from the UK. Despite all these caveats, however, the constitutional future of Scotland remains on a knife-edge.

In attempting to unite all the various potential constitutional futures and reforms, it is possible to lose sight of one fundamental question – can the Union of Great Britain and Northern Ireland work, and be seen to work, better for its citizens? A repeat of the previous lost decade of austerity,[104] identity politics and the divisive politics of grievance, the self-harm of Brexit, and declining public services could be fatal for the Union. However, if, instead, one of the most successful economies and multicultural unions in the world can be seen to deliver security, prosperity and a sense of belonging successfully, it could yet be remade.

Epilogue

Profound uncertainty regarding the survival of the United Kingdom of Great Britain and Northern Ireland has become an accepted and strangely normalised fact of British political life for over a decade now. The 2021 elections to Holyrood and 2022 elections to Stormont confirmed the extent of the challenges the Union faces, and underlined key arguments made in this book: namely, the significant connections and interplay between the politics and cultures of the two places, and the centrality of Scottish and Northern Irish politics to the future of the UK. These are not issues contained within the condescended 'Celtic periphery', but instead are existential to a permanent member of the UN Security Council. Pro-Union responses to this state of affairs continue to swing often between complacency and fatalism, while Scottish and Irish nationalists now commonly express variations of an inevitability thesis – a belief that the arc of history bends unavoidably towards victory. However, as we have detailed, there was nothing inevitable about the shape of the Union's past, and its future remains up for grabs.

The Holyrood election of May 2021 granted a renewed mandate for Nicola Sturgeon's leadership, and the formation of an SNP–

Green coalition government represented a pro-independence majority of MSPs.[1] In the final stages of the election campaign, Sturgeon appealed to non-nationalists to vote SNP, saying: 'Thursday is not an independence referendum, it's not asking people to vote yes or no';[2] but a year later she set the scene for renewed demands for a second referendum and a legal battle with the British government by stating: 'Last May the people of Scotland said Yes to an independence referendum by electing a clear majority of MSPs committed to that outcome.'[3] The UK government rejected calls for a new referendum, so Sturgeon took the issue to the UK Supreme Court, arguing that conducting such a referendum on 19 October 2023 is within her government's competence. With pro-Union Scottish parties stating they would boycott any such move, the spectre of Catalonia's 2017 unconstitutional referendum and subsequent Spanish legal battles, arrests and street protests haunts the thoughts of some in Scotland.

With legal opinion suggesting that the Supreme Court is unlikely to rule in the Scottish government's favour, Sturgeon's Plan B is to assert additional political pressure on the UK government by framing the next Westminster general election as a de facto referendum. The echoes of Northern Irish political culture grow louder. Presenting complex elections at the local, devolved and Westminster levels as single-issue constitutional referendums – regardless of the electoral systems and the attitudes of other parties – sounds very familiar to Northern Irish ears, and is a good working definition of the process of Ulsterisation that many voices in Scotland still refuse to acknowledge has happened there.

Sturgeon's legal and 'Plan B' gambles are high risk, and a change from the cautious and gradualist approach she had shown previously. While an impatient nationalist base may be energised by such tactics, and many Scots undoubtedly are angry at a London block on another referendum, this confrontational approach also has the potential to alienate 'the persuadables' in Middle Scotland. Many Scots may view the next general election through the lens of another single issue – getting rid of a Conservative government riven with divisions after deposing a fourth prime minister in six years. The possibility of a UK Labour government could substantially change the dynamics of Scottish politics, and also empower a reappraisal of the constitutional architecture of the wider devolved UK. What is certain is that Scotland will again be centre stage across the UK during the next general election, with the Tories repeating their campaign line from 2015 that a weak Labour government would be in the pocket of Scottish nationalists. Aiming to kill this narrative, Keir Starmer has ruled out any coalition or deal with the SNP, again seeking to sharpen the choice anti-Conservative Scottish voters face when electing to Westminster. Whether it is this approach by Starmer or Sturgeon's de facto referendum that succeeds in defining the Westminster election in Scotland will be key for the future of both Labour and the Union: the path to a Labour government and renewed hope for the Union both run through Labour regaining a significant voice in Scotland.

However the short-term politicking is conducted between now and the aftermath of the next Westminster election, a fundamental question remains: can a majority of Scots be convinced that their future best lies in the Union? There are clear merits to the Conservative and Labour position of opposing a 2023 Scottish referendum: there is no polling evidence that suggests a clear majority of Scots want either independence or a referendum in the current circumstances and there has not been a substantial sustained change of opinion on the issue since the 'once in a generation' referendum held nine years prior to the SNP's proposed sequel. But in the longer term the Union obviously needs the consent of a majority of Scots, and they remain deeply and evenly split on its future. As we have detailed, the conception of the Union as a partnership has been fundamental to Scottish unionism since its inception, and also to its previously successful maintenance of both Scottish distinctiveness and broad identification with the Union. Simply saying no to another referendum is not an answer to the question of how this partnership and positive identification can be renewed.

While Nicola Sturgeon was finalising her Plan B intervention, in May 2022, Northern Ireland went to the polls and returned Sinn Féin as the largest party. The potency of this hugely symbolic moment may have been diluted by the lack of any immediate likelihood of a new Stormont Executive actually forming, due to the DUP's refusal to operate the institutions under the current Northern Ireland Protocol arrangements, but the result powerfully conveyed the reality of the new Northern Ireland. Traditional unionism, those voters aligned with explicitly unionist political parties, is now one of three minority electoral groupings.

Global headlines understandably focused on an Irish nationalist party winning more seats than any of its rivals in a Northern Ireland election for the first time,[4] and on the extraordinary journey of Sinn Féin. However, the results were not a surge in support for Irish nationalism. Instead the election was defined by the three-way split in unionism, a 3 per cent fall in the combined unionist vote compared to 2017 and a 6.7 per cent fall in the DUP vote.[5] The combined nationalist share of the vote, now only 1 per cent behind the unionist total, remained essentially static, as it has since 1999, with Sinn Féin's vote share up 1 per cent from 2017 and the SDLP falling by 3 per cent.

Alliance's consolidation as the third force in Northern Irish politics, with 13.5 per cent of the vote and 20 per cent of the seats, highlighted again the 'others' as the key demographic in any future border poll. Alliance's stance on Brexit and support for the Protocol has not, as yet, damaged its support in middle-class, traditionally unionist areas, and the party continues to break some new ground in traditionally nationalist areas. In taking all of the Green Party's remaining seats, Alliance is now the sole representative of the 'others' at Stormont. The social class dynamics of the growth of the 'others' is worthy of note – this is a largely middle-class phenomenon.[6] One consequence of this dynamic is a parallel working-class tilt in the support base of unionist parties. One can speculate on the role of Brexit in alienating the professional and business classes from the DUP, or perhaps see a Northern Irish version of the wider European and North American embourgeoisement of progressive politics.

That the DUP's loss of support was primarily to the hard-line Traditional Unionist Voice (TUV) highlights the anger in other sections of the unionist community at the Protocol. If the party had not stated its opposition to devolution returning under the existing Protocol, it is clear the DUP vote would have collapsed further. The spread of unionist – or previously unionist – voters across the spectrum from Alliance to TUV conveyed the failure of the DUP's leadership of unionism during the chaotic years of the Brexit process. The UUP's attempt to offer a liberal unionist alternative has so far stalled, but it did manage to hold its own in what was a febrile election.

Unionism can therefore highlight many qualifications to a narrative of unstoppable nationalist growth in Northern Ireland, and polling evidence of a surge in support of a border poll or an end to Northern Ireland is currently scarce. But the failure of the DUP to coalesce unionist voters, even when playing the familiar tune of stopping a republican first minister, and the failure of the two major unionist parties to win back significant support from Alliance, must raise alarm bells for the unionist cause. Old strategies of unionist unity are, as we have discussed, not the answer to the new electorate of Northern Ireland, but alternative strategies to broaden the appeal of the Union have to be built in the context of the division and uncertainty caused by Brexit and the Northern Ireland Protocol.

How the machinations of the unstable UK–EU relationship are finally resolved, and how much damage is done economically and politically until then, will do much to frame how the politics of Northern Ireland develop. With a UK government unilaterally breaking from the basis, as well as the letter, of an international treaty they previously lauded, the trust required between London, Dublin, Belfast and Brussels to resolve these issues will be tough to build. Furthermore, the potential impact of the 'full fat' Protocol – minus the grace periods and other temporary concessions agreed or ignored by either party to the agreement – remains unpredictable economically and politically. Legal confrontations between the EU and the UK risk a return to an EU agenda of rigorously implementing an agreement which was accepted by all sides in early 2022, including, quietly, the pro-Protocol parties, as not implementable as originally intended. The boasts of Boris Johnson and his successors that they 'got Brexit done' remain a cruel joke in Northern Ireland.

The response in Scotland to the Stormont elections was significant. Strikingly the SNP leadership has moved closer than ever before to acknowledging shared interests with Sinn Féin. Immediately prior to the election, John Swinney, SNP Deputy First Minister, expressed hopes that a Sinn Féin First Minister would work well with the SNP 'to challenge the United Kingdom government on many aspects of its policy approach'.[7] After the votes were counted, Sinn Féin was warmly congratulated by Nicola Sturgeon, who soon met with First Minister designate Michelle O'Neill in Edinburgh. Surveying Britain and Ireland after the meeting, Sturgeon noted:

> There's no doubt there are big fundamental questions being asked of the UK as a political entity right now ... They're being asked here in Scotland, they're being asked in Northern Ireland, they're being asked in Wales, and I think we're going to see some fundamental changes to UK governance in the years to come and I am certain one of those changes is going to be Scottish independence.[8]

Similarly, the leader of Plaid Cymru, Adam Price, met with 'our friends' Mary Lou McDonald and Michelle O'Neill, noting their 'shared journeys to realising our potentials as independent nations'.[9]

If 'Celtic nationalism' expresses such common cause, then the SNP and Plaid Cymru will have to address not only uncomfortable conversations about Northern Ireland's future, but also the ties and fault-lines within their societies and these islands that can be traced to Ulster. Conversations that were largely absent from the political mainstream in Great Britain through the period of the Troubles and beyond are now heard loud and clear. The public warmth evident between the SNP and Sinn Féin would have been unimaginable without the new generation of Sinn Féin leaders, who are largely personally untainted by the Troubles, but while some scars have healed, there remains a political risk for the SNP in linking Irish and Scottish nationalism, given the delicate balance of how it has sought to utilise and negotiate Irish passions and prejudices in Scotland. One unionist Scottish newspaper responded to the O'Neill–Sturgeon meeting by listing the forty-nine members of Scottish regiments murdered by the Provisional IRA.[10]

Across the political spectrum more voices are beginning to address the Scottish–Northern Irish dynamics in this period of intense political flux. The unionist Northern Irish commentator Newton Emerson noted that: 'it is still striking how little attention each pays to the other's politics. Scotland sees Northern Ireland as a warning but not one worth following in detail.'[11] As an example Emerson noted the lack of commentary after legislation passed at Westminster protecting both the Irish language and what is now defined in law as 'the Ulster Scots and Ulster British tradition' in Northern Ireland.

The Ulster-Scots component of the culture, heritage and language of the north of Ireland has long been misunderstood or frankly treated with hostile ridicule, often in class-ridden terms from within unionist communities, but it reflects many of the ties that culturally bind the two places together. Significantly there is something of an

Ulster-Scots literary revival under way, with writers such as Steve Dornan, Angeline King, Angela Graham, Robert Campbell, Al Millar and Anne McMaster writing fiction and poetry utilising, or playing with, variations of Ulster-Scots. While some see Ulster-Scots simply as a cultural strand of contemporary unionism, in its history and culture it also has the potential to challenge unionist versus nationalist culture wars – it can be a gateway to understanding the United Irishmen, multiple migrations between Scotland and Ireland, or minority language rights, as much as it is essential to understanding the lineage of the Ulster Covenant. Dornan, a County Down-born poet living in Aberdeenshire, powerfully argues that: 'It is a feature of Ulster-Scots, and arguably one of its key virtues, that it has the potential to problematise limiting binaries ... Ulster-Scots can be a liminal space that offers an alternative to essentialist thinking as it's by definition hybrid and spliced: it speaks to east–west archipelagic connections and yet is of the island of Ireland.'[12]

In an age of political polarisation where, for example, crude discourse describing contemporary unionists in Northern Ireland as Planters is used by social media trolls and leading American Congressmen alike, challenges to 'limiting binaries' are to be welcomed.

As we have explored, the shock 2011 Holyrood victory of Alex Salmond's SNP began an era, which paused only briefly after the 2014 referendum, when the fragility of the Union has been an almost constant presence in a turbulent age of political polarisation and international crises. Long accustomed to constitutional instability emanating solely from Northern Ireland, centres of power and opinion-formers in Great Britain have struggled to respond coherently to the intertwined challenges now emanating from Belfast and Edinburgh. The approach of successive UK governments to the shaky architecture of a devolved UK has too often been fragmented, piecemeal, lacking in long-term strategy, and unwilling to think seriously about what connects the constituent parts of the UK. Similarly Scottish nationalism, too, has failed to seriously engage with what its project would mean for the part of these islands it historically has most in common with, the north of Ireland. This book has sought to break many of these silences and connect artificially segregated debates that highlight a shared history and common contemporary challenges for two constituent parts of the UK. In doing so we have brought centre stage conversations, including uncomfortable ones, about what divides and unites Scotland and Northern Ireland.

Regardless of the shape future political settlements take, there is a need for wider and better-informed public conversations concerned with the relationships across Britain and Ireland. For those who want the Union to prosper, there is an urgent need for a new approach and a new framework, inclusive of Wales and economically struggling regions of England that have largely been outside the remit of our study. Any new UK political or constitutional framework requires a unifying language and an agenda of common citizenship and shared endeavours, which offers an alternative to the politics of grievance and the ever-decreasing silos of identity politics that have so marked the previous decade. An era of profound international crises of health, security, climate, energy and the economy ensures that there will be no easy choices, but this hostile world suggests the continuing need for the pooling and sharing of resources, and a state with more capacity to provide security for its citizens.

In his poem 'Jaa Banes', Steve Dornan writes: 'Ulster an Scotland, sib an sindert/At yinst forenent an throuither', which he translates as: 'Ulster and Scotland, closely related but divided, at the same time standing opposite each other but all mixed up.'[13] Whatever the political and constitutional future holds for both Northern Ireland and Scotland – be it the status quo, the break-up of the UK or a remade Union – this mixing will continue. The deep ties evident in the people, heritages and cultures of both places remain; as does an interdependent economic and geopolitical future across the narrow sea.

Endnotes

INTRODUCTION

1   Newton Emerson, 'Does the intellectual collapse of the exhausted SNP hint at Sinn Féin's future?', *The Irish Times*, 30 June 2022.

2   Graham Walker, *Intimate Strangers: Political and Cultural Interaction Between Scotland and Ulster in Modern Times* (Edinburgh: John Donald, 1995).

CHAPTER 1:
SHARED HISTORY ACROSS THE NARROW SEA

1   *The Irish Times*, 26 January 2019.

2   Ian Adamson, *The Cruthin: The Ancient Kindred* (Belfast: Pretani Press, 1974); *The Identity of Ulster: The Land, the Language and the People* (Belfast: Pretani Press, 1982); Garry R. Watson, *The Ulster Covenant and Scotland* (Belfast: DCAL, 2013).

3   Edna Longley, *From Cathleen to Anorexia: The Breakdown of Irelands* (Dublin: Attic Press, 1990).

4   Jonathan Bardon, *A Narrow Sea: The Irish–Scottish Connection in 120 Episodes* (Dublin: Gill Books, 2018), Preface.

5   Finlay Holmes, 'The Scots', in Pat Loughrey (ed.), *The People of Ireland* (Belfast: Appletree Press, 1988).

6   The scholarly literature on the Plantations is voluminous. Jonathan Bardon's recent study *The Plantation of Ulster: The British Colonisation of the North of Ireland in the Seventeenth Century* (Dublin: Gill & Macmillan, 2011) challenges many myths and commonly held views surrounding it.

7   David Stevenson, *Scottish Covenanters and Irish Confederates: Scottish–Irish Relationships in the Mid-seventeenth Century* (Belfast: Ulster Historical Foundation 1981), p. 305.

8   W. McAfee and V. Morgan, 'Population in Ulster, 1660–1760', in Peter Roebuck (ed.), *Plantation to Partition: Essays in Ulster History in Honour of J.L. McCracken* (Belfast: Blackstaff Press, 1981); John R. Young, 'Scotland and Ulster in the seventeenth century: The movement of peoples across the North Channel', in William Kelly and John R. Young (eds), *Ulster and Scotland, 1600–2000: History, Language and Identity* (Dublin: Four Courts Press, 2004); Marianne Elliott, *When God Took Sides: Religion and Identity in Ireland – Unfinished History* (Oxford: Oxford University Press, 2009), Ch. 5; M.W. Heslinga, *The Irish Border as a Cultural Divide: A Contribution to the Study of Regionalism in the British Isles* (Assen: Van Gorcum, 1979). A famous poem first published in 1836, 'Willy Gilliland: An Ulster Ballad' by Sir Samuel Ferguson, celebrates the bravery and daring of a Scottish Covenanter on the run in Ulster. It recalls the highly emotive folk images of the persecuted Covenanters on the Scottish moors and includes the lines: 'And for persecuted kirk, and for her martyrs dear/And against a godless church and king he spoke up loud and clear.'

9   Bryan Fanning, 'Why it is now time to reassess the story of the Plantation of Ulster', *Belfast Telegraph*, 5 March 2018. See also Bryan Fanning, *Migration and the Making of Ireland* (Dublin: UCD Press, 2018).

10 D.M. McRaild and M. Smith, 'Migration and Emigration, 1600–1945', in Liam Kennedy and Philip Ollerenshaw (eds), *Ulster Since 1600: Politics, Economy, and Society* (Oxford: Oxford University Press, 2013).

11 The Ulster-Scots Agency, based in Belfast, has produced a steady stream of pamphlet literature on historical and cultural topics since the late 1990s. See also Wesley Hutchinson, *Tracing the Ulster-Scots Imagination* (Belfast: Ulster University Press, 2018).

12 Heslinga, *The Irish Border*, pp. 165–6; Rory Fitzpatrick, *God's Frontiersmen: The Scots–Irish Epic* (London: Weidenfeld & Nicolson, 1989).

13 A.T.Q. Stewart, *The Shape of Irish History* (Belfast: Blackstaff Press, 2001), pp. 121–2.

14 James Greer and Graham Walker, *Ulster-Scots' Contribution to Political Thought* (Belfast: Queen's University, 2018); James Dingley, *Francis Hutcheson. His Life and Work: An Introduction* (Belfast: Francis Hutcheson Institute, 2014).

15 The quote is popularly attributed to United Irishmen leader Wolfe Tone.

16 'Mary Ann McCracken: Revolutionary, radical and tireless activist', in Bardon, *A Narrow Sea*, Episode 82.

17 See A.T.Q. Stewart, *The Summer Soldiers: 1798 United Irishmen Rebellion in Antrim and Down* (Belfast: Blackstaff, 1995).

18 Elaine McFarland, *Ireland and Scotland in the Age of Revolution* (Edinburgh: Edinburgh University Press, 1994).

19 John Hewitt, *The Rhyming Weavers* (Belfast: Blackstaff Press, 1974).

20 'An Industrial Hub: Belfast and Glasgow', in Bardon, *A Narrow Sea*, Episode 91.

21 Sidney Pollard, 'British and World Shipbuilding, 1890-1914. A Study in Comparative Costs', *The Journal of Economic History*, vol. 17, no. 3 (1957), pp. 426-44.

22 R. Geary and W. Johnson, 'Shipbuilding in Belfast, 1861-1986', *Irish Economic and Social History*, vol. 16 (1989), pp. 42-64.

23 Andrew R. Holmes, 'Union and Presbyterian Ulster Scots: William McComb, James McKnight, and "the Repealer Repulsed"', in Gerard Carruthers and Colin Kidd (eds), *Literature and Union: Scottish Texts, British Contexts* (Oxford: Oxford University Press, 2018), pp. 165-91.

24 Donald Akenson, *Between Two Revolutions: Islandmagee, County Antrim 1798-1920* (Dublin: Academy Press, 1979).

25 Graham Walker, 'The Protestant Irish in Scotland', in Tom Devine (ed.), *Irish Immigration and Scottish Society in the 19th and 20th Centuries* (Edinburgh: John Donald, 1991).

26 McFarland, *Ireland and Scotland*.

27 Elaine McFarland, *Protestants First! Orangeism in 19th Century Scotland* (Edinburgh: Edinburgh University Press, 1991).

28 Ian Meredith, 'Irish Migrants in the Scottish Episcopal Church in the Nineteenth Century', in Martin Mitchell (ed.), *New Perspectives on the Irish in Scotland* (Edinburgh: John Donald, 2008), pp. 44-64.

29 Alan Campbell, *The Lanarkshire Miners: A Social History of their Trade Unions, 1775-1874* (Edinburgh: John Donald, 1979).

30 Kyle Hughes, *The Scots in Victorian and Edwardian Belfast: A Study in Elite Migration* (Edinburgh: Edinburgh University Press, 2013).

31 Isabella M.S. Tod, 'Myth and Fact', *The Liberal Unionist*, 1 June 1887.

32 Good examples of the scholarly literature on this topic are Alvin Jackson, *Home Rule: An Irish History 1800-2000* (London: Weidenfeld and Nicolson, 2003), and Alan O'Day, *Irish Home Rule, 1867-1921* (Manchester: Manchester University Press, 1998).

33 John Kendle, *Federal Britain: A History* (London: Routledge, 1997); Arthur Aughey, *Nationalism, Devolution and the Challenge to the United Kingdom State* (London: Pluto Press, 2001).

34 Brian Walker, *Ulster Politics: The Formative Years, 1868-1886* (Belfast: Institute of Irish Studies, 1989).

35 Andrew R. Holmes, 'Covenanter Politics: Evangelicalism, Political Liberalism and Ulster Presbyterians, 1798–1914', *English Historical Review*, cxxv, no. 513 (2010), pp. 340–69.

36 Graham Walker, 'Thomas Sinclair: Presbyterian Liberal Unionist', in Richard English and Graham Walker (eds), *Unionism in Modern Ireland: New Perspectives on Politics and Culture* (Basingstoke: Macmillan, 1996); Graham Greenlee, Gordon Lucy and William J. Roulston, *Thomas Sinclair: 'Ulster's Most Prominent Citizen'* (Belfast: Ulster Historical Foundation, 2016).

37 David Livingstone and Ronald Wells, *Ulster–American Religion: Episodes in the History of a Cultural Connection* (Indiana: University of Notre-Dame Press, 1999).

38 See later in this chapter regarding Sinclair's part in drawing up the Ulster Covenant.

39 Mike Mecham, *William Walker: Social Activist and Belfast Labourist 1870–1918* (Dublin: Umiskin Press, 2019); Terence Bowman, *People's Champion: The Life of Alexander Bowman, Pioneer of Labour Politics in Ireland* (Belfast: UHF, 1997); Torquil Cowan, *Labour of Love: The Story of Robert Smillie* (Glasgow: Neil Wilson Publishing, 2012).

40 David Howell, *British Workers and the Independent Labour Party 1888–1906* (Manchester: Manchester University Press, 1983).

41 Myrtle Hill, 'Women, War and Welfare: The Co-operative Crusades of Margaret Taylor McCoubrey, 1880–1956', *Familia: Ulster Genealogical Review*, vol. 32 (2016), pp. 38–59.

42 Richard McMinn, *Against the Tide: J.B. Armour, Irish Presbyterian Minister and Home Ruler* (Belfast: PRONI, 1985).

43 Rev. Hugh Hanna, *Scotland, Ulster and Home Rule for Ireland: A Letter Addressed to a Friend in Scotland* (Dublin: Irish Loyal and Patriotic Union, 1888).

44 See discussion in Peter Dunn, 'Forsaking their "own flesh and blood"? Ulster unionism, Scotland and home rule, 1886–1914', *Irish Historical Studies*, vol. xxxvii, no. 146 (2010), pp. 203–20.

45 Special mention might be made in this regard of the eminent Belfast-born Glasgow University scientist William Thomson, Lord Kelvin (1824–1907).

46 McFarland, *Protestants First!*; Walker, *Intimate Strangers*, Ch. 2.

47 See speeches at the 1892 unionist convention, quoted in Gordon Lucy, *The Great Convention: The Ulster Unionist Convention of 1892* (Lurgan: The Ulster Society, 1995).

48 Quoted in Walker, *Intimate Strangers*, p. 31.

49 David Officer and Graham Walker, 'Protestant Ulster: Ethno-history, memory, and contemporary prospects', *National Identities,* vol. 2, no. 3 (2000), pp. 293–307.

50 Gordon Lucy, *Understanding the Ulster Covenant* (Belfast: Ulster-Scots Agency, 2012).

51 See especially David Miller's classic study *Queen's Rebels: Ulster Loyalism in Historical Perspective* (Dublin: Gill & Macmillan, 1978). At the 1892 Convention Thomas Sinclair proclaimed: 'We are the children of the [1688] Revolution' (see note 47 above).

52 Colin Kidd, *Union and Unionisms: Political Thought in Scotland, 1500–2000* (Cambridge: Cambridge University Press, 2008).

53 Watson, *The Ulster Covenant.*

54 John Buchan, *What the Home Rule Bill Means* (Peebles: Neidpath Press, 1912).

55 See, for example, J.B. Woodburn, *The Ulster Scot: His History and Religion* (London: H.R. Allenson, 1914), published at the height of the Home Rule controversy. See also discussion in Colin Reid, 'Democracy, Sovereignty and Unionist Political Thought during the Revolutionary Period in Ireland, 1912–1922', *Transactions of the Royal Historical Society,* vol. xxvii (2017), pp. 211–32.

56 T.M. Devine, *Scotland's Empire: The Origins of the Global Diaspora* (London: Penguin, 2012).

57 These themes will be discussed in more depth in Chapter 3.

58 Graham Walker, 'Varieties of Protestant identity', in T.M. Devine and R.J. Finlay (eds), *Scotland in the 20th Century* (Edinburgh: Edinburgh University Press, 1996).

59 For Connolly's role in these events, and that of another Scot, Margaret Skinnider, see Kirsty Lusk and Willy Maley (eds), *Scotland and the Easter Rising: Fresh Perspectives on 1916* (Edinburgh: Luath Press, 2016).

60 Philip Orr, *The Road to the Somme* (Belfast: Blackstaff Press, 1987); Officer and Walker, 'Protestant Ulster'.

61 Alan Parkinson, *A Difficult Birth: The Early Years of Northern Ireland, 1920–25* (Dublin: Eastwood Books, 2021).

62 The Conservatives and Liberal Unionists had formally merged in Scotland in 1912 when both were pre-occupied with the struggle against Irish Home Rule.

63 Steve Bruce, *Conservative Protestant Politics* (Oxford: Oxford University Press, 1998), Ch. 4.

64 Ewen Cameron, *Impaled Upon a Thistle: Scotland since 1880* (Edinburgh:

Edinburgh University Press, 2010), pp. 68–9; see also Scotland First Minister Donald Dewar's address in Dublin in 2000, reproduced in David Dickson (ed.), *Ireland and Scotland: Nation, Region, Identity* (Dublin: Centre for Irish-Scottish Studies, TCD, 2001).

65 See Walker, *Intimate Strangers*, Ch. 3 for full discussion.

66 Steve Bruce, 'Sectarianism in Scotland: A contemporary assessment and explanation', *Scottish Government Yearbook* 1988, pp. 150–65.

67 Tom Gallagher, *Edinburgh Divided: John Cormack and No Popery in the 1930s* (Edinburgh: Polygon, 1987) for 'Protestant Action'. Stewart J. Brown, '"Outside the Covenant": The Scottish Presbyterian Churches and Irish Immigration, 1922–38', *Innes Review*, vol. 42, no. 1 (1991), pp. 19–45, remains the best treatment of the Church's campaign.

68 Scottish Record Office (SRO) 37110/1.

69 Angela McCarthy, *Personal Narratives of Irish and Scottish Migration, 1921–1965* (Manchester: Manchester University Press, 2007), pp. 51–2.

70 Tom Gallagher, *Glasgow: The Uneasy Peace: Religious Tension in Modern Scotland* (Manchester: Manchester University Press, 1987), p. 92.

71 SRO HH55/65.

72 SRO HH55/68.

73 See discussion in Paul Bew, *Ideology and the Irish Question: Ulster Unionism and Irish Nationalism 1912–1916* (Oxford: Oxford University Press, 1994).

74 Graham Walker and James Greer, 'Religion, Labour, and National Questions: The 1924 General Election in Belfast and Lanarkshire', *Labour History Review*, vol. 84, no. 3 (2019), pp. 217–39.

75 Walker, *Intimate Strangers*, Ch. 3; Richard J. Finlay, 'The Interwar crisis: The failure of extremism', in T.M. Devine and Jenny Wormald (eds), *The Oxford Handbook of Modern Scottish History* (Oxford: Oxford University Press, 2012).

76 James Greer and Graham Walker, '"Awkward Prods": Biographical studies of progressive Protestants and political allegiance in Northern Ireland', *Irish Political Studies*, vol. 33, no. 2 (2018), pp. 167–83; Edna Longley, 'Progressive Bookmen: Politics and Northern Protestant Writers since the 1930s', *Irish Review*, no. 1 (1980), pp. 50–9; S. Alex Blair, 'W.F. Marshall: Profile of an Ulsterman', *Bulletin of the Presbyterian Historical Society of Ireland*, no. 24 (1995), pp. 1–20.

77 See Chapter 2.

78 Bob Purdie, '"Crossing Swords with W.B. Yeats": Twentieth Century Scottish Nationalist Encounters with Ireland', *Journal of Irish and Scottish Studies*, vol. 1, no. 1 (2007), pp. 191–210.

79 See Chapter 3.

80 See Bill Murray, *The Old Firm: Sectarianism, Sport and Society in Scotland* (Edinburgh: John Donald, 2000).

81 The most detailed treatment of the APL remains Edna Staunton, *The Nationalists of Northern Ireland, 1918–73* (Dublin: Columba Press, 2001), Chs 11 and 12.

82 *The Scotsman*, 8 September 1948.

83 See Henry Patterson, *Ireland Since 1939* (Oxford: Oxford University Press, 2002), Ch. 4; Troy Davis, *Dublin's American Policy* (Washington DC: The Catholic University of America Press, 1998), especially Ch. 3.

84 Brian Barton, *Northern Ireland in the Second World War* (Belfast: UHF, 1995).

85 See Graham Walker, *A History of the Ulster Unionist Party: Protest, Pragmatism, Pessimism* (Manchester: Manchester University Press, 2004), pp. 100–4 for the example of APL secretary and nationalist MP Malachi Conlon.

86 In general terms the Irish experience in post-war Britain compared favourably to that of Commonwealth immigrants – see Clair Wills, *Lovers and Friends: An Immigrant History of Post-War Britain* (London: Penguin, 2018), p. 67.

87 For the APL and Labour, see Russell Rees, *Labour and the Northern Ireland Problem 1945–1951* (Dublin: Irish Academic Press, 2009).

88 *The Glasgow Herald*, 18 October 1948. On the same day as de Valera spoke in Glasgow, Cahir Healy (a Northern nationalist MP) made a similar population movement suggestion at an APL meeting in London: see PRONI HA/32/1/900. This suggests clearly that it was APL policy. De Valera's biographers have been generally silent on his speeches at this time although Ronan Fanning, *Éamon de Valera: The Will to Power* (London: Faber and Faber, 2015), p. 227, concedes that they were 'inflammatory'. See also John Bowman, *De Valera and the Ulster Question* (Oxford: Clarendon Press, 1982), Ch. 7.

89 See Bowman, *De Valera*, p. 276, for the comments critical of the APL and its Catholic sectarian character by Ernest Blythe and Thomas Johnson; also, Bob Purdie, 'The Irish Anti-Partition League, South Armagh and the Abstentionist Tactic, 1945–58', *Irish Political Studies*, vol. 1 (1986), pp. 67–77.

90 Walker, *A History of the Ulster Unionist Party*, pp. 100–4.

91 This is evident in the recrudescence of 'planters' as a pejorative term used in public discourse. Arguably, there has also been a tendency – in response to the so-called 'revisionist' turn in Irish history writing – towards what might be called 'plantation reductionism' in parts of academia. The post-colonialism

turn in the academic sphere has obscured the advances and insights of the earlier 'revisionism' phase and given new life to the much older 'Four Green Fields' school of Irish nationalist history. See Newton Emerson, 'Academic rhetoric more dangerous than declined invitation', *The Irish Times*, 23 September 2021. One of the most popular historians (certainly in terms of book sales) in Ireland, Tim Pat Coogan, concluded his book *Wherever Green is Worn* (London: Hutchinson, 2000) with the observation that the 'energy of the Celts' would overcome the unionist obstacle to a united Ireland.

92   *The Glasgow Herald*, 18 October 1948.

93   *The Scotsman*, 4 September 1948.

94   *The Glasgow Herald*, 26 October 1948. The MPs were the Rev. J.G. MacManaway (Ulster Unionist) and Norman Porter (Independent) respectively.

95   *Evening Times* (Glasgow), 14 September 1998.

CHAPTER 2:
SCOTLAND, NORTHERN IRELAND AND DEVOLUTION

1   David Reynolds, *Island Stories: Britain and its History in the Age of Brexit* (London: William Collins, 2019), p. 165. See also Colin Kidd 'Independence and Union Revisited: Recent interpretations in Scottish History, Literature, and Politics', in Gerry Hassan (ed.), *The Story of the Scottish Parliament* (Edinburgh: Edinburgh University Press, 2019).

2   See Iain McLean, *What's Wrong with the British Constitution?* (Oxford: Oxford University Press, 2012), Ch. 8.

3   Stein Rokkan and Derek Urwin (eds), *The Politics of Territorial Identity: Studies in European Regionalism* (London: Longman, 1982); James Mitchell, *Strategies for Self-Government: The Campaigns for a Scottish Parliament* (Edinburgh: Polygon, 1996), Ch. 1, fn. 10; Iain McLean and Alistair McMillan, *State of the Union: Unionism and the Alternatives in the United Kingdom Since 1707* (Oxford: Oxford University Press, 2005).

4   James Mitchell, *Devolution in the UK* (Manchester: Manchester University Press, 2009); Michael Keating, *Plurinational Democracy: Stateless Nations in a Post-sovereignty Era* (Oxford: Oxford University Press, 2001).

5   See discussion in David Powell, *Nationhood and Identity: The British State Since 1800* (London: I.B. Tauris, 2002), Introduction.

6   Lindsey Paterson, *The Autonomy of Modern Scotland* (Edinburgh: Edinburgh University Press, 1994).

7   Some examples of the work in this area of Bernard Crick can be found in his *Political Thoughts and Polemics* (Edinburgh: Edinburgh University Press, 1990).

8   Vernon Bogdanor, *Devolution* (Oxford: Oxford University Press, 1979), p. 2.

9   See Kendle, *Federal Britain*.

10   Alvin Jackson, *The Two Unions: Ireland, Scotland, and the Survival of the United Kingdom, 1707–2007* (Oxford: Oxford University Press, 2012), p. 193.

11   See discussion of Dicey's thinking and influence in Richard Bourke, *Peace in Ireland: The War of Ideas* (London: Bloomsbury, 2003), Ch. 9.

12   McLean, *What's Wrong with the British Constitution?*, Ch. 8.

13   John Kendle, *Ireland and the Federal Solution* (Kingston and Montreal: McGill-Queens University Press, 1989), pp. 46–7.

14   See Tam Dalyell, *The Question of Scotland: Devolution and After* (Edinburgh: Birlinn, 2016).

15   See later in this chapter.

16   See Mitchell, *Strategies for Self-Government*, Ch. 3, for the Scottish Home Rule Association and other pressure groups of this era.

17   See Jackson, *The Two Unions*, p. 232.

18   Adam Evans, 'A Lingering Diminuendo? The Conference on Devolution, 1919–20', *Parliamentary History*, vol. 35 (2016), pp. 315–35.

19   Graham Walker, *Thomas Johnston (Lives of the Left)* (Manchester: Manchester University Press, 1988), p. 71.

20   Mitchell, *Strategies for Self-Government*, Ch. 2.

21   See John Kendle, *Walter Long, Ireland, and the Union, 1905–1920* (Dún Laoghaire: Glendale Publishing, 1992).

22   Alvin Jackson, '"Tame Tory Hacks"? The Ulster Party at Westminster, 1922–72', *Historical Journal*, vol. 54, no. 2 (2011), pp. 453–75.

23   For more on this, see later in chapter.

24   See Graham Walker and Gareth Mulvenna, 'Northern Ireland Representation at Westminster: Constitutional Conundrums and Political Manoeuvres', *Parliamentary History*, vol. 34, no. 2 (2015), pp. 237–55.

25   See discussion in Walker, *A History of the Ulster Unionist Party*, Chs 2 and 3; Patrick Buckland, *James Craig* (Dublin: Gill and Macmillan, 1980); Paul Bew et al., *The State in Northern Ireland: Political Forces and Social Classes* (Manchester: Manchester University Press, 1979).

26   See Bryan Follis, *A State Under Siege: The Establishment of Northern Ireland* (Oxford: Oxford University Press, 1995), Ch. 6, for a detailed account of these developments.

27   G.C. Duggan, series of articles in *The Irish Times* between 19 April and 3 May 1950.

28   McLean, *What's Wrong with the British Constitution?*, p. 164.

29 Report of the *Royal Commission on the Constitution*, Cmnd 5460 (London: HMSO, 1973). See, for example, p. 175, para 578.

30 McLean, *What's Wrong with the British Constitution?*, Ch. 8.

31 Donald Dewar, 'Devolution and Local Government Reform', in Neil MacCormick (ed.), *The Scottish Debate: Essays on Scottish Nationalism* (Oxford: Oxford University Press, 1970).

32 Report of *Royal Commission on Scottish Affairs*, 1952–54, Cmnd 9212 (London: HMSO, 1954).

33 Walker, *Intimate Strangers*, Ch. 3.

34 David Torrance, *The Scottish Secretaries* (Edinburgh: Birlinn, 2006), pp. 135–45.

35 Walker, *Thomas Johnston*, Ch. 6.

36 Torrance, *The Scottish Secretaries*, pp. 248–69; see also Bernard Donoughue, *Downing Street Diary, Vol. 1* (London: Pimlico, 2006), p. 290.

37 Ian Levitt, 'Britain, the Scottish Covenant Movement and Devolution, 1946–1950', *Scottish Affairs* 22 (1998), pp. 33–57.

38 The quotations that follow are sourced in Graham Walker, 'Scotland, Northern Ireland and Devolution, 1945–79', *Journal of British Studies*, vol. 49, no. 1 (2010), pp. 117–42. See also Graham Walker, 'Scotland, Northern Ireland and Devolution: Past and Present', *Contemporary British History*, vol. 24, no. 2 (2010), pp. 235–56.

39 The Scottish Grand Committee was central to the distinctive arrangements for Scottish business at Westminster.

40 David Torrance, *Standing Up for Scotland: Nationalist Unionism and Scottish Party Politics* (Edinburgh: Edinburgh University Press, 2022).

41 Indeed, the Labour government's unwillingness to ensure that Northern Ireland came into line with the local government franchise changes for the rest of the UK in 1946 might also be explained by a desire to dampen down discussion of devolution and constitutional matters. The more the government engaged with Northern Ireland, and if it attempted to override the Stormont government, the more the Scottish case could boil up.

42 This literature includes: Arthur Turner, *Scottish Home Rule* (Oxford: Blackwell, 1952); F.N. Newark (ed.), *Devolution of Government: The Experiment in Northern Ireland* (London: Allen and Unwin, 1953); Thomas Wilson (ed.), *Ulster Under Home Rule: A Study of the Political and Economic Problems of Northern Ireland* (Oxford: Oxford University Press, 1955).

43 Woodburn review of Wilson (ed.), *Ulster Under Home Rule*, in NLS Acc. 7656 Box 22/3.

44 Keith Robbins, '"This grubby wreck of old glories": the United Kingdom and

the end of the British Empire', *Journal of Contemporary History*, 15 (1980), pp. 81–95; Jimmi Ostergaard Nielsen and Stuart Ward, '"Cramped and restricted at home": Scottish separatism at Empire's end', *Transactions of the Royal Historical Society*, 25 (2015), pp. 159–85.

45   See Chapter 3 on Britishness.

46   Quoted in Walker, 'Scotland, Northern Ireland and Devolution'.

47   See Marc Mulholland, *Terence O'Neill* (Dublin: UCD Press, 2013); also, speeches collected in Terence O'Neill, *Ulster at the Crossroads* (London: Faber and Faber, 1969); Walker, *A History of the Ulster Unionist Party*, pp. 150–4.

48   Powell, *Nationhood and Identity*, p. 196.

49   For an examination of the significance of what was called 'The Declaration of Perth', see Gordon Pentland, 'Edward Heath, the Declaration of Perth, and the Scottish Conservative and Unionist Party, 1966–70', *Twentieth Century British History*, vol. 26, no. 2 (2015), pp. 249–73.

50   See the recollections of Cabinet minister Douglas Hurd in his *An End to Promises: Sketch of a Government 1970–74* (London: Collins, 1979), p. 7 and p. 102 regarding the urgency of the NI issue and the time it took up.

51   See Walker, *A History of the Ulster Unionist Party*, p. 223. The quote is from a UUP document published in 1976.

52   See Gordon Wilson, *SNP: The Turbulent Years 1960–1990* (Stirling: Scots Independent, 2009), p. 97.

53   Walker, 'Scotland, Northern Ireland and Devolution'; Walker and Mulvenna, 'Northern Ireland Representation'.

54   See Ivor Trewin (ed.), *The Hugo Young Papers* (London: Allen Lane, 2008), pp. 37–9, regarding Lord Hailsham's comments about the UWC strike contributing to contemporary political instability and threats to democracy.

55   Walker, 'Scotland, Northern Ireland, and Devolution'. It should be noted that the Labour Party in Scotland, fiercely antagonistic to the SNP, had to be dragged to a position of support for a Scottish Parliament with many in their ranks viewing this as effectively a recipe for encouraging outright separatist sentiment in the long run.

56   See Walker, 'Scotland, Northern Ireland, and Devolution'.

57   *Our Changing Democracy: Devolution to Scotland and Wales*, Cmnd 6348 (London: HMSO, 1975).

58   For an analysis of the Convention see Michael Kerr, *The Destructors: The Story of Northern Ireland's Lost Peace Process* (Dublin: Irish Academic Press, 2011), Ch. 10.

59   See the recollections of MPs Gordon Wilson of the SNP and Tam Dalyell of Labour in their respective books, op. cit.

60   See the recent scholarly study of Powell's career, including his Ulster years, by Paul Corthorn, *Enoch Powell: Politics and Ideas in Modern Britain* (Oxford: Oxford University Press, 2019).

61   Simon Heffer, *Like the Roman: The Life of Enoch Powell* (London: Bloomsbury Press, 1998), p. 719.

62   Walker and Mulvenna, 'Northern Ireland Representation', fn. 34.

63   See Trewin (ed.), *The Hugo Young Papers*, pp. 55–6. Harold Wilson had admitted that keeping Scottish representation at Westminster at the same level would make it easier for the central government to assert, if need be, 'override powers'; see also comments by Francis Pym (Tory spokesman on devolution) in Trewin (ed.), *The Hugo Young Papers*, p. 104.

64   Walker and Mulvenna, 'Northern Ireland Representation'.

65   See Bernard Donoughue, *Downing Street Diary*, Vol. 2 (London: Jonathan Cape, 2008), p. 314.

66   Tam Dalyell, *Devolution: The End of Britain* (London: Jonathan Cape, 1977), p. 285.

67   See in particular Paul Arthur, 'Northern Ireland: Devolution as Administrative Convenience', *Parliamentary Affairs*, 30 (1977), pp. 97–106.

68   See W.D. Birrell, 'The Mechanics of Devolution', *Political Quarterly*, 49 (1978), pp. 304–21; also, Graham Walker, 'John P. Mackintosh, Devolution and the Union', *Parliamentary Affairs*, 66 (2013), pp. 557–8.

69   See Graham Walker, 'The "Scotland is British" campaign against devolution, 1976–8', *Scottish Affairs*, 61 (2007), pp. 74–100.

70   See Graham Walker, *The Labour Party in Scotland: Religion, the Union and the Irish Dimension* (Basingstoke: Palgrave, 2016), Ch. 3; see also Chapter 4 of this book.

71   Jackson, *The Two Unions*, p. 278.

72   Charles Moore, *Margaret Thatcher: The Authorised Biography*, Vol. 1 (London: Penguin, 2014) pp. 619 and 596.

73   See discussion in Chapter 3 about the unionists' sense of Britishness, and of belonging and citizenship entitlements.

74   Sir David Goodall, 'Hillsborough to Belfast: Is it the final lap?' in Marianne Elliott (ed.), *The Long Road to Peace in Northern Ireland* (Liverpool: Liverpool University Press, 2002), pp. 120–8.

75   See for example James Cornford, 'Constitutional Reform in the UK', in S. Tindale (ed.), *The State and the Nations: The Politics of Devolution* (London:

Institute for Public Policy Research, 1996); Crick, *Political Thoughts and Polemics.*

76 Graham Walker, 'Scotland and Northern Ireland: Constitutional Questions, Connections, and Possibilities', *Government and Opposition*, vol. 33, no. 1 (1998), pp. 21–37.

77 Paterson, *The Autonomy of Modern Scotland.*

78 Margaret Thatcher, *The Downing Street Years* (London: HarperCollins, 1993), pp. 618–24; David Torrance, *'We in Scotland': Thatcherism in a Cold Climate* (Edinburgh: Birlinn, 2009), p. 159.

79 David Torrance, *George Younger: A Life Well Lived* (Edinburgh: Birlinn, 2008), Ch. 12; also, Torrance *'We in Scotland'.*

80 Dalyell, *The Question of Scotland*, Ch. 10.

81 Mitchell, *Strategies for Self-Government*, pp. 99–105.

82 Andrew Dickson, 'The Scots: National Culture and Political Action', *Political Quarterly*, vol. 59, no. 3 (1988), pp. 358–68.

83 James Mitchell, 'The evolution of devolution: Labour's home rule strategy in opposition', *Government and Opposition*, 33 (1998), pp. 479–96; Dalyell, *The Question of Scotland.*

84 Cook quoted in Walker, *Intimate Strangers*, p. 162.

85 Bernard Crick, 'If Scotland fights might Ulster be righted?', *Fortnight*, no. 282 (March 1990); also, his 'Sovereignty of Parliament and the Irish Question' in Crick, *Political Thoughts and Polemics.*

86 Walker, 'Scotland, Northern Ireland and Devolution: Past and Present'.

87 Trewin (ed.), *The Hugo Young Papers*, p. 378.

88 David McCrone, *Understanding Scotland: The Sociology of a Stateless Nation* (London: Routledge, 1992); see also Richard Kearney, *Postnationalist Ireland: Politics, Culture, Philosophy* (London: Routledge, 1997); Gerard Delanty, 'Northern Ireland in a Europe of the Regions', *Political Quarterly*, vol. 67, no. 2 (1996), pp. 127–34.

89 See Owen Dudley Edwards (ed.), *A Claim of Right for Scotland* (Edinburgh: Polygon, 1989); Kenyon Wright, *The People Say Yes* (Glendaruil: Argyll Press, 1997); see discussion of Scottish interpretations of sovereignty in Kidd, *Union and Unionisms*, especially p. 231 regarding the 'Claim of Right' of 1842 which led to the 'Great Disruption' and was also concerned to place limits on parliamentary sovereignty.

90 See Wright, *The People Say Yes*, pp. 121–2.

91 See ibid., Ch. 22.

92 A parallel referendum for Wales saw a paper-thin majority in favour of the

more limited devolution scheme for that country.

93 See Walker, *History of the Ulster Unionist Party*, pp. 242–3.

94 See Chapter 3.

95 See the writings in particular of Will Hutton, an important 'New Labour' political thinker and commentator.

96 For Major's account of the Scottish and Northern Irish issues, see his *The Autobiography* (London: HarperCollins, 2000), Chs 18 and 19.

97 Powell, *Nationhood and Identity*, p. 216; Mitchell, *Strategies for Self-Government*, pp. 286–7; Kidd, *Union and Unionisms*, p. 126 – 'Devolution ... closer to the spirit of true unionism'.

98 See Trewin (ed.), *The Hugo Young Papers*, p. 443 (Cook) and p. 482 (Dewar).

99 For a scholarly treatment of this set of constitutional changes see Aughey, *Nationalism, Devolution and the Challenge*.

100 This was its main attraction for UUP leader David Trimble. See Dean Godson, *Himself Alone: David Trimble and the Ordeal of Unionism* (London: HarperCollins, 2004), p. 293.

101 The agreement was endorsed in separate referendums in the North and South of Ireland in June 1998.

102 House of Commons Debates, 14 July 1997, vol. 298, cc. 656–7.

103 See Chapter 4.

104 House of Lords Select Committee on the Constitution, the Union and Devolution. HL Paper 2016; Peter Hennessey, *The Kingdom to Come* (London: Haus, 2015), p. 31 (quoting Lord Smith).

105 A good example of this kind of scholarship is Chris Bryant, *The Nations of Britain* (Oxford: Oxford University Press, 2006). A recent corrective to it is Reynolds, *Island Stories*.

106 House of Lords report (see note 104); Charlie Jeffery, 'Devolution in the United Kingdom: Problems of a Piecemeal Approach to Constitutional Change', *Publius*, vol. 39, no. 2 (2009), pp. 289–313.

107 See Chapter 5.

108 Regular monitoring and commentary regarding the devolution process has been supplied by the Constitution Unit, a group led by the scholar Robert Hazell and set up following the advent of devolution. The unit's website contains information on the many publications and reports produced so far.

109 Alan Trench (ed.), *The State of the Nations 2008* (Exeter: Imprint Academic, 2008), Ch. 9. See also Trench's website: devolutionmatters.com.

110 *Glasgow Herald*, 13 October 2007.

111 See Edna Longley, Eamonn Hughes, Des O'Rawe (eds), *Ireland (Ulster) Scotland: Concepts, Contexts, Comparisons* (Belfast, 2003); Graham Walker,

'Ireland and Scotland: From Partition to Peace Process', in Angela McCarthy (ed.), *Ireland in the World: Comparative, Transnational, and Personal Perspectives* (London: Routledge, 2015), pp. 181–97.

112 John Barry, 'Northern Ireland: From Power-sharing to Power being Shared Out', *Green European Journal* (2017).

113 See introduction to Hassan (ed.), *The Story*; Jim Gallagher, 'Devolution: An Assessment' in Hassan (ed.), *The Story*, pp. 242–51; Tom Gallagher, *Scotland Now: A Warning to the World* (Edinburgh: Scotview Publishing, 2016) for the SNP and use of patronage.

114 *Belfast Telegraph*, 1 July 2019; Gallagher, 'Devolution: An Assessment'.

115 The Calman (2009) and Smith (2015) Commission Reports have led to significant extensions of the powers of the Scottish parliament, including over income tax; Gallagher, 'Devolution: An Assessment'.

116 David Gover and Michael Kenny, *Finding the Good in EVEL: An Evaluation of 'English Votes for English Laws' in the House of Commons* (Constitution Unit, 2017); Michael Kenny, 'English Nationalism, the 2019 Election and the Future of the British State', *Political Insight*, vol. 11, issue 1 (March 2020), pp. 24–7. Scottish representation in the House of Commons was cut from seventy-two to fifty-eight in 2003.

117 *The Herald*, 13 July 2021.

118 See discussion in Brice Dickson, *Writing the United Kingdom Constitution* (Manchester: Manchester University Press, 2019).

CHAPTER 3:
THE BRITISH QUESTION

1 Hugh Kearney, *The British Isles: A History of Four Nations* (Cambridge: Cambridge University Press, 1989); Keith Robbins, *Nineteenth-Century Britain: Integration and Diversity* (Oxford: Clarendon, 1988). Bernard Crick in his 'The English and the British', in idem (ed.), *National Identities: The Constitution of the United Kingdom* (Oxford: Blackwell, 1991), criticises Robbins' neglect of Ireland, and says that Kearney's is the 'only fully integrative account'. See also Kearney's chapter 'Four Nations or One?' in the Crick edited volume.

2 Ian McBride, 'Ulster and the British Problem', in English and Walker (eds), *Unionism in Modern Ireland*.

3 Linda Colley, *Britons: Forging the Nation 1707–1837* (London: Pimlico, 1992).

4 On this point, see Aughey, *Nationalism, Devolution and the Challenge*, pp. 17–20.

5   Kidd, *Union and Unionisms*.

6   See the various works of John M. McKenzie, especially John M. McKenzie and Tom M. Devine (eds), *Scotland and the British Empire* (Oxford: Oxford University Press, 2011), and his 'David Livingstone: The construction of the myth', in Graham Walker and Tom Gallagher (eds), *Sermons and Battle Hymns: Protestant Popular Culture in Modern Scotland* (Edinburgh: Edinburgh University Press, 1990); Walker, *Intimate Strangers*, Ch. 2.

7   'Britain' and 'British' have thus functioned as shorthand for the whole UK in most public and academic discussion. Terms such as 'UK-ness' have, unsurprisingly, never caught on.

8   See Paul Bew, 'Britishness and the Irish Question', in Matthew D'Ancona (ed.), *Being British: The Search for the Values That Bind the Nation* (Edinburgh and London: Mainstream Publishing, 2009).

9   Kidd, *Union and Unionisms*.

10 Kidd, 'Independence and Union Revisited', pp. 219–28.

11 Jackson, *The Two Unions*, pp. 40–2; see also Chapter 1.

12 Ian Bradley, *Believing in Britain: The Spiritual Identity of Britishness* (Oxford: Lion Books, 2008), p. 150.

13 The most recent scholarly study is James W. McAuley, Jon Tonge and Andrew Mycock, *Loyal to the Core? Orangeism and Britishness in Northern Ireland* (Dublin: Irish Academic Press, 2011).

14 High-profile attempts were made to organise the Conservatives in Northern Ireland in the 1980s and 1990s: see Colin Coulter, 'The Character of Unionism', *Irish Political Studies*, vol. 9 (1994), pp. 1–24; for the subject of Labour organisation see Hugh Roberts, '"Sound stupidity": The British Party System and the Northern Ireland Question', *Government and Opposition*, vol. 22, no. 3 (1987), pp. 315–35.

15 See Walker, *Intimate Strangers*, p. 86; see also Chapter 2.

16 Bryant, *The Nations of Britain*, p. 239.

17 Varun Uberoi and Iain McLean, 'Britishness: A Role for the State?' in Andrew Gamble and Tony Wright (eds), *Britishness: Perspectives on the British Question* (Chichester: Wiley-Blackwell, 2009).

18 Gerry Hassan and Eric Shaw, *The People's Flag and the Union Jack: An Alternative History of Britain and the Labour Party* (London: Biteback Books, 2019).

19 Kearney, *The British Isles*; Bernard Crick, *Crossing Borders: Political Essays* (London: Continuum, 2001), Chs 1–5; Paul Ward, *Unionism in the United Kingdom, 1918–1974* (Basingstoke: Palgrave-MacMillan, 2005); Reynolds, *Island Stories*.

20 See Andrew Marr, *The Day Britain Died* (London: Profile Books, 2000), p. 81.

21 Miller, *Queen's Rebels*.

22 See discussion in Graham Walker, 'The Ulster Covenant and the pulse of Protestant Ulster', *National Identities*, vol. 18, no. 3 (2016), pp. 313–25. Strictly speaking women signed a separate document, although to the same effect.

23 See Chapter 1. Also, Cathal McCall, 'Arise Therefore Ulster Scot', in R.J. Morris (ed.), *Scotland and Ireland: Order and Disorder, 1600–2000* (Edinburgh: Birlinn, 2005); Linda Hagen, 'The Revival of the Ulster-Scots Cultural Identity at the Beginning of the 21st Century', *Journal of Irish and Scottish Studies*, vol. 1, no. 1 (2007), pp. 271–82.

24 Bradley, *Believing in Britain*, p. 38.

25 Kidd, *Union and Unionisms*; see also Jonathan Hearn, *Claiming Scotland: National Identity and Liberal Culture* (Edinburgh: Edinburgh University Press, 2000).

26 See Mackintosh article, 'The New Appeal of Nationalism', in Lindsay Paterson (ed.), *A Diverse Assembly: The Debate on a Scottish Parliament* (Edinburgh: Edinburgh University Press, 1998).

27 See Kidd, *Union and Unionisms*.

28 Jackson, *The Two Unions*.

29 Hassan and Shaw, *The People's Flag*.

30 See Nicola McEwan, 'State Welfare Nationalism: The Territorial Impact of Welfare State Development in Scotland', *Regional and Federal Studies*, vol. 12 (2002), pp. 66–90; also David McCrone, '"Who do you say you are?" Making sense of national identities in Modern Britain', *Ethnicities*, vol. 5 (2002), pp. 301–20; Frank Bechhofer and David McCrone, 'The End of Being British?', *Scottish Affairs*, vol. 2, no. 3 (2014), pp. 309–22.

31 McLean and McMillan, *State of the Union*, passim; Murray Leith, 'Governance and identity in a Devolved Scotland', *Parliamentary Affairs*, vol. 63, no. 2 (2010), pp. 286–301.

32 See discussion in Walker, *The Labour Party in Scotland*, Ch. 3; also see following chapters in this volume.

33 Quoted in Walker, *Intimate Strangers*, p. 160; Brown was speaking in a debate about the Conservative proposal for 'English Votes for English Laws', which he strongly opposed.

34 Hassan and Shaw, *The People's Flag*, p. 4.

35 See Kidd, *Union and Unionisms*; Graeme Morton, *Unionist Nationalism: Governing Urban Scotland, 1830–1860* (East Linton: Tuckwell Press, 1999). The exclusion of the Orange Order from the 'Better Together' campaign

(see Ch. 4) was an indication of the desire to keep the case free of hyper-British and religious associations.

36 But see Michael Keating's comments about unionism increasingly taking on a British nationalist character as the Brexit issue unfolded, *The Herald*, 6 July 2020. See discussion in Chapter 5.

37 See Marianne Elliott, *Hearthlands: A Memoir of the White City Housing Estate in Belfast* (Belfast: Blackstaff Press, 2018).

38 See fuller discussion in Walker, *Intimate Strangers*, Ch. 4.

39 The most informative works in this area are Aaron Edwards, *A History of the Northern Ireland Labour Party: Democratic Socialism and Sectarianism* (Manchester: Manchester University Press, 2009), and Terry Cradden, *Trade Unionism, Socialism, and Partition* (Belfast, 1993). It might be noted that in the British general elections of 1964 and 1966, the NILP won over 100,000 votes.

40 See Richard Bourke, *Peace in Ireland: The War of Ideas* (London: Bloomsbury, 2003), Ch. 7.

41 See McAuley et al., *Loyal to the Core*; also, Eric Kaufmann, *The Orange Order: A Contemporary Northern Irish History* (Oxford: Oxford University Press, 2007).

42 See the elegiac essays in Ian Jack, *The Country Formerly Known as Great Britain* (London: Jonathan Cape, 2009).

43 Ward, *Unionism in the United Kingdom*, p. 183.

44 This argument is pursued in Graham Walker, 'John P. Mackintosh, Devolution, and the Union', *Parliamentary Affairs*, vol. 66, no. 3 (2013), pp. 557–8 and Christopher Farrington and Graham Walker, 'Ideological Content and Institutional Frameworks: Unionist Identities in Scotland and Northern Ireland', *Irish Studies Review*, vol. 17, no. 2 (2009), pp. 135–52.

45 Walker, *History of the Ulster Unionist Party*, pp. 250–5.

46 See Chapter 5.

47 BFI booklet accompanying release of DVD of film in 2008.

48 Bernard Crick, 'An Englishman looks at his passport', in Crick, *Crossing Borders*.

49 The film may also have been influenced by contemporary debates about British 'decline' and texts that predicted the end of the UK, such as Tom Nairn's *The Break-Up of Britain: Crisis and Neo-Nationalism* (London: Verso, 1977).

50 There may be echoes of Orwell here: see Bernard Crick, *George Orwell: A Life* (London: Penguin, 1980); also, discussion in Marr, *The Day Britain Died*.

51 This is not, of course, to overlook the miscarriages of justice that resulted

from the bombings in Guildford and Birmingham.

52 See article in BFI booklet (fn. 47 above) by Sukhda Sandhu, 'Border Zones'.

53 See Des Shaw, 'Bowie's Berlin', *World Histories*, iss. 7 (Dec 2017/Jan 2018), pp. 62–7.

54 See Eve Hepburn and Peter McLoughlin, 'Celtic nationalism and supranationalism: Comparing Scottish and Northern Ireland party responses to Europe', *British Journal of Politics and International Relations*, vol. 13, no. 3 (2011), pp. 383–99.

55 Quoted in Walker, *A History of the Ulster Unionist Party*, p. 244.

56 Edna Longley, 'Multi-culturalism and Northern Ireland', in Edna Longley and Declan Kiberd, *Multi-culturalism: The View from the Two Irelands* (Cork: Cork University Press, 2001).

57 See essays in Paul Bew, *The Making and Remaking of the Good Friday Agreement* (Dublin: The Liffey Press, 2007).

58 This famous phrase was uttered by John Smith while Labour leader.

59 See discussion in Arthur Aughey, 'The British Question: Between Contract and Solidarity', *Political Quarterly*, vol. 72, no. 4 (2001), pp. 473–9.

60 A flavour of such thinking can be found in essay collections such as Angus Calder, *Scotlands of the Mind* (Edinburgh: Luath Press, 2002) and Christopher Harvie, *Mending Scotland: Essays in Economic Regionalism* (Glenaruel: Argyll Publishing, 2004).

61 'Choosing Scotland's Future: A National Conversation' (Scottish Government, 2007); see also David Torrance, *Salmond: Against the Odds* (Edinburgh: Birlinn, 2011), pp. 378, 383–4, 456 (fn. 23).

62 The SNP also fed off the writings of nationalist intellectuals like Tom Nairn, who argued precisely in this vein. See, for example, Nairn's *After Britain: New Labour and the Return of Scotland* (London: Granta, 2000), especially Ch. 2.

63 See, for the Scottish context, the writings of political journalist Iain Macwhirter, for example his book *Road to Referendum* (Glasgow: Cargo Publishing, 2013).

64 Gallagher, *Scotland Now*.

65 See discussion in Chapter 4.

66 See Graham Walker, 'The "Scotland is British" campaign against devolution, 1976–78', *Scottish Affairs*, no. 61 (2007), pp. 74–100.

67 'Scottish Independence: Could it be a "Ticking Time Bomb" for Northern Ireland?', *Huffington Post*, 22 August 2014.

68 Alex Salmond, *The Dream Shall Never Die* (London: William Collins, 2015); Torrance, *Salmond*, pp. 407–9.

69 See Chapter 4.

70 Graham Walker, 'The British–Irish Council', in Rick Wilford (ed.), *Aspects of the Belfast Agreement* (Oxford: Oxford University Press, 20001); Tom Nairn, 'Gordon Brown: Bard of Britishness', in Jamie Maxwell and Pete Ramand (eds), *Tom Nairn: Old Nations, Auld Enemies, New Times* (Edinburgh: Luath Press, 2014) for a discussion of the BIC within a critique of New Labour.

71 Paul Teague, 'Brexit, the Belfast Agreement and Northern Ireland: Imperilling a Fragile Political Bargain', *Political Quarterly*, 89 (2019), pp. 1–15.

72 Bernard Crick, 'Interrelations', *Political Quarterly*, 79 (2008), pp. 71–9.

73 Marr, *The Day Britain Died*, p. 215.

CHAPTER 4:
THE ULSTERISATION OF SCOTTISH POLITICS

1 See Graham Walker, 'Religion and the Political Parties', in Michael Keating (ed.), *The Oxford Handbook of Scottish Politics* (Oxford: Oxford University Press, 2020).

2 John McCaffrey, 'Roman Catholics in Scotland; Nineteenth and Twentieth Centuries', in C. MacLean and K. Veitch (eds), *Scottish Life and Society: A Compendium of Scottish Ethnology*, vol. 12 (Edinburgh: John Donald, 2006).

3 See discussion in Walker, *The Labour Party in Scotland*, Ch. 1.

4 See Chapter One. See also essays in David Torrance (ed.), *Whatever Happened to Tory Scotland?* (Edinburgh: Edinburgh University Press, 2012).

5 See David Seawright, *An Important Matter of Principle: The Decline of the Scottish Conservative and Unionist Party* (Aldershot: Ashgate, 1999).

6 See Chapter 2.

7 See Jack Brand, *The National Movement in Scotland* (London: Routledge, 1978), pp. 150–4; William Miller, *The End of British Politics? Scots and English Political Behaviour in the Seventies* (Oxford: Oxford University Press, 1981), pp. 94, 144–7.

8 Some of these individuals are featured in the documentary *The War Next Door* produced by Tern TV and broadcast on BBC Scotland in the autumn of 2019.

9 See Ian S. Wood, *Crimes of Loyalty: A History of the UDA* (Edinburgh: Edinburgh University Press, 2006), Ch. 13; also, the fictional treatment of the matter in Liam McIlvaney, *All the Colours of the Town* (London: Faber and Faber, 2009).

10 See Walker, *The Labour Party in Scotland*, pp. 15–21; Edward Burke, *An Army of Tribes: British Army Cohesion, Deviancy and Murder in Northern Ireland* (Liverpool: Liverpool University Press, 2018), in particular pp. 107–9 for an

account of the cross-community bonds within the Argyll and Sutherland Regiment serving in Northern Ireland.

11 Brown quoted in Walker, *Intimate Strangers*, p. 160. The term 'Billy and Dan' is used in Scotland to mean 'Protestant and Catholic'.

12 See discussion in Chapter 2.

13 Tom Gallagher, 'Scotland and the Anglo-Irish Agreement: The Reaction of the Orange Order', *Irish Political Studies*, 3 (1988), pp. 19–31.

14 See Steve Bruce, Tony Glendinning, Iain Paterson and Michael Rose, *Sectarianism in Scotland* (Edinburgh: Edinburgh University Press, 2004), pp. 96–7.

15 Speech reprinted in Dickson (ed), *Ireland and Scotland*.

16 See discussion of Smith and Monklands in Mark Stuart, *John Smith: A Life* (London: Politicos, 2005), pp. 350–65.

17 See Walker, *The Labour Party in Scotland*, p. 35.

18 See, for example, *Scotland on Sunday*, 23 October 1994.

19 MacMillan's lecture is reproduced in Tom M. Devine (ed.), *Scotland's Shame? Bigotry and Sectarianism in Modern Scotland* (Edinburgh: Mainstream Publishing, 2000), along with articles both in support of and in opposition to his thesis.

20 See discussion in Martin Steven, 'The Place of Religion in Devolved Scottish Politics', *Scottish Affairs*, 58 (2007), pp. 96–110; Norman Bonney, 'Religion and the Scottish Independence Referendum', *Political Quarterly*, vol. 84, no. 4 (2013), pp. 478–85.

21 See Stephen McGinty, *This Turbulent Priest: The Life of Cardinal Winning* (London: HarperCollins, 2003), Ch. 20, for discussion of 'Section 28 or 2a'. At the time of the controversy, Winning referred to homosexuality as 'perversion'. He died in 2001.

22 See *Glasgow Herald*, 23 March 1992.

23 See Walker, *The Labour Party in Scotland*, Ch. 2. For acknowledgement of the guidance of NBM on the part of several MSPs see 'Tackling Religious Hatred: Report of the Cross-Party Working Group on Religious Hatred' (Scottish Executive, 2002).

24 Bruce et al., *Sectarianism in Scotland*. By the early twenty-first century around half of marriages of those under thirty-five in Scotland were of the 'mixed' variety.

25 Walker, *The Labour Party in Scotland*, Ch. 2; see also John MacKay, *Notes of a Newsman: Witness to a Changing Scotland* (Edinburgh: Luath Press, 2015), p. 128.

26 Henry McLeish, *Scotland First: Truth and Consequences* (Edinburgh: Main-stream Press, 2004), pp. 162–3; see also Owen Dudley Edwards, 'Ireland and the Liddell Re-conquest of Scotland', *Scottish Affairs*, 35 (2001), pp. 25-34.

27 As well as Bruce et al., *Sectarianism in Scotland*, see Lindsay Paterson and Christina Iannelli, 'Religion, social mobility and education in Scotland', *The British Journal of Sociology*, vol. 57, no. 3 (2006), and Michael Rosie, 'The Sectarian Iceberg?' *Scottish Affairs*, vol. 24, no. 3 (2015), pp. 328–50.

28 'Sectarianism in Glasgow – Final Report' (Glasgow City Council, 2003).

29 Torrance, *Salmond*, pp. 207–9, 210, 215; Rob Johns and James Mitchell, *Takeover: Explaining the Extraordinary Rise of the SNP* (London: Biteback, 2016), pp. 34–41.

30 See later discussion of identity politics in this chapter.

31 'Tackling sectarianism and its consequences in Scotland' (Scottish Government, 2015).

32 The Netherlands is one such example.

33 See Bonney, 'Religion'. There are a handful of other faith schools in Scotland; however, the situation stands in complete contrast to other societies, including England and Wales, where there are many such schools of different faiths.

34 'Tackling Sectarianism' report.

35 See discussion in Walker, *The Labour Party in Scotland*, Ch. 3.

36 Executive Summary of Interim Report of Advisory Group on Tackling Sectarianism published by the Scottish government in December 2013.

37 Jonathan Bardon, *The Struggle for Shared Schools in Northern Ireland* (Belfast: UHF, 2012). It should be noted that a leading member of the Alliance Party of Northern Ireland, which supports integrated schooling in Northern Ireland, Duncan Morrow, the Chair of the Scottish Government's Advisory Group on tackling sectarianism, apparently saw no reason to support the same measure in Scotland.

38 J. Liechty and C. Clegg, *Moving Beyond Sectarianism* (Dublin: Columba Press, 2000); Elliott, *When God Took Sides*.

39 *The Scotsman*, 1 January 2016; see also discussion in Gregor McClymont, 'The Nationalist Interpretation of Scottish History', *Renewal*, vol. 22, nos 1–2 (2014), pp. 146–55. McClymont is a former Scottish Labour MP.

40 See the remarks of Michael Kelly, a former Catholic Lord Provost of Glasgow, Labour Party figurehead, and Celtic FC director that 'the vast majority of Scots rejected bigotry'. *The Scotsman*, 1 September 2011. Kelly and Brian Wilson were among the few to realise the potential damage to Labour of a political preoccupation with identity matters.

41 The Offensive Behaviour at Football and Threatening Communications (Scotland) Act 2012. For a critique see Stuart Waiton, *Snobs' Law: Criminalising Football Fans in an Age of Intolerance* (Dundee: Take a Liberty, 2012).

42 James Robertson, *And the Land Lay Still* (London: Penguin, 2011), p. 297.

43 Emphasis in original. The written submissions on the Bill were published on the Justice Committee's website.

44 Labour promised to repeal the Act should they come back to power in Scotland. See *The Herald*, 5 November 2014.

45 For example, Humza Yousaf, who went on to become a controversial SNP Justice Minister.

46 See Gallagher, *Scotland Now*, pp. 47–9.

47 See Graham Walker, 'From Darlings to Pariahs: Rangers and Scottish National Pride', in Alan Bissett and Alasdair McKillop (eds), *Born Under a Union Flag: Rangers, Britain, and Scottish Independence* (Edinburgh: Luath Press, 2013).

48 See reflections of journalist and broadcaster – and pro-Union campaigner – Archie McPherson in his book *More than a Game: Living with the Old Firm* (Edinburgh: Luath Press, 2020), especially Epilogue.

49 See Peter Geoghegan, *The People's Referendum: Why Scotland Will Never Be the Same Again* (Edinburgh: Luath Press, 2015), Chs 1 and 7; also, Tom Devine, *Independence or Union: Scotland's Past and Scotland's Present* (London: Penguin, 2016), pp. 224–5.

50 Iain Macwhirter, *Tsunami: Scotland's Democratic Revolution* (Glasgow: Freight Books, 2015).

51 Alex Massie, 'Wha's Like Us? Scots win at Identity Politics', *The Times*, 4 November 2018.

52 Examples include Scottish Television (STV) journalist Aidan Kerr, author and journalist David Torrance – see *The Herald* 9 May 2016 – and journalist Andy McIver – see *The Herald*, 28 December 2019.

53 Gerry Hassan, 'DIY Scotland', *Scottish Review*, 11 May 2016.

54 *The Herald*, 15 May 2016.

55 Jamie Maxwell, 'Referendum to deepen Anglo-Scottish political gap', *The Irish Times*, 6 April 2016.

56 For an account of the debate over faith schools, particularly in relation to England, see David Conway, *Disunited Kingdom: How the Government's Community Cohesion Agenda Undermines British Identity and Nationhood* (London: Civitas, 2009).

57 See Dominic Brown, 'Apartheid in the schools', *Scottish Review*, 10 February 2016; also, *The Herald*, 14 March 2014.

58 See coverage of the issue in *The Irish News*, 28 January 2015 and 4 February 2015.
59 *The Irish News*, 4 February 2015. Both the GAA and INTO are steeped in a history of Irish nationalist politics.
60 *The Irish News*, 26 March 2012.
61 *Belfast Telegraph*, 12 May 2016. The teacher's social media accounts also featured pictures of IRA gunmen. The 'Ra' is a colloquial reference to the IRA.
62 See *Scottish Catholic Observer* (SCO), 18 January 2019. See also *The Herald*, 10 March 2017, regarding the angry response to the criticisms made by another SNP politician, Tommy Shepherd. The SCO campaign in defence of Catholic schools has dominated its pages in recent years.
63 *The Sunday Times* (Scotland), 17 November 2019.
64 *The Herald*, 19 November 2019.
65 See Brian Wilson's comments in *The Herald*, 21 March 2017.
66 See *The Herald*, 14 January 2015.
67 See Chapter 2.
68 A good example of academic work produced to serve the cause of promoting Irish identity in Scotland is that of Joseph Bradley. See, in particular the series of books under his editorship entitled *Celtic-Minded*, and published by the Argyll Press in Scotland.
69 *Daily Record*, 3 April 2017.
70 *Sunday Herald,* 12 and 19 February 2017.
71 Owen Dudley Edwards, 'Ireland: The Elephant in the Room', in Owen Dudley Edwards and Jamie Maxwell (eds), *Why Not? Labour and Scottish Independence* (Edinburgh: Luath Press, 2014).
72 *The Scotsman*, 1 February 2017.
73 *Scottish Review*, 14 February 2017.
74 Poster going by 'RBRFC' on Follow Follow (Rangers supporters) website: www.followfollow.com/forum/forums/the-bear-pit/ (accessed 25 November 2019).
75 *The Herald*, 24 February 2016.
76 *The Scotsman*, 23 February 2016 regarding the North Lanarkshire Council; *The Herald*, 23 February 2016 regarding the protests promised by a group calling themselves 'The Regimental Blues'.
77 *The Herald*, 13 September 2016.
78 *The Herald*, 12 September 2019. See also the article 'On the March' in *The Economist*, 13 July 2019.
79 Follow Follow (accessed 1 May 2019). The pub reference relates to an

election campaign set-piece involving then First Minister Alex Salmond and government minister Humza Yousaf.

80 *Scottish Review*, 10 May 2017.
81 *The Herald*, 21 March 2017.
82 See statement issued by the dissident republican group Saoradh, reproduced in *The Herald*, 2 September 2019.
83 *News Letter* (Belfast), 25 January 2020.
84 See Iain Macwhirter commentary in *The Herald*, 12 February 2020; also, Marisa McGlinchy in the *Belfast Telegraph*, 14 January 2020, on Irish republicans and Scotland.
85 *Think Scotland*, 20 April 2020.
86 *The Herald*, 28 January 2020. See Also Mark Smith on Govan in *The Herald*, 9 and 11 November 2019.
87 See Chapter 5.
88 See the Scottish political feature in *The Economist*, 30 November 2019.
89 *Guardian Briefing*, 27 August 2018.
90 A feature in the Scottish Sunday newspaper, *The Sunday Post*, 22 September 2019, 'Sectarian violence threat after a no-deal Brexit', included the following statement from North Ayrshire Council: 'The legal status of the Irish border in a no-deal is unclear, danger of recurrence of Irish troubles. Greater sectarian tensions in the West of Scotland including North Ayrshire.' In January 2020 the proceedings of the Scottish parliament were disrupted by a protester denouncing SNP 'support for the IRA', see *News Letter*, 25 January 2020.
91 This 'ultra' form of nationalism, which sees anything British as 'Other', pervades the pages of the daily newspaper *The National* in Scotland.
92 *The Herald*, 19 March 2019. This pressure group has received strong backing in the Catholic Church publication *Scottish Catholic Observer*.
93 Edwards, 'Ireland: The Elephant in the Room'.
94 Tony Judt, *The Memory Chalet* (London: Vintage Books, 2011), pp. 189–91, 201–2.
95 For scholarly treatments see Francis Fukuyama, 'Against Identity Politics', *Foreign Affairs*, vol. 97, no. 5 (2018), pp. 90–114; Mark Lilla, *The Once and Future Liberal: After Identity Politics* (London: Hurst and Co., 2018).
96 Anne Applebaum, *Twilight of Democracy: The Failure of Politics and the Parting of Friends* (London: Penguin, 2020), pp. 106–7, 117–18.
97 *The Herald*, 15 June 2021: 'SNP MSP branded a "fool" after "making up bigotry about Edinburgh"'.
98 See Eric Kaufmann, *Whiteshift: Populism, Immigration and the Future of*

White Majorities (London: Penguin, 2019), p. 314.

99   See critique of 'Call It Out' claims by academics Tom Devine and Michael Rosie in *The Herald*, 29 May 2021.

100 See discussion in Kaufmann, *Whiteshift*, pp. 338–41.

101 See, for example, 'There's more than one form of hatred in Scotland', published and accessed 31 August 2021 on the 'Lily of St Leonards' website. The article was accompanied by a photograph of a banner displayed by Celtic fans which read 'Know your place hun scum'. 'Hun' is used in both Scotland and Northern Ireland to refer in a derogatory way to Protestants: www.effiedeans.com/2021/08/theres-more-than-one-form-of-hatred-in. html.

102 *News Letter*, 11 May 2021.

103 *The Herald*, 30 September 2021. MacKay claimed that he was viewed with suspicion, on account of being from Northern Ireland, by both nationalists and unionists in Scotland.

104 *The Herald*, 3 May 2021.

105 *The Herald*, 31 May 2021. The commentator was political expert Mark Smith.

CHAPTER 5:
LEAVING, REMAINING AND REMAKING

1   James Greer 'The Paisleyites: From protest movement to electoral breakthrough', *The Sixties: A Journal of History, Politics and Culture*, vol. 2, issue 2, (2009), pp. 187–205.

2   Paul Bew, 'Confessions of a disappointed Irish unificationist', Royal Irish Academy, 26 November 2021.

3   *Irish Independent*, 18 November 2003.

4   Paul Anderson, 'The 2016 Scottish Parliament election: A nationalist minority, a Conservative comeback and a Labour collapse', *Regional & Federal Studies*, vol. 26, no. 4 (2016), pp. 555–68.

5   *The Observer*, 13 September 2015.

6   For a sceptical appraisal of the transformative power of the Northern Irish identity see Kevin McNicholl, 'The Northern Irish Identity is No New Dawn', *The Detail*, 3 April 2017, https://thedetail.tv/articles/the-northern-irish-identity-is-no-new-dawn (accessed 8 June 2022).

7   Sam McBride, *Burned: The Inside Story of the 'Cash-for-Ash' Scandal and Northern Ireland's Secretive New Elite* (Dublin: Merrion Press, 2019).

8   Tony Judt, *Postwar: A History of Europe Since 1945* (London: Vintage, 2010), pp. 153–9.

9   Ibid., pp. 305–9.

10   David Butler and Uwe Kitzinger, *The 1975 Referendum* (London: Macmillan, 1976), pp. 2–3.

11   Duncan Weldon, *Two Hundred Years of Muddling Through: The Surprising Story of Britain's Economy from Boom to Bust and Back Again* (London: Little Brown, 2021), pp. 213–17.

12   In addition to Butler and Kitzinger, *The 1975 Referendum*, see Robert Sanders, *Yes to Europe! The 1975 Referendum and Seventies Britain* (Cambridge: Cambridge University Press, 2018).

13   Michael Geary, *An Inconvenient Wait: Ireland's Quest for Membership of the EEC* (Dublin: Institute of Public Administration, 2009).

14   Charles Haughey speech to Galway students, 14 December 1962, quoted in: Katy Hayward, *Irish Nationalism and European Integration* (Manchester: Manchester University Press, 2009), p. 130.

15   Paul Arthur, *Northern Ireland: A Crucial Test for a Europe of Peaceful Regions?* (Norway: Norwegian Institute of International Affairs, 1993), p. 56.

16   Sinn Féin (Provisional), *EEC No! Why Ireland Should not join the Common Market*, 1972: Linen Hall Library, Belfast, Northern Ireland Political Collection (NIPC); Provisional Prisoners for No poster, Linen Hall Library NIPC.

17   Richard Roberts, 'Back to the Future? Britain's 1975 Referendum on Europe', *New Statesman*, 23 January 2015.

18   *Evening Standard*, 24 March 1975, referenced in Butler and Kitzinger, *The 1975 Referendum*, p. 167.

19   Valeria Tarditi, 'The Scottish National Party's changing attitude towards the European Union', EPERN Working Paper, No. 22, February 2010.

20   For analysis of the economic impact of the oil industry on Scotland and the UK see C.H. Lee, *Scotland and the United Kingdom: The Economy and the Union in the Twentieth Century* (Manchester: Manchester University Press, 1995), pp. 148–52.

21   Tarditi, 'The Scottish National Party's changing attitude', p. 11.

22   Robert Sanders, '"An auction of fear": The Scotland in Europe referendum, 1975: An earlier referendum in which Scotland's place in a larger political union was at stake', *Renewal*, vol. 22, issue 1–2 (Spring 2014), pp. 87–95.

23   *Dictionary of Irish Biography*, 'Con O'Neill': www.dib.ie/biography/oneill-sir-con-douglas-walter-a6917 (accessed 10 June 2022).

24   Ciaran Hanna, *Northern Ireland Political Attitudes to the European Economic Community*, 1970–75 (Belfast: QUB Institute of European Studies, 2001); 'European Economic Community United Kingdom Application for Membership 1967: Papers 1962–70', Northern Ireland Public Record Office, COM/62/1/1385.

25 Hanna, *Northern Ireland Political Attitudes*, p. 29.

26 Terence O'Neill, *Ulster at the Crossroads* (London: Faber and Faber, 1969), pp. 187–91. Speech given in Bonn, 2 April 1967.

27 John Harbinson, *The Ulster Unionist Party, 1882–1973: Its Development and Organisation* (Belfast: Blackstaff, 1974).

28 Shaun McDaid, *Template for Peace: Northern Ireland 1972–75* (Manchester: Manchester University Press, 2013).

29 *Ballymena Guardian*, 29 May 1975: 'Traditional Protestantism has no future in the EEC – Says Paisley'.

30 Ulster Vanguard, *Ulster a Nation* (Belfast, 1972); Garry Watson, '"Meticulously Crafted Ambiguities": The Confused Political Vision of Ulster Vanguard', *Irish Political Studies*, vol. 28, issue 4 (2013) pp. 536–62.

31 Hanna, *Northern Ireland Political Attitudes*, p. 19.

32 Obituary of Anthony Alcock, *The Guardian*, 12 December 2006.

33 Anthony Alcock, 'Britain, Europe and a Changing World: Text of address delivered by Dr A. Alcock to the Irish Association', Linen Hall Library NIPC P2198.

34 *Derry Journal*, 3 June 1975.

35 Camilla Schofield, *Enoch Powell and the Making of Postcolonial Britain* (Cambridge: Cambridge University Press, 2013).

36 Powell speech in Banbridge, Co. Down, 25 September 1974; quoted in Paul Corthorn, 'Enoch Powell, Ulster Unionism and the British Nation', *The Journal of British Studies*, vol. 51, no. 4 (2012), pp. 967–97.

37 Corthorn, 'Enoch Powell'.

38 James Greer, 'Typical Unionists? The Politicians and their People', in Paul Burgess and Gareth Mulvenna (eds), *The Contested Identities of Ulster Protestants* (Hampshire: Palgrave, 2015).

39 Fintan O'Toole, *Heroic Failure: Brexit and the Politics of Pain* (London: Apollo, 2018). For a rebuttal of O'Toole's 'imperial nostalgia' thesis see John Lloyd, 'Why Fintan O'Toole has got Brexit all wrong', *The Irish Times*, 23 January 2019.

40 Timothy Snyder, 'Europe's dangerous creation myth', *Politico*, 1 May 2019: www.politico.eu/article/europe-creation-project-myth-history-nation-state/ (accessed 4 September 2022).

41 For the development of the AES see Noel Thompson, *Left in the Wilderness: The Political Economy of British Democratic Socialism Since 1979* (London: Acumen, 2002), pp. 29–69.

42 Tony Benn, *Against the Tide: Diaries 1973–76* (London: Hutchinson, 1989), p. 302.

43   David Willets, 'How Thatcher's Bruges speech put Britain on the road to Brexit', *Financial Times*, 31 August 2018.

44   *The Irish News*, 3 March 2017. The much less wealthy UUP also spent zero on the campaign, and outside of the DUP's controversial £10,000, spending of all Northern Irish parties was low in 2016.

45   *The Irish Times*, 27 February 2016.

46   See Henry McDonald, 'Higgins confirms my fears of a less tolerant Ireland', *News Letter*, 20 September 2021. McDonald wrote: 'Living and working south of the border from around 2016 I detected ... the return of a more revanchist nationalism in the air.'

47   Paul Nolan, 'Breaking up the UK', *Fortnight*, no. 480 (January 2021), pp. 6–7.

48   Colin Coulter, Niall Gilmartin, Katy Hayward and Peter Shirlow (eds), *Northern Ireland: A Generation After Good Friday* (Manchester: Manchester University Press, 2021), Ch. 8.

49   See discussion in Bernard Crick, 'The Politics of British History', in Crick's collection of essays, *Crossing Borders*.

50   See Kidd, *Union and Unionisms*; Morton, *Unionist Nationalism*.

51   See Maria Sobolewska and Robert Ford, *Brexitland: Identity, Diversity and the Reshaping of British Politics* (Cambridge: Cambridge University Press, 2020). See also John Lloyd, *Should Auld Acquaintance be Forgot: The Great Mistake of Scottish Independence* (Cambridge: Polity, 2020), Ch. 2.

52   Fintan O'Toole, 'British government must accept messy compromises', *The Irish Times*, 23 September 2017.

53   Michael Keating, 'Plurinational Democracy', in Denis Galligan (ed.), *Constitution in Crisis* (London: I.B. Tauris, 2017).

54   Seamus Mallon, *A Shared Home Place* (Dublin: Lilliput, 2019). Lloyd in *Should Auld Acquaintance* makes the same point in the book's conclusion in relation to any second referendum in Scotland that may take place.

55   NI Assembly, Official Report (Hansard) vol. 4, 17 January 2000, p. 90.

56   David Reynolds, 'A Union Built on Blood', *New Statesman*, 22–28 November 2019.

57   *ITV News*, 9 June 2016: www.itv.com/news/2016-06-09/tony-blair-sir-john-major-eu-referendum-northern-ireland (accessed 5 September 2022).

58   *The Guardian*, 9 June 2016. 'Tony Blair and John Major: Brexit would close Irish border'.

59   *The Sunday Times*, 2 January 2021: Alex Massie, 'Britain is Splintering Beneath the Brexit King'. Regarding the SNP's dilemmas over Brexit, see also Ben Jackson, *The Case for Scottish Independence: A History of Nationalist*

Political Thought in Modern Scotland (Cambridge: Cambridge University Press, 2020), p. 160.

60   The Executive Office, 'Letter to the Prime Minister Rt Hon. Theresa May', 10 August 2016. Joint Foster–McGuinness letter: www.executiveoffice-ni.gov. uk/publications/letter-prime-minister-rt-hon-theresa-may-mp (accessed 5 September 2022).

61   Katy Hayward, *What Do We Know and What Should We Do about the Irish Border* (London: Sage, 2021), p. 46.

62   *The Irish Times*, 9 January 2017.

63   John Garry, 'The EU referendum Vote in Northern Ireland: Implications for our understanding of citizens' political views and behaviour', Northern Ireland Assembly Knowledge Exchange Seminar Series, 2016–17, p. 2.

64   *News Letter*, 19 October 2019, for coverage of the UK–EU Protocol agreement and of Johnson's 2018 speech to the DUP conference.

65   For an in-depth analysis of the governance, structures and processes of the Northern Ireland Protocol as originally agreed by the UK and EU, see: Katy Hayward, David Phinnemore and Milena Komarova, with Conor Campbell and James Greer, 'Anticipating and Meeting New Multilevel Governance Challenges in Northern Ireland after Brexit' (Queen's University Belfast & The UK in a Changing Europe, May 2020).

66   *BBC News*, 7 September 2020: www.bbc.co.uk/news/uk-northern-ireland-54056890 (accessed 5 September 2022).

67   See *News Letter*, 8 September 2021 for summary of a batch of UUP proposals and unionist opposition to these plans.

68   Hayward, *The Irish Border*, pp. 33–40.

69   *The Irish Times*, 17 September 2021 'President's refusal of Armagh invitation "unexpected", say Church Leaders'.

70   Poll conducted by *Ireland Thinks* for the *Irish Mail on Sunday*, 19 September 2021. Analysis of poll *Newstalk*, 19 September 2021: www.newstalk.com/news/overwhelming-public-support-for-presidents-decision-not-to-attend-ni-event-poll-1253762 (accessed 4 September 2022).

71   'Jeremy Corbyn, Britain's unlikely EU Warrior, makes last stand on Brexit', *Reuters*, 9 September 2019: www.reuters.com/investigates/special-report/britain-eu-corbyn/ (accessed 4 September 2022).

72   For example, Corbyn opposed the Anglo-Irish Agreement from an Irish republican perspective. See 'Fact Check – Corbyn and Northern Ireland', *Channel Four News*, 13 May 2017: www.channel4.com/news/factcheck/factcheck-corbyn-on-northern-ireland (accessed 4 September 2022).

73   *The Spectator*, 30 October 2019. Alex Massie: 'I am convinced Corbyn is

intensely relaxed about Scottish independence and the break-up of the United Kingdom because the majority of people in Scotland who agree with Corbyn on most things are so relaxed about independence they voted for it in 2014. I have no doubt whatsoever Corbyn would have done so too had he been living in Scotland five years ago.'

74 'Further Trade Rules Relaxed Between GB and Ireland', *BBC News*, 5 March 2021: www.bbc.co.uk/news/uk-northern-ireland-56294309 (accessed 4 September 2022).

75 Rory Montgomery, 'Protocol problems for both parts of Ireland: North and South', *Fortnight*, issue 481, pp. 2–5.

76 *The Irish Times*, 18 October 2018.

77 Lee Reynolds, 'Sink Michael Gove's Irish Sea Border', *The Critic*, 4 February 2022: https://thecritic.co.uk/sink-michael-goves-irish-sea-border/ (accessed 4 February 2022).

78 N. McEwen and Mary C. Murphy, 'Brexit and the union: Territorial voice, exit and re-entry strategies in Scotland and Northern Ireland after EU exit', *International Political Science Review*, March 2021.

79 *The Herald*, 4 December 2017. See Iain Macwhirter's criticisms of the SNP around the issue Europe and borders in his 'Sturgeon's border problems', *The Herald*, 11 April 2021. Macwhirter made the following point about the relevance of Northern Ireland: 'There has never been a direct read across from the troubles in the province to Scotland. But Northern Ireland is only 12 miles away, and closer culturally and politically than we'd like to think.'

80 *The Irish Times*, 28 April 2021.

81 The 2021 Census found that the population either Catholic or brought up Catholic is 45.7 per cent, compared to 43.48 per cent Protestant. *BBC News*, 22 September 2022, www.bbc.co.uk/news/uk-northern-ireland-62980394 (accessed 23 September 2022).

82 University of Liverpool, 'Northern Ireland General Election Survey 2019': www.liverpool.ac.uk/humanities-and-social-sciences/research/research-themes/transforming-conflict/ni-election-survey-19/ (accessed 5 September 2022).

83 University of Liverpool, '2017 Northern General Election Study' (Economic and Social Research Council): www.liverpool.ac.uk/politics/research/research-projects/2017-election-study/ (accessed 4 September 2022).

84 Ailsa Henderson and James Mitchell 'Referendums as Critical Junctures? Scottish Voting in British Elections', *Parliamentary Affairs*, vol. 71, no. 1 (2018), pp. 109–24.

85 Sobolewska and Ford, *Brexitland*, p. 275.

86 Michael Keating, 'The SNP's Brexit Dilemma', *UK in a Changing Europe*, 11 October 2019.

87 Sobolewska and Ford, *Brexitland*, p. 254.

88 Ibid., p. 12.

89 Henry Hill, 'Putting Muscle Behind the Union', *The Critic*, November 2021.

90 *The Guardian*, 16 November 2020.

91 For the high level of support for devolution in Northern Ireland see analysis of the *Northern Ireland Life and Times Survey* by Katy Hayward and Ben Rosher, 'Political attitudes at a time of flux', ARK Research Reports, 2020, which found majority support for the principles of power-sharing and devolution. A University of Liverpool survey conducted in October 2021 found that 65 per cent of respondents wanted Stormont to function until the election of May 2022, despite differences regarding the Protocol: University of Liverpool, *The Ireland/Northern Ireland Protocol: Consensus or Conflict?* (University of Liverpool: 2021). A 2021 YouGov poll measured support for abolishing devolution in Scotland at only 20 per cent, with 66 per cent in support of maintaining Holyrood, and measured 27 per cent of Welsh voters in favour of ending devolution, which is in line with the figures consistently found in 'Welsh Political Barometer' polling. See YouGov, 'Who supports abolishing the devolved parliaments, and why?', 4 May 2021: https://yougov.co.uk/topics/politics/articles-reports/2021/05/04/who-supports-abolishing-devolved-parliaments-and-w (accessed 31 August 2022).

92 Ciaran Martin, 'Can the Union Survive Muscular Unionism?', *Political Insight*, December 2021, pp. 36–9.

93 Institute for Government, 'Coronavirus and Devolution', 20 March 2020: www.instituteforgovernment.org.uk/explainers/coronavirus-and-devolution (accessed 31 August 2022).

94 Stuart McIntyre and Graeme Roy, 'Has devolution led to differing outcomes during the Covid-19 crisis?' *Economics Observatory*, 12 February 2021: www.economicsobservatory.com/has-devolution-led-to-different-outcomes-during-the-covid-19-crisis (accessed 31 August 2022).

95 Alex Nurse, 'Andy Burnham's standoff with London was about more than money', *The Conversation*, 23 October 2020: https://theconversation.com/andy-burnhams-standoff-with-london-was-always-about-more-than-just-lockdown-money-148594 (accessed 31 August 2022).

96 *The Guardian*, 21 June 2021.

97 'Metro Mayors', *Institute for Government*, 9 February 2022: www.instituteforgovernment.org.uk/explainers/metro-mayors?gclid=EAIaIQo

bChMl2t75yK327glVjJftChо_mgkUEAAYASAAEgl2bfD_BwE (accessed 31 August 2022).

98 Robert Hazell, 'The English Question comprises two broad questions, with half a dozen different answers', *The Constitutional Unit*, 25 September 2014: https://constitution-unit.com/2014/09/25/the-english-question-comprises-two-broad-questions-with-half-a-dozen-different-answers/ (accessed 31 August 2022).

99 Arthur Aughey, 'Anxiety and injustice: the anatomy of contemporary English nationalism', *Nations and Nationalism*, vol. 16, iss. 3, pp. 506–24.

100 Douglas Dowell, 'The Union of 1707 and the art of the deal', 21 February 2021: https://dijdowell.medium.com/the-union-of-1707-and-the-art-of-the-deal-ca89cb5dfaca (accessed 31 August 2022).

101 Gordon Brown, 'How to Save the United Kingdom?', *New Statesman*, 20 November 2020.

102 Tom McTague, 'Will Britain Survive?', *The Atlantic*, 5 January 2022.

103 An April 2022 poll, by the Institute of Irish Studies at the University of Liverpool, conducted for *The Irish News*, 5 April 2022, found support for immediate Irish unity/Northern Ireland leaving the UK to be only 30 per cent, rising only to 33 per cent if the change happens after ten to fifteen years. The same poll, this time funded by the Economic and Social Research Council in 2020, similarly found 29 per cent in favour of Irish unity: *Belfast Telegraph*, 'Just 29% in Northern Ireland would vote for unity, major study reveals', 18 February 2020.

104 Resolution Foundation, *The Living Standards Outlook* 2022, resolution foundation.org. For a long-term perspective on the 'lost decade' of the 2010s and gloomy predictions for a 2020s' fall in household disposable incomes, see p. 49: 'FIGURE 15: This Parliament risks being the worst on record for real household income growth' (accessed 31 August 2022).

EPILOGUE

1 The SNP fell one seat short of an outright majority but formed a pro-independence majority coalition with the eight returned Green MSPs. In the constituency and regional list votes within the same election the electorate voted 49/51 per cent and 51/49 per cent for unionist and nationalist parties: 'Scottish Election 2021, Results in maps and charts', *BBC News*, 9 May 2021: www.bbc.co.uk/news/uk-scotland-scotland-politics-57028315 (accessed 14 September 2022).

2 *The Scotsman*, 2 May 2021.

3 *Scottish Government*, 'Independence referendum: First Minister's statement

– 28 June 2022': www.gov.scot/publications/ministerial-statement-independence-referendum/ (accessed 14 September 2022).

4   It is often forgotten that the SDLP were the largest party by votes, though not seats, in the Assembly election of 1998.

5   'NI Election Results 2022', *BBC News*: www.bbc.co.uk/news/election/2022/northern-ireland/results (accessed 1 September 2022).

6   Lucid Talk Tracker Poll, April 2022: www.lucidtalk.co.uk/single-post/lt-ni-tracker-poll-april-2022 (accessed 1 September 2022). Demographic breakdown for each party – 'ABC1/C2DE' social class figures – shows Alliance receiving twice as much support from middle-class voters as from working-class supporters. Both the UUP and DUP were found to have more support proportionately among the working class. The DUP were found to have the most working-class support base of any Northern party.

7   'Scottish local elections: SNP "could work with Republicans to challenge UK government"', *The Times*, 6 May 2022.

8   Louise Wilson, 'Sinn Féin's victory is not the anti-Union win nationalists paint it as', *Holyrood*, 22 May 2022: www.holyrood.com/inside-politics/view,sinn-feins-victory-in-stormont-is-not-the-antiunion-win-scottish-nationalists-paint-it-as (accessed 1 September 2022).

9   Adam Price, Twitter, @Adamprice, 9 July 2022 (accessed 4 September 2022).

10   'Nicola Sturgeon's dalliance with Sinn Féin will infuriate many ordinary Scots', *Scottish Daily Express*, 9 May 2022.

11   'Does the intellectual collapse of the exhausted SNP hint at Sinn Féin's future?', *The Irish Times*, 30 June 2022.

12   Author interview with Steve Dornan, 26 June 2022.

13   *Dig With It*, issue 4 (Spring 2021).

Acknowledgements

We wish to thank all at Irish Academic Press for helping us navigate the challenges of writing a contemporary history in uncertain times, and for all their efforts in producing this volume. We are especially grateful to Wendy Logue for her guidance and hard work, and for saving us from several errors.

Parts of this book grew out of research funded by the Northern Ireland Department for Communities, when the authors collaborated in the School of History, Anthropology, Philosophy and Politics at Queen's University Belfast.

We benefited greatly from discussions with friends and colleagues. Our thanks to Steve Dornan, John Erskine, Jack Foster, Ryan Mallon, Gareth Mulvenna, Massimiliano Nastri, and Mark Thompson.

The main text of this book was completed in September 2022 during a period of rapid change when the political architecture, culture and economy of the United Kingdom often appeared to be shifting significantly on a daily basis. The death of Queen Elizabeth and the tragicomedy of the Liz Truss premiership were just two of the more prominent events highly relevant to our study that we watched unfurl in the ensuing weeks. This continuing volatility has underlined the issues this book has raised regarding the direction of travel taken in recent years by Northern Ireland, Scotland and the UK as a whole.

Graham Walker was, once again, inspired and sustained throughout by Elda Nikolou-Walker and Alexander Walker.

James Greer wishes to thank his partner Elodie Fabre for her support and scholarly insights. Finally, he remembers with love the encouragement and support of his late parents, Dorothy and Harry, whose lives and family speak of the importance of ties between Northern Ireland and Scotland.

Index

Catholicism, Presbyterian perception of 9

Catholics: anti-Catholicism in Scotland 29, 127, 134; Britishness and 100; emigration to Scotland 15, 29; Liberal Unionists and 22; nationalism 11; in Northern Ireland 7–8, 51, 100, 195–6; penal laws and 8; politicisation of 12–13; poverty and 14; radicalism and 9; in Scotland 15, 27, 29, 71–2, 133–4, 155; Scottish Presbyterian incomers and 7–8; SNP, support for 127, 132–3, 147

Celtic nationalism 169, 214–15

Celtic Tiger 86

Chichester-Clark, James 168

Church of Ireland 7–8, 11, 18–19

Church of Scotland 17, 29, 130, 134, 135

civil rights campaign, Northern Ireland and 62, 126

Civil War (1922–23) 32, 33

Coal and Steel Community 163

Colley, Linda 91, 94, 97; *Britons* 90

Collins, Michael 31

commemorations, sectarianising of 149

Common Market 163, 165, 170, 172; opposition to 166, 174, 175; UK and 163, 167–8

Commonwealth 34, 35, 37, 60, 171

communism 36, 119

Connolly, James 25

Conservative governments: Brexit and 189; Heath government 63, 64, 68; Northern Ireland, Major and 80–1

Conservative Party 21–2, 27, 47, 78; divisions within 210; EEC membership referendum (1975) 166; Europe, attitude towards 175; Protestants in Scotland 120, 121, 122; in Scotland 28, 76, 124, 152–3, 154; Scottish devolution 63; Ulster Unionist Party and 50, 67

Conti, Mario, Archbishop of Glasgow 130

contractarianism 8, 23

Cook, Robin 76–7, 81

Cooke, Revd Henry 12

Corbyn, Jeremy 190

Corthorn, Paul 174

Costello, John A. 34

Council of Ireland 26, 48, 49

Covenanters 9, 18, 22

COVID pandemic 201–2

Craig, James 52, 54, 55

Craig, William (Bill) 170, 171

Crick, Bernard 41, 77, 94, 106, 117

Crowther, Geoffrey, Baron 61

'Cruthin' people 4

Cullen, Alice 36

Cullen, Chris 147–8

Dalyell, Tam 45, 71, 75–6, 83, 123; *Devolution: The End of Britain* 70

Davitt, Michael 27

de Gaulle, General Charles 163, 168

de Valera, Éamon 31, 33–4, 36, 37, 38, 164

Delors, Jacques 175

Democratic Unionist Party (DUP) 86, 160, 196, 206; Brexit and 103, 177, 178, 179, 184, 185, 186, 191; Britishness and 103; EEC membership, opposition to 170; elections (2022) 212; General Election (2016) 160; Good Friday Agreement and 109, 187; Irish Sea Border and 186; leadership failures, Brexit and 212; Northern Ireland Protocol and 211; power-sharing institutions and 161, 211; Renewable Heat Incentive (RHI) and 162; Sinn Féin and 114; voters, failure to coalesce 213

Irish unity 35, 37, 93, 180; SNP and 149, 151, 152; *see also* United Ireland
Irish Volunteers 9–10
Irish-Scottish links 125

Jackson, Alvin 42, 92, 97
James I, King (James VI of Scotland) 5–6
Jenkins, Roy 166
Johnson, Boris 88, 201; Brexit and 189, 191, 198, 214; Irish Sea Border and 189, 191; Northern Ireland Protocol and 186, 187; Scottish devolution, views on 199
Johnston, Thomas 56
Joint Ministerial Committees (JMCs) 85
Judt, Tony 155–6

Kearney, Hugh 89, 94, 117
Keating, Michael 180
Kelly, James 140
Kidd, Colin 90, 92, 96
Kilbrandon Commission (1968–73) 54, 60, 61–2, 65, 68
Kilbrandon, James Shaw, Baron 61, 65, 68
King, Angeline 216
Knox, John 17–18

Labour governments: anti-partitionist campaign, attitude towards 35; constitutional reform 82, 98; devolutionary reforms (1990s) 41, 43, 81, 82; government (1923–24) 120; government (1964–70) 50, 61, 68; government (1974–79) 65–7, 68–9, 72; government (1997–2007) 82, 84, 98, 110, 176; minority government (1924) 47, 52; Northern Ireland and 60, 65–7; post-Second World War reforms 100; post-war Scotland and 57, 58, 59; Scotland Act (1998) 79; Speaker's conference 68, 69; welfare state measures 55

'Labour Nation', concept of 97–8
Labour Party: Alternative Economic Strategy 174–5; conference (1906) 20; constitutional reform 175; devolution for Scotland and Wales 175; EEC membership referendum (1975) 166; Europe, attitude towards 175; Iraq war and 133; Irish unity, support for 35, 124; landslide victory (1997) 81; leadership 189–90; New Labour 82–8, 98, 175–6, 199; in Northern Ireland 28; Scottish nationalists and 210
Labour Party (Irish) 165
Labour Party in Scotland 31, 32, 47, 70–1, 76, 98, 118; by-election (1994) 126–7; Catholic support for 27, 119, 121, 126–7, 132; devolution and 72, 83; future of 210; General Election (1987) 124; General Election (2015) 142–3, 146; identity politics and 137–8; Irish communities and 36, 119; 'Loyalist' working class and 135–6; perception of 138; Protestants and 126; Scottish Constitutional Convention and 78, 79; sectarianism and 126–7, 137–9
Labour-Liberal Democrat government 129–30
land reform 9, 19, 22, 27–8
Liberal government (1912) 46
Liberal Party 16, 17, 18, 27, 119, 120
Liberal Unionism 21, 22
Liberal Unionist Association 16
Livingstone, David 90
Lloyd George, David 27
Locke, John 8
Long, Naomi 158
Long, Walter 48
Longley, Edna 4
loyalists: flag protests 112–13, 161; in Northern Ireland 25, 58, 95, 105, 110,